THE ETHICS OF
ECONOMIC RATIONALISM

D1713993

JOHN WRIGHT is a philosopher and teaches in the areas of History of Philosophy, Metaphysics, Philosophy of Religion and Philosophy of Science at the University of Newcastle, Australia. He has previously written books on the Philosophy of Science and on Metaphysics and is now working on a book on rationality and scientific method.

THE ETHICS OF ECONOMIC RATIONALISM

John Wright

A UNSW Press book

Published by
University of New South Wales Press Ltd
University of New South Wales
UNSW Sydney NSW 2052
AUSTRALIA
www.unswpress.com.au

National Library of Australia
Cataloguing-in-Publication entry:

Wright, John, 1956– .
The ethics of economic rationalism.

Bibliography.
ISBN 0 86840 661 9.

1. Economics — Australia — Moral and ethical aspects.
2. Australia — Social policy. 3. Australia — Economic
policy. I. Title.

338.994

Printer Griffin Press

CONTENTS

Preface   vii

Acknowledgments   xi

PART ONE: THE ECONOMIC CASE FOR ECONOMIC RATIONALISM   1

1 What is economic rationalism?   3

2 The foundations of economic rationalism in classical economics   19

3 Economic rationalism, efficiency and the free market   38

PART TWO: THE ETHICAL CASE FOR ECONOMIC RATIONALISM   63

4 Rationality and morality   64

5 Utilitarianism   74

6 The arguments from desert   100

7 Social Darwinism   123

8 The argument for the free market from the notion
   of voluntary exchange   138

9 Economic democracy and the maximisation of liberty   151

10 Conservatism, the free market and economic rationalism   167

11 Summary and Conclusions   181

Notes   187

Bibliography   199

Index   202

PREFACE

The expression 'economic rationalism' was first used in 1991 by the sociologist Michael Pusey in his monograph *Economic Rationalism in Canberra*. Pusey wanted to give a name to an approach to economic management, and to government generally, which he felt had come to dominate in Australia. We define economic rationalism in more detail later in this book, but very briefly, an important part of it is the idea that governments should increase efficiency by leaving as much as possible up to the 'free market'. What this means in practice is that, according to the rationalists, government should *stop* doing many of the things they have traditionally done, or at least they should *reduce* their own activities as much as they can. So, for example, rationalists might say governments should stop, or reduce, the aid they give to the poor and the unemployed, to health care, schools and universities, or to the Arts. They should stop worrying about the gap between the rich and the others, and they should stop giving help to struggling industries. In brief, Governments should 'wind back' their own activities and leave more up to free enterprise.

Why do economic rationalists think this? The short answer is that they think doing this will, in the long term, make Australia wealthy. In fact, they believe economic rationalism will eventually *maximise* the amount of wealth in the country. Just why they think this is a fairly complicated story, and the aim of the first part of this book is to explain in non-technical terms why it is thought economic rationalism will do this.

When Pusey coined the expression 'economic rationalism', he was using it to describe a movement he felt had become dominant within Australia. Although the *term* 'economic rationalism' is peculiarly

Australian, the set of ideas that make it up are not. In the United States of America, a related set of ideas are sometimes referred to as 'neo-conservatism' or 'neo-liberalism'; less flatteringly, it has also been called 'economic fundamentalism'. Economic rationalism also has 'Thatcherism' in the United Kingdom and 'Reaganomics' in the United States as its 'close cousins'.

Should we adopt economic rationalism? It is tempting to think that the answer to this question must be 'Yes'; after all, if it is going to (eventually) maximise wealth, isn't that what we all want? However, there is also a 'downside' to economic rationalism. Although it may maximise the *total* wealth of a community, even many of its most prominent advocates concede it is likely to increase the gap between rich and poor. And if there is reduced aid for the poor and the jobless, won't their lives be made more miserable? How does that fit with *fairness*, and with a belief in egalitarianism? Also, economic rationalism means less government aid for struggling industries. Companies that previously might have received help from the government will have to sink or swim. That is likely to reduce job security and make competition more intense. So, stress and a sense of uncertainty may increase. This may in turn affect people's health. As we will see later in the book, the impact that economic rationalism has on stress and health is very real. And if there is also less government assistance for health and medical care, these problems may become even worse.

So, it seems as though there is likely to be both a case *for* economic rationalism, and a case *against* it. The case for it is that, according at least to its advocates, it maximises wealth; the case against concerns, among other things, its effects on fairness and equality, security, stress and health. And so we are confronted with a problem: is the case for economic rationalism, on balance, stronger than the case against it? It is with this problem — or, rather, with one aspect of it — that we will be concerned in this book.

There is a moral dimension to the debate between the advocates and the opponents of economic rationalism. Is it better for a country to go down the path of maximising its total wealth, even if that may mean increasing the gap between the 'haves' and the 'have-nots', or should it rather take steps towards ensuring a degree of equality or fairness, even though that may mean *decreasing* total wealth? Is it right to take steps that will maximise total wealth, even if that is also likely to increase the stress and insecurity of the poor, the jobless and those working in struggling industries? But on the other hand, if a government were to interfere with the running of the free market, would it thereby be reducing the freedom of its citizens? Could such a reduction in freedom be justified, or would such a government be guilty of imposing its own values on people? Questions like these cannot be answered *just* by doing economics: they also have an ethical, or moral, aspect to them, and so to address them we need to consider ethical, or moral arguments.

This book addresses the *moral*, or *ethical* (we will be using these terms interchangeably), dimension of the arguments for and against economic rationalism. The first part of the book explains, in nontechnical terms, the *economic* case for economic rationalism. In the second part we look at the various attempts that have been given to provide an *ethical* justification of economic rationalism. Some of these arguments are: that economic rationalism maximises total human happiness; that it gives to each individual the amount of wealth they deserve; that economic rationalism is 'natural' because it enables the (economically) fit to thrive; that it inevitably brings about a distribution of wealth which, although unequal, is nevertheless *just*; that it maximises freedom, or liberty; and that it can be defended on conservative grounds. But we will also be concerned to *critically evaluate* these attempts to give a moral justification of economic rationalism. By the end of the book the reader will have a broad knowledge of the strengths and the weaknesses of the attempts to morally justify economic rationalism.

ACKNOWLEDGMENTS

Many people provided assistance in the writing of this book. The lectures of Professor CA Hooker introduced me to the topic of the economic arguments for economic rationalism. My colleagues at the University of Newcastle: Mr A Arposio, Dr J Atkins, Dr W Christensen, Dr J Collier, Dr DW Dockrill, Dr C Falzon, Dr R Farrell, Ms Y Gao, Rev. G Garnsey, Mr B Greetham, Dr W Herfel, Dr B Hodges, Mr M Mays, Dr J Mintoff, Ms M Purcell, Mr AW Sparkes and Dr C Wilks provided a congenial and stimulating place for work. Particular thanks must go to Dr Heath Gibson, a professional economist, for reading and supplying me with helpful comments on chapter three of the book. I would also like to thank Professor Bill Mitchell, Head of the Department of Economics at the University of Newcastle, for some thought provoking discussions on some of the themes dealt with here. I would like to thank Mrs S Bowcock for typing some parts of the manuscript. I also need to thank many persons whose names I do not know: in preparing for this book I spoke to a wide range of Australians about what they took 'economic rationalism' to be, and how they felt about it. Thank you to everyone who gave me their views. Special thanks must go to John Elliot of UNSW Press, and Natalie D'Enyar, whose encouragement and careful attention to detail were extremely helpful. Finally, I would like to thank Judith Fielsen, my parents, Edmund and Shirley, my brother Peter and sister Helen for helping me to realise that the subject matter of this book really is more important than the questions of metaphysics and epistemology I usually write about.

PART ONE

THE ECONOMIC CASE FOR ECONOMIC RATIONALISM

1
WHAT IS ECONOMIC RATIONALISM?

As a first approximation, we can say that economic rationalism is the doctrine that the primary role of government should be to ensure that *economic efficiency* within a country is maximised. What is economic efficiency? We will give a technical definition of economic efficiency in the third chapter, but for a start the following definition is satisfactory. *Maximising* efficiency involves:

1 *minimising* expenditure or outlay required to obtain an end product — the expenditure or outlay could be money, or resources such as raw materials, time or energy; and

2 *maximising* the output of the desired end-product, which may be valuable goods such as food, cars, television sets or services.

More briefly, we can say maximising efficiency, and so being economically rational, is maximising the ratio of desired end-product to expenditure. Surprisingly, many people are not aware that this is what economic rationalism *is*, as indicated by the following definitions of economic rationalism offered by typical Australians. (None of the people approached were economists, but some were tertiary qualified professionals and business people.)

Economic rationalism was thought to be:

• being narrow and logical in looking at how economics works — money must not be invested unless you get a return;

• when money has been distributed to the states and so on in a rational, logical way;

- ensuring that any decision concerning what to do falls within the bounds of what the available funds allow;
- when they break things up, bit by bit;
- when they take more for themselves and leave less for you;
- restructuring industries so they can compete overseas;
- making sure businesses can show a profit, or don't get into debt; or
- laying off people if it is the only way to make a business profitable.

It should be noted that about one sixth of the people approached confessed they did not know what the expression 'economic rationalism' meant at all. 'I just hear it on the news and "roll with it"' was one comment. Even those who did offer a definition tended to be uncertain about whether they understood the term correctly. And many gave what could be called a repetitive definition: 'it means just what it says' or 'just what those words mean' were common responses. Only one person out of about twenty-five (a post-graduate university student) gave a definition that was correct and more than just a repetition. *Nevertheless, most people asked described it in basically positive terms.* On the face of it, it is rather odd that most people should feel that economic rationalism is a good thing even though they do not quite know what it is. It seems to be assumed that because the word 'rational' appears in it, whatever it is precisely, it must be something basically good. Indeed, most people seemed to think it amounted to little more than being *responsible*, *sensible*, *logical* and *rational* about money matters. Moreover, most of those approached who did not have a basically 'pro' view did not doubt that it was 'rational' or 'logical'; rather, they were concerned that being rational or logical meant being somehow narrow and heartless. One wonders to what extent economic rationalism would be generally accepted as a 'good thing', or even as 'harsh but necessary medicine', if it was given another name such as 'economic efficiency-ism', 'neo-classical economics' or 'economic fundamentalism'.

If a political party were to emerge which named itself 'The Party of Health, Wealth and Happiness' we would either be extremely sceptical about the claims implicit in the name, or — perhaps more likely — we would regard it as some kind of a joke. So, why have people been so ready to accept the claims of a movement that says it is simply making *rational* decisions about economics? I think the answer lies in the fact that economics is widely accepted to be a *science*, and in scientific matters we non-experts feel we should defer to what the experts have to say. If a scientist tells us Jupiter is 400 000 000 miles from Earth, we would simply accept it; a public debate would be neither necessary nor appropriate. Or if doctors tell us that drug X will have such and such effects, we will, by and large, accept what they say. However, politics is different. If a *politician* tells us a particular thing is what the public needs, we may or may not accept what the politician says, and a public debate on the topic may be a part of the process of democracy. We do not accept the politician in the same *uncritical* way we will accept a scientist, and neither should we. However, we are perhaps inclined to accept the judgments of *economists* in more or less the same way we are inclined to accept the judgments of scientists. They are experts. If we are told something is economically rational, we are perhaps inclined to say, 'Well, I guess they know, and if something is the rational thing to do we should do it.' But if exactly the same proposal had been defended by conventional political arguments then we may have felt more inclined to express our own opinion and engage in public debate.

If a course of action is 'economically rational' — that is, if it *maximises economic efficiency* — does that mean it really is rational to adopt that course of action? If something maximises economic efficiency, does that thereby mean it is *the right thing to do*? These are the questions we will be looking at in this book.

WHY MAXIMISING EFFICIENCY CERTAINLY SEEMS TO BE RATIONAL

As we have already noted, maximising economic efficiency consists of two parts: (a) minimising the amount of money (or other valued thing) that is spent, and (b) maximising the *outcome* that is a result of spending that money or other valuable resources. This outcome could be goods or services produced, or some other desired thing. Clearly, this certainly *seems* to be rational. Suppose you are considering buying a car. You draw up a list of the features you would like your car to have: that it will reliably get you from A to B, that it would be able to go 'off-road', that it can comfortably seat six people, that it can tow a boat and so on. You will want to *maximise* the number of good qualities that the car has — that is, you will want to maximise the number of things on your list that you get with the car. But you will also want to *minimise* the amount of money you spend. In other words, you will try to *maximise economic efficiency*. This seems perfectly sensible, or 'rational'; indeed, we would regard any one who did not attempt to do this as being rather odd.

The same points apply to the owner of a company. The owner will try to minimise their expenditure; that is, they will try to minimise the quantity of raw materials they use, as well as other expenses involved in making their products. They will also try to maximise output, or the number of items they produce. In other words, the company owner will try to maximise economic efficiency. In this way they hope to success-fully compete against other companies making similar items.

So, in summary, it seems that the whole enterprise of trying to maximise efficiency is just common sense. No wonder it is called eco-nomic *rationalism*. On the face of it, it does indeed seem to be irra-tional to do anything else. But, of course, things are not always that simple. Pursuing efficiency might be *obviously* rational for an individual deciding how to spend their own money, or a manager trying to run a company. But matters become rather more complicated when we con-sider a whole *country*. Some people think that trying to maximise effi-ciency when running a country is misguided. This is where economic rationalists disagree: for them the pursuit of efficiency is appropriate at all levels — at the level of individuals, companies, governments or whole countries. We can begin to see why this disagreement should exist by considering a simple, imaginary country and looking at some of the problems that might arise as the country develops.

THE STORY OF XLAND

We will imagine a simple imaginary country called 'Xland'. This coun-try trades with its neighbours by ship, but is surrounded by a danger-ous reef resulting in many ships running aground on it with the loss of large quantities of goods. What should the Xlanders do? A natural sug-gestion is that they should build a lighthouse. But let us consider: could an individual, or a company, *make money* by building a lighthouse? If the individual or the company had enough money and raw materials they could, of course, *construct* the lighthouse. But how would they then go about using the lighthouse to make a profit? The difficulty is that *every* ship sailing in the vicinity of the lighthouse gains the benefit of being informed where the reef is *whether they have paid money to the lighthouse owners or not*. Are the owners of the lighthouse to pursue every ship sailing past and extract a fee from the captain? What if the ship was in no danger of heading towards the reef in the first place? What if the captain of the ship had no prior agreement to pay for the benefits of the lighthouse?

Pretty clearly, then, there is no way the owners of the lighthouse could *exclude* ships from seeing the light, and thus gaining the benefit of being told about the reef. The good offered by the lighthouse is therefore, in economists' terminology, *non-excludible*. Obviously, it is hard to make a profit by providing to the public a non-excludible good such a lighthouse. People can gain the benefit of the good even if they have not paid the owner for it and there seems to be no way the owner can stop them. Why then should we expect them to pay the owner?

There is another feature of the lighthouse that makes it different from those goods from which it is possible to make a profit. One ship seeing the light, and thus gaining the benefit of being told about the reef, does *not prevent another* ship from seeing the light. Both ships can be sailing by and be informed of the reef by the light. But in this respect, the lighthouse is rather different from the goods that we typically buy and sell. Suppose two people enter a shop, both wishing to buy a hamburger. If they *both* want a (whole) hamburger then, obviously enough, they will each have to buy their own hamburger. And so the shop owner will get to sell two hamburgers. The two persons plainly cannot both eat the same hamburger (at least if they want a whole one). In this respect, they are *rivals* for the consumption of a particular hamburger.

However, the two ships sailing by are not rivals for the good provided by the lighthouse. One ship's gaining the benefit from the light does not prevent another ship from gaining the same benefit. In the terminology of economists, the benefit offered by the lighthouse is *non-rival*, that is, one person gaining the benefit does not prevent another person gaining the same benefit. Again, it is clear that it would be very difficult indeed to make a profit by supplying to the public a *non-rival* good. (It is because one person eating a hamburger prevents anyone else from eating that particular hamburger that the shop owner gets to sell *many* hamburgers. But the lighthouse owner only has to provide one lighthouse, and an indefinite number of ships can gain the benefit of it.)

Any good that has the features of being *non-excludible* and *non-rival* is called by economists a 'public good'. Lighthouses, then, are examples of public goods. We will return to the notion of a public good from time to time later in the book. However, here we need to note: it is generally not possible for a privately owned company to make a profit by providing a public good.

So, how would the lighthouse be funded? One suggestion is that perhaps all the ship owners would get together and 'chip in' to pay for it. But would this work? Two difficulties are likely to arise. First, a ship owner may say: 'Look, I agree that we would all benefit from having a lighthouse on those rocks, but what assurance can you give me that, if I put my bit in, others will also contribute? I don't want to be the *only* one to give you money, because in that case the lighthouse will not get built and my donation will be wasted. So what assurance can you give me that enough people will contribute money for the lighthouse to be built?' Of course, those trying to collect the money can give no assurance: the collector does not have any power to *force* people to hand over the money. So, the ship owner may decide, on these grounds, not to give any money. This problem is called the *assurance problem*.

The second problem arises when the ship owner reasons to himself in the following way: 'Obviously, whether this lighthouse gets built or not is not going to depend on whether *I* contribute. Suppose, it does not get built; then I will have wasted my money if I give it to this collector. Yet suppose it does get built. Then I will still be able to make use of it even if I have not made a contribution. They can't stop a ship *seeing* the lighthouse. So, I might as well *not* make a contribution. I will let others pay for the lighthouse, and then, when it is built they won't be able to stop me using it.' We can say that this person decides to take a 'free ride' on the benefits that come about as a result of contributions made by others. This is called the *free rider problem*. We will discuss both the assurance and free rider problems from time to time later in this book.

Now, whatever we may think of the ethics of these ship owners (and I think we are particularly likely to have some doubts about the ethics of the second one), their behaviour is quite *rational*. If you cannot be given any assurance that enough people will contribute to guarantee that the lighthouse will be built, and hence that you will not be wasting your money if you contribute, it does seem to be rational to *not* contribute. And if you will be able to *use* the lighthouse *whether or not* you pay, it does seem to be irrational to pay. Hence it is rational to *not* pay. What all this means, of course, is that it is likely that the lighthouse will not get built. The idea of all the ship owners *voluntarily* chipping in to pay for the construction and running of the lighthouse runs up against the assurance and free rider problems. So, how *does* a lighthouse ever get built? One answer is that the government pays for the lighthouse — out of *taxes*.

Why is it that the government would be able to succeed when the other methods fail? We saw that a private company would not be able to construct and run a lighthouse because it was not possible to make a profit out of it. However, a government does not need to make a profit. The idea of ship owners voluntarily chipping in probably would not work because they might (perfectly rationally) decide *not* to chip in. But a government can *compel* people to pay taxes. People do not choose or decide to pay taxes, they pay them because they have to, because they know they will go to jail if they do not. It is because governments can compel people to pay taxes that the construction *by governments* of lighthouses — and some other things in the public benefit — does not run up against the assurance and free rider problems.

So, let us suppose that in Xland the government uses taxes to build the lighthouse. The whole community benefits from it: the seas are safer for those travelling on them, fewer goods are lost as a result of ships crashing on the rocks, and so trade increases. Society as a whole benefits. The cost of the construction of the lighthouse was 'worth it' in terms of the benefits that went to society. But still, it was something that had to be constructed by the government because, due to the nature of this particular case, it was not possible for a privately owned company to make a profit from it and neither could it have been financed by a group of freely co-operating individuals.

GOODS THAT CANNOT BE PROVIDED BY THE FREE MARKET (OR PROVIDED ONLY WITH DIFFICULTY)

There are many other things that have the feature of providing a valuable service to people but which, for one reason or another, could not be provided by the operation of the free market. One such example is the footpath. It would be very difficult for a private company to make a profit by constructing footpaths and charging people for walking on them. How would it be done? By constructing turnstiles outside everyone's front gate and charging them a fee before allowing them to walk down the street? Clearly this would not be practical. Like a lighthouse, the benefit provided by a footpath is available to anybody who chooses to use it, not just those who have helped pay for its construction. Some other examples include the lighting of public streets, the construction of (most) roads, drains, public parks and so on. (These are all public goods, in the sense that they are non-excludible and non-rival.) A private company that tried to offer these services to the public would be unable to make a profit, and any attempt to pay for them by people voluntarily 'chipping in' would run up against the assurance and free rider problems. So, if we are to have these services at all they need to be paid for by taxes, which people are compelled to pay.

Two particularly important examples of *services* that could not be provided just by the operation of the free market are the army and the police. Imagine a private company putting out an advertisement saying, for example, 'You pay us $50 a year and we will protect *you* if the country is invaded.' What would happen if someone chose not to pay their fee to the army? Would it be possible for the army to *not* defend from attack that particular house, while defending all the other houses in the country? Clearly not. So, the householder will likely argue: 'This private company can't *force* people to pay. So I have no assurance that others will pay even if I do.' They might also argue: 'The army will *defend the whole country*, and therefore my own house, against attack whether I pay the fee or not. So there is no reason for me to pay.' And of course the same logic could be used by *all* the householders in the country. Consequently, it is at least very doubtful whether the private company could make a profit by running an army designed to protect a country.

What we have here, of course, are the assurance and free rider problems over again.

It appears, then, that it would not be viable for a private company to set up an army with the job of defending a country against attack. Of course, there *are* some armies run by private companies. We sometimes call these 'mercenaries' and they can also be employed by private individuals and companies to do a particular job. However, in those cases, the employer of the mercenaries is the sole beneficiary of the services performed by the mercenaries, and the employer would not have received that service if they had not paid the mercenaries. In such a case, the assurance and free rider problems do not emerge, and so a private, profit-seeking company can run an army. Where private enterprise won't work is where those who are to pay for the service believe that the service will be performed, and they will benefit from it, *whether they pay for it or not*. In such cases, many (at least) *won't* pay and therefore a private company could not make a profit and so would not be workable.

The same applies to at least many of the services performed by the police. Consider 'random breath tests': these have the effect of removing drunken drivers from the road, and so make the roads safer, benefiting us all from this. Yet note, a person would still benefit from having drunken drivers removed from the road even if they had not paid a 'fee' to police for performing this service. So many people (at least) would, perfectly rationally, decide not to pay if doing so were voluntary.

The services we have looked at so far would be impossible, or at least very impractical, for a private company to offer. But not all government provided services are of this character — consider education. Our society believes it is worthwhile for everyone to be educated. If a significant proportion of the population were not educated, their lives would be worse off: not only would they find it almost impossible to get a job, they would also be confronted with all sorts of difficulties in their everyday life, from reading a map, to following written directions, to performing simple operations with money. The country as a whole benefits from having an educated workforce. So in our society universal education, up to a particular level, is considered desirable. But if education is to be universal, it must also be compulsory, for if it were not compulsory then inevitably a proportion of parents would choose not to have their children educated. However, if it is compulsory, then necessarily, there must also be *free* education available. If there were no free education, but it was still compulsory, then *poor* parents would be placed in an intolerable position: they would be *compelled* to pay for something they could not afford. As a result, in our society free education is available, although of course, it is also possible for parents to send their children to non-government, fee-accepting schools. If (some) education is free, then, quite obviously it is not possible for a private company to make a profit out of it. So free education must be run by the government and paid for out of taxes.

The case of education is a little different from the other cases we have looked at so far. By their very nature, a lighthouse, a footpath or an army are not the type of thing that a private company could make a profit constructing or running. Education is different; private companies can, and do, make a profit offering educational services. If we have government run schools, it is not because it is impossible for private companies to make a profit running schools, but because it is believed that *certain types* of education (free, compulsory education) are of sufficient value to society to have our governments provide them.

There are other activities in our society which are (rightly or wrongly) considered worthy of government assistance. One such area is 'the Arts'. It is almost impossible to make a living as an artist in our society. The vast majority of fine arts graduates find employment in occupations other than that of practising artist, and the small minority who do persist as practising artists barely sustain themselves from their art. Yet it is felt (at least by some) that society as a whole benefits from having an active and healthy artistic community. So the government provides assistance to the Arts, in the form of grants to artists and subsidies to artistic bodies.

Yet another activity which receives government assistance is scientific and medical research. No-one disputes that scientific and medical research benefits society, but for a variety of reasons private companies are reluctant to employ scientists to do research. One reason is simply the timelag that can occur between the discovery in the laboratory of some new form of technology and its eventual appearance in the shops. Private companies like to show a profit on their activities within two or three years; after all, they need regular profits to ensure that their shareholders continue to invest in their company. If they do not, their shareholders may take their money elsewhere. But many forms of technology take much more than just a few years to pass through all the stages of research in the laboratory, development into a marketable product, sales, and eventual production of profit. The 'research' phase alone can sometimes take several years. Also, if it takes five or more years for research to bear fruit, the executive who suggests or initiates the plan to engage in the research may no longer be around to get the credit for the success of their plan. If they are unlikely to get the credit, what incentive is there for them to initiate the research in the first place?

A version of the free rider problem can also dissuade company owners from paying people to do research. The results of research will often become publicly available, either through being published in scientific journals or when the applications of the research become available as a purchasable product. Why should a company owner pay for one of their own employees to do the research when they can get the benefits of some other company doing it instead? And if the company owner *does* pay for research, there is the danger other companies will use the results to make *their* products better. Of course, a company owner can try to take out a patent on the results of research, but that takes time and money, and may not even be successful. This line of thought has led many (particularly Australian) businessmen to see financing research as 'not making good business sense'.

In summary, there are many reasons why private businesses can be reluctant to spend money on scientific or medical research. However, research benefits the community. Without it we might still have kerosene lanterns, the horse and buggy, or steam trains, and we would still be vulnerable to small pox, tuberculosis and many other diseases. Thus, governments will pay for some research out of taxes.

ACTIVITIES IN XLAND

Provided by private companies and individuals as profit making businesses	Partly provided by private companies, and partly provided by government	Provided by government, not as profit making enterprises
Food		
	Hospitals	Lighthouses
	Medical Services	
Cars Housing		Footpaths
Appliances	The Arts	Army
Clothing	Utilities	Police
	Electricity	
Television stations	Gas	
	Scientific research	
	medical research	
Tends to use less government activity, more private activity; more emphasis on making a profit		Tends to use more government activity, less private activity, less emphasis on making a profit

Figure 1.1 Activities in Xland

ECONOMIC RATIONALISM CLARIFIED

We have considered some of the activities which a society may decide to have paid for by the government. In some cases (lighthouses, footpaths) it is not possible for a private company to make a profit by offering the service in question. In other cases (education, the Arts, scientific research) it is possible to make a profit, but for a variety of reasons it may be felt that society as a whole benefits from the government giving assistance to those activities.

Now let us suppose that, as it develops, Xland decides it is best to have some activities entirely run by the government and not as profit-making enterprises, other activities entirely left up to private enterprise, and still others somewhere in between. After a while, the situation in Xland resembles that found in Figure 1.1.

The idea behind this table is that the further to the *left* the service indicated is on the table, the greater the extent to which the production of that service is left up to private individuals or companies operating within the free market, whereas the further to the *right*, the greater the extent of government involvement in the offering of that service. This 'government involvement' may take the form of the government itself, and its employees, directly offering the service (for example, government employees constructing footpaths), or it may take the form of the government offering assistance to individuals or companies engaged in that activity (for example, the provision of government grants to practising artists). Alternatively, it may take a number of other forms, some of which are described below.

Suppose some *economic rationalists* get into power in Xland. They reform Xland in accordance with the principles of economic rationalism. But what, *specifically*, do they actually do? *They will tend to move the activities on the above table towards the left of the table.* For example, they may eliminate government assistance to the Arts, and so force artists to rely solely on selling their work to the public as the means of getting money. They may reduce funding to universities, thereby increasing the proportion of scientific research that is carried out by private companies. They may try to make hospitals function more like private companies, or they may turn public utilities that were previously government owned into privately owned companies.

It is very important to note that probably no *actual* economic rationalist will want to move *all* activities to the extreme left of the diagram. Almost certainly, they will retain the police force as a government funded institution. And, regarding our original example, they would probably have no choice but to keep lighthouses government funded and may retain a fair measure of government run hospitals and schools.

Economic rationalists typically do not advocate moving *everything* to the far left of the diagram, but almost certainly they will advocate moving many activities a considerable distance to the left. In this respect, *economic rationalism* needs to be distinguished from *extreme free marketeerism*. An extreme free marketeer would say every activity in Xland should either be moved to the extreme left of the diagram — that is, turned into a privately owned profit making private business — or else eliminated altogether.

Extreme free marketeers are not common — no prominent Australian would fit that description. The position is, however, not unknown in the United States. One extreme free marketeer group is the anti-socialist John Birch Society, which advocates the eventual removal of all government activity.

Extreme free marketeerism is sometimes called right wing market anarchy. It is worthwhile briefly digressing to consider the rationale for this extreme position. First, we need to make clear the meaning of the word 'anarchy'. It does not mean, as is sometimes thought, 'chaos' or 'total mess and absence of order'; rather, it means '*absence of authority*'.

Anarchists believe *authority* should be abolished, they do not necessarily believe order should be abolished. Let us recall why a government was able to construct the lighthouse while private enterprise and voluntary co-operation between individuals could not. Ultimately, it came down to the fact the government was able to *compel* people to pay taxes. The government is able to demand that you pay it money in the form of taxes and if you do not comply the government can back up its demand with guns and imprisonment. But if anybody else used the threat of guns and imprisonment to extract money from us we would regard them as thieves or extortionists. Anarchists regard the government's use of the threat of force to extract money from us as such a bad thing it should not be accepted. Right wing *market* anarchists would have the only institutions in society run by voluntary co-operation between individuals operating within the free market.

So, in summary, it is only right wing market anarchists who say that *all* institutions should be moved to the extreme left of our diagram. Economic rationalists will tend to say activities should be moved *towards* the free market side, but they will retain some government activities. This raises two questions.

1 How many activities will economic rationalists say should be moved to the free market end, and how far should they be moved in that direction?

2 *Why* do economic rationalists say activities should be moved to the free market end?

The answers to the two questions take us to the core of what economic rationalism is about.

Economic rationalists believe that activities should, in general, be moved towards the free market end of the spectrum because typically that will lead to *an increase in economic efficiency.*

How far should activities be moved towards the free enterprise end of the spectrum? As a first approximation, we can say:

Economic rationalists believe that activities should be moved to that point in the spectrum which maximises *the overall economic efficiency of society.*

Note that the above statement is only true *as a first approximation.* It is useful here to distinguish between what we will call *pure* or *strict* economic rationalism, and economic rationalism as a *tendency.* A *pure* economic rationalist says that there should be one and only one aim of government activity: to maximise economic efficiency. Roughly speaking, a pure economic rationalist will say all possible activities in a country *ought* to be brought within the free market, because that maximises efficiency.[1] But it is not quite accurate to say that all economic rationalists will say that all activities that *can* be carried out by the free market *should* be carried out by the free market. Rather, the typical economic rationalist will allow some activities (such as teaching), which can be carried out by the free market, to also be carried out by governments, if doing so increases the overall economic efficiency of society. For the economic rationalist, the important question is always: what will maximise economic efficiency?

The economic rationalist *also* believes that very often, although not always, the best way to increase economic efficiency is to have as many activities as possible carried out by the free market. A *pure* economic rationalist can allow that there are some activities which, of their very nature, cannot be brought within the free market, but which are nevertheless essential for the efficient running of a free market. A pure economic rationalist will permit such activities but insist they be carried out with maximum economic efficiency. So if, for example, having lighthouses helps to maximise economic efficiency, a pure economic rationalist will permit the existence of (government run) lighthouses, but insist that they be run as efficiently as possible. If having police helps an economy to run more efficiently (by encouraging people to work rather than engage in unproductive activities such as theft), a pure economic rationalist will permit a (government run) police force, but will, again, insist it be as economically efficient as possible.

There is one more type of government activity that an economic rationalist will allow. We have already noted that, unlike the running of a lighthouse or a police force, it is possible to make a profit out of offering educational services in the free market. But an economic rationalist can allow some degree of government funded education. Let us imagine what it would be like if there were no government funded schools. The only schools would be private schools, which are expensive. Therefore only the well-off would be able to afford to have their children educated. This would in turn mean that much of the population would be unable to read or write, or possess basic mathematical skills. It is obvious that this would mean the total productivity of the country would be greatly reduced. The total economic output of the country is, therefore, greatly increased by having government funded schools. For this reason, an economic rationalist can permit government funded schools, even though it is possible to make a profit out of education in the free market. For the economic rationalist, the important question is always: will this increase economic efficiency? If it will, then the (pure) economic rationalist will approve of it.

We can define a *pure* economic rationalist as follows:

> A pure economic rationalist says all activities should be brought within the free market except for those activities which, (a) by their very nature cannot be brought within the free market but which are nevertheless essential for the efficient running of the free market, or (b) although they can be brought within the free market, government activity is necessary to ensure the level of those activities which maximise the overall economic efficiency of society. The pure economic rationalist will say all such activities should be carried out in as economically efficient a manner as possible.

Some economists are pure economic rationalists, but it is rather unlikely that any elected government would fully implement pure economic rationalism.[2] What governments in this country have done, and are likely to continue doing, is adopt economic rationalism as a *tendency*. To adopt economic rationalism as a tendency is to move a country *towards* pure economic rationalism. Such a government would increase the number of activities that are to be undertaken by the free market, while making more efficient the remaining essential governmental activities. Economic rationalism has been present in Australia *as a tendency* since about 1976.[3]

One question is: how far should we go along the path to pure economic rationalism? Of course, many people will say we have *no choice* but to continue going down the path of economic rationalism *if we are to be competitive in the global economy*, that is, in an economy in which producers are competing not just against others in the same region, state or country, but against similar producers throughout the world. We should note here that 'being competitive in the global economy' is not an all-or-nothing matter: there are degrees of competitiveness. How competitive should Australian companies become? Again, many might be tempted to say, 'There is no real question here; we should aim for maximum possible competitiveness.' As we will see in chapter three, there is very good reason to believe that adopting pure economic rationalism is the way to get to maximum possible competitiveness, but it is at just this point that we encounter the issues to be discussed in this book. *The fact is that moving closer and closer to pure economic rationalism has many different consequences; some of them are good, others are not.* One consequence will be an increase in efficiency, but another — which, as we will see in a later chapter, is already occurring — is that the gap between rich and poor is likely to increase. Another consequence is decreased job security. Another is likely to be longer work hours, and for some, at least, this will mean increased stress, which in turn may affect health. Other consequences may have an impact on the natural environment.

The path towards pure economic rationalism has good and bad consequences. Will the benefits always outweigh the costs, or will there come a point when the benefits that come from further increasing our efficiency become less than the costs of a society divided into rich and poor, increased stress, insecurity and environmental damage? The aim of this book is not to give a definite 'Yes' or 'No' answer to this question, but to simply lay out, as clearly as the author can, the arguments on both sides of the issue. Yet the book also has a narrower emphasis: it focuses primarily on the moral or ethical aspects of the debate. Very briefly, defenders of economic rationalism and the free market emphasise its importance in maintaining and increasing the efficient production of wealth in a country. Opponents of economic rationalism are more inclined to stress the importance of equality, egalitarianism and 'quality of life', which may not necessarily equate with the quantity of material wealth. However, questions such as: Should we aim for the maximum quantity of wealth or a more even distribution of wealth? Which is more important, maximising economic freedom or maximising fairness? are questions of an essentially *ethical* nature. It is these and similar questions that we consider in this book. We look at what famous economists, leading businessmen and prominent ethicists, political theorists and philosophers have had to say about these questions.

ECONOMIC RATIONALISM AND RELATED 'ISMS'

Whilst the term 'economic rationalism' is a peculiarly *Australian* term, closely related systems have sometimes been advocated, and implemented, in other countries. In America, much the same system is sometimes called 'neo-liberalism'. An economic rationalist and a neo-liberal will very often agree on what governments ought to do; in particular, they will agree that governments ought to reduce their own activities and leave as much as possible up to the free market. But when they come to explain *why* they think governments ought to do this, economic rationalists and neo-liberals might give rather different answers. The economic rationalist will emphasise the role that the free market has in increasing efficiency and creating wealth. But a neo-liberal might instead emphasise the ways in which, by cutting back on their own activities, governments can thereby maximise the liberty of their citizens. The economic rationalist will emphasise efficiency, the neo-liberal, freedom. We should also note that this difference is also likely to only be one of *emphasis*: the economic rationalist will be quite happy to acknowledge that an additional benefit of their position is that it increases people's liberty, while an advocate of neo-liberalism will be quite happy to point out that their position also tends to increase efficiency and wealth.

Although advocates of neo-liberalism and of economic rationalism might *nearly always* agree on what governments should do, we can imagine some possible situations in which they might disagree. Suppose some possible course of action by a government was likely to increase efficiency, while at the same time taking away a little from people's economic freedom. Then an economic rationalist might approve of that government action, while the neo-liberal would disapprove; but generally, the two positions are very similar.

Also very closely related to economic rationalism is 'free market economics'. Indeed, some economic rationalists themselves are prepared to define 'economic rationalism' as 'free market economics', but it is probably better to see 'free market economics' as a more general term.[4] A person can subscribe to free market economics for many reasons: because it increases efficiency (as the economic rationalist believes), because it ensures freedom (as the neo-liberal believes), or for a range of other reasons, many of which are discussed in this book. Economic rationalists are *one type* of adherent to free market economics.

As we noted at the start of this chapter, economic rationalists believe the primary goal of government should be the maximisation of economic efficiency. *Moving activities towards the free enterprise end of the spectrum is for them the primary means of increasing efficiency.* Of course, all this raises a further question: *Why* do economic rationalists believe that moving activities towards the free enterprise end will increase efficiency? The precise answer to this question is rather complex, but, in outline, the reason was seen by the great economist Adam Smith in the eighteenth century. Smith's ideas form the focus of the next chapter.

2

THE FOUNDATIONS OF ECONOMIC RATIONALISM IN CLASSICAL ECONOMICS

Modern economic rationalism has its intellectual foundations in a branch of economics known as neo-classical economics. As the name 'neo-classical' suggests, this is a new or modern version of classical economics. So it is appropriate to start by briefly looking at classical economics.

CLASSICAL ECONOMICS AND THE WEALTH OF NATIONS

The work of classical economics to which modern economic rationalists most generally appeal is Adam Smith's *An Inquiry Into The Nature and Causes of The Wealth of Nations*, usually known more briefly as *The Wealth of Nations*. Adam Smith was an eighteenth century Scottish philosopher and economist. For most of his career he was Professor of Moral Philosophy at the University of Glasgow and his *Theory of Moral Sentiments* (1759) was highly regarded by his contemporaries. He retired from university life in 1764 and, after a brief period acting as tutor to the Duke of Buccleuch, commenced work on *The Wealth of Nations*. It took him ten years to write and was published in 1776, the same year as the American Declaration of Independence. Some prominent authors see parallels between the two documents: the former explains the principles of economic freedom, the later of political freedom.[1]

The Wealth of Nations has had a huge impact. The conservative social theorist and politician Edmund Burke said of Smith's book that 'in its ultimate result this is probably the most important book that has ever been written'.[2] It is surely no exaggeration to say that, at least for economists who are inclined to stress the value of the free market, Smith's book is as important as Darwin's *Origin of Species* is for biologists.

Smith was working during a period of European expansion and discovery. North America was developing, and new lands were being discovered in Central and South America, and in the Pacific; Captain Cook was making his great voyages. Smith noted that there were sometimes huge differences in the relative wealth of countries. While Great Britain, and much of Europe, was comparatively wealthy, many other countries in the world were poor. Smith sought an explanation of this fact, and so conducted his 'inquiry into the nature and causes of the wealth of nations'.

THE KEY IDEAS OF THE WEALTH OF NATIONS

Smith considered the plausible idea that it was the presence or absence of natural resources which determined the level of wealth of a country, but rejected this because he found that there were some rich countries with very few natural resources and some very poor countries with immense natural resources.[3] Some other factor, or factors, must therefore be responsible for the creation of wealth. But what were they? The parts of Smith's book that form the basis of the key ideas of both neoclassical economics and economic rationalism are those parts in which he discusses the importance of *voluntary exchange* between individuals.

Suppose you go into a bakery to buy a loaf of bread. You hand over, let us say, a dollar and the baker gives you a loaf of bread. This exchange is, of course, purely voluntary. You did not have to go into the bakery and offer a dollar, and the baker could have refused to accept your dollar. Yet the exchange did take place. Smith's key idea is that a *voluntary* exchange between individuals will take place only if both parties benefit from it. *You* are better off with the loaf of bread rather than keeping the dollar coin. (If you weren't, you would not offer the coin to the baker in exchange for the bread.) The baker is better off with the dollar than with the loaf of bread, of which he has more than he can possibly eat. He needs the dollar so he can buy things other than bread. In modern terminology, the exchange is a win–win situation. Smith's point is that voluntary exchanges in the free market are win–win situations — if they weren't they would not take place at all.

Now let us consider some small businessperson, (such as, for example, our baker) trying to make a profit. Obviously enough, if the baker is to make a profit, he must at least *sell* that which he produces. He can only sell what he produces if people are prepared to buy it. So, under what circumstances will people buy what the baker makes? Obviously, only if it is good value for money: his bread must be as cheap as that which is produced by other bakers or of a similar quality, or both, since people want bread that is cheap and good. So, obviously enough, if the baker is to sell his produce, *he must give people what they want*. The baker is motivated by his own desire to make a profit, but if he is to do this he must give his customers what they want, and as cheaply as he can, if he is to persuade them to buy their bread from him. The same applies, of course, to any producer of goods who hopes to sell them. The crucial point, for Smith, is that although the baker (or any other producer) intends only his own gain, he ends up 'producing and selling the goods which satisfy the greatest needs of the people ... [I]ntending his own gain, he contributes nonetheless to the general welfare.'[4] In a famous passage from *The Wealth of Nations,* Smith himself expresses the idea as follows:

> Every individual is continually exerting himself to find out the most advantageous employment for whatever capital he can command. It is his own advantage, indeed, and not that of society which he has in view. But the study of his own advantage naturally, or rather necessarily, leads him to prefer that employment which is most advantageous in society.[5]

> He generally, indeed, neither intends to promote the public interest, nor knows how much he is promoting it ... he intends only his own security ... only his own gain ... and he is in this led by an invisible hand to promote an end which was no part of his intention. By pursuing his own interest he frequently promotes that of society more effectually than when he really intends to promote it.[6]

Smith's idea of the 'invisible hand' is a key notion of *The Wealth of Nations,* and (in a somewhat more mathematically sophisticated form) it is at the centre of the modern, neo-classical case for economic rationalism. The 'invisible hand' is a striking and memorable phrase, but it is also misleading. It has led some unsympathetic critics to assert that Smith thinks there is an additional, unseen and benevolent force which ensures that the efforts of businesspeople to make a profit will also result in the general population benefiting as well.[7] But there is no need to postulate an additional force, benevolent or otherwise. The benefits that go to the general population are simply a direct consequence of the fact that any voluntary exchange between two individuals must be a win–win situation. In order to get people to freely or voluntarily buy what is produced the businessperson offers for sale what people want, or what satisfies their needs, as cheaply as possible and is therefore led to act in *their* interests.

Clearly, the motivating force in all this is *self-interest*. The baker, for example, will offer for sale to the public the type of bread they want not out of altruism, but because he has the self-interested desire for profits. For Smith, self-interest, *when operating in the free market,* has the *unintended consequence* of leading to the benefit of the general public. It provides the energy or driving force which improves the public welfare via the 'invisible hand'. As Smith says in another part of *The Wealth of Nations*:

> It is not from the benevolence of the butcher, the brewer, or the baker that we expect our dinner, but from their regard to their own interest.[8]

Since selfishness, or self-interest, has (unintended) beneficial side-effects, there is a sense in which Smith would agree with the character Gordon Gekko in the film *Wall Street* that 'greed is good'. (We will say more about the apparently inverted or topsy-turvy conception of morality that exists in free market economics later in this chapter.)

THE DEVELOPMENT OF SMITH'S IDEAS

RESOURCES

Let us now explore Smith's views in a little more detail. Imagine a village containing perhaps twenty or thirty families. One family, let us say, grows potatoes. Since they grow far more potatoes than they can eat by themselves, and since they need more to live on than just potatoes, they trade with others for goods such as meat, clothes and firewood. Another family may raise sheep and exchange wool for bread, building materials and so on. Now let us suppose a new family moves into the area and tries to make a living. At first they might try growing oats; but it turns out that the particular patch of land they have is not well suited to that purpose: it only produces few oats of poor quality. No-one wants to buy their oats or exchange them for other goods. So, this new family will, at least if they are sensible, turn to growing something else — for example, cabbages. Let us suppose that their soil is very good for growing cabbages: they grow large quantities of high quality cabbages which everybody wants to buy. So, of course, the family will decide to stick with growing cabbages. There are two things we need to note here.

1   The family *themselves* are better off growing cabbages — since they are now growing large quantities of something everyone wants to buy, they are making a greater profit.

2   The village community as a whole is better off because they now have available to them a large quantity of high quality cabbages. The village is better off with the new family growing cabbages than it would have been had they stuck with oats.

That is, both the new family, *and* the rest of the village, are better off. Of course, it may turn out that when the family tries to grow cabbages the land is no good for that either. In that case they will have to continue to look for something the land is good for. The important point is that, if they want to maximise their own profit, they will look until they find that use for which the land is best suited. This use of the land will be the best for them, because it will maximise their own profits, and it will also maximise the benefit to the other members of the village by providing them with something they want to buy. They may not have intended to benefit the village but they are, as Smith said, 'led by an invisible hand' to promote an end which was no part of their intention.

What we have just said about the new family coming into the area will also apply to all the other families already there. Each family in this village will put their own land to the use which generates the most profit for them, and this will, according to Smith, be the use that also produces the most benefit for the community of which they are a part. This is true not just of land, but of whatever else they can use to sell to others: wood, stone, metal or resources of any kind. In a system of voluntary exchange, each individual will put the resources they have to that use which maximises their profitability, and this will be the use that also maximises the benefit to the community with whom they trade.

SKILLS

Let us now suppose that a new person moves into the village. He buys a house near the centre of the village and sets up shop as a bootmaker. Unfortunately, it turns out he has poor skills as a bootmaker, producing boots of poor quality, and few people want to buy them. He decides he doesn't have what it takes to be a good bootmaker and so turns his hand to being a blacksmith. He discovers he is a good blacksmith — the quality of the things he makes is very high and people are happy to buy them. He makes a good profit and satisfies the needs of the people in his community. This simple story illustrates that the point we just made about resources also applies to people's talents and abilities. In a system of voluntary exchange, people will put to use those *talents* which maximise their own profit, and these will be the abilities that maximise the benefit they render to the community as a whole. Summarising this line of thought, we can say, following Smith:

> In a system of free exchange between individuals, it will inevitably occur that resources and skills will be put to those uses which bring the maximum benefit to the community.

THE CREATION OF WEALTH IN A COMMUNITY

What factors are responsible for creating wealth in a community, whether that community be a small village or an entire nation? Obviously, there will be some factors over which people have no control. For example, whether a region receives high or low rainfall, has naturally fertile soil, or contains valuable minerals is something that is not subject to human control. Some factors that help to determine wealth are just due to nature and we can't do anything about them. But, given that nature has given us certain resources, what will determine the wealth of a community? Obviously, it will be determined by *how those resources are used*. But we have just seen that, in a system of free exchange, according to Smith, resources and abilities will be put to that use which most benefits the community as a whole. So, Smith concludes, the system of free exchange between individuals (or the 'free market'), via the operation of the 'invisible hand', is responsible for generating the wealth of nations.

SMITH ON THE ROLE OF THE 'DIVISION OF LABOUR' AND THE CREATION OF WEALTH

It is worth noting that although the operation of the 'invisible hand' in the free market plays a *conceptually* central role in Smith's account, it is not the factor to which he gives pride of place in his book. The factor which, in Smith's opinion, is responsible for the 'greatest improvement in the productive powers of labour [is] the division of labour'. In a famous discussion at the very beginning of *The Wealth of Nations*, Smith examines the manufacture of pins.[9] He points out that making pins involves many operations: drawing out wire, straightening it, cutting it, sharpening the end, making the head, and so on — all in all, he calculates, about eighteen distinct operations. In the pin making industry in Smith's day, where each man performed only one or two of these operations, he observed that a team of ten men could produce 48 000 pins a day, or about 4800 pins a day each. But, Smith said, if a single man, working by himself, tried to make pins he would be lucky to make twenty pins in a day, and may even be unable to make a single pin.

How can this be? If ten men can make 48 000 pins, why can't one man make about 4800? The answer, Smith said, lies in the division of labour. By dividing the process of pin making up into a number of simple steps, such as sharpening the point, each man is able to devote his energies to perfecting that operation, so with time he is able to perform that operation with much greater speed and skill than a person who tries to do everything. It is this division of labour, operating throughout all industries, which Smith saw as the greatest single factor in increasing output. He also included in this *mechanisation*, or the performing of very simple tasks by machines rather than humans. (Even in Smith's day mechanisation was a factor in increasing productivity.)

It is important to note that, although Smith gives the division of labour and mechanisation 'pride of place' in his book, these are *not* factors which exist independently of the mechanism of free exchange. On the contrary, they arise as *consequences* of it as they facilitate the creation of wealth in the community. A manufacturer who wishes to make a profit from selling pins will try to make them as cheaply as possible. Now, if he does *not* employ the method of division of labour but has, say, ten men each performing *all* of the operations, then (if Smith is correct) they could only hope to make somewhere between about 20 and 400 pins per day. Yet if they use division of labour, then the same number of men will produce about 48 000 pins per day. Either way, the employer is paying the wages of ten men, but it is very obvious that he will be able to sell pins much more cheaply if it takes the wages of ten men to make 48 000 rather than to make a few hundred. So, if the employer is going to get people of their own free will to voluntarily buy *his* pins, rather than those of his rivals, there will be a strong incentive on him to use the division of labour. The same remarks apply, of course, to mechanisation. The division of labour and mechanisation also lead to benefits for the general population, since they make available products that are much cheaper. The most important point is that division of labour and mechanisation are not factors independent of voluntary exchange and the 'invisible hand', they are a *consequence* of the competition that develops under free exchange and they increase the general welfare that is an unintended consequence of the efforts to make a profit.

Let us continue with our story of the imaginary village. Suppose that a pin manufacturer decides to set up business in this small village. Should the pin manufacturer use the division of labour to enable him to produce cheap pins? It would *seem* from the considerations just given that he should. However, we do not have to think about things for very long to see there is a problem. Our imaginary village contains, let us say, only twenty or thirty families: maybe a hundred or so people in all. A company making 48 000 pins a day would probably, in just a few days, supply the village with its entire pin needs for several centuries. So, it seems as though the pin manufacturer would have to conduct a much smaller operation if setting up in the village. Instead of employing ten people with each one performing one or two of the operations of pin making, it would seem much more sensible to employ just one person — or, more realistically, perhaps, making pins would be something the blacksmith could do as a sideline. *But*, if pin making was just something the blacksmith did 'as a sideline', pins would become vastly more expensive — there would be no division of labour and the vastly reduced costs it brings about. Assuming that labour is the bulk of the cost in pin production, pins would become (on Smith's own reckoning) at least 140 times more expensive, and perhaps as much as 4800 times as expensive as they would be if division of labour were employed.

THE ROLE OF TRANSPORT AND LARGE POPULATIONS IN CREATING WEALTH

The simple points just made illustrate a principle which is, if anything, even more important today than it was when Smith wrote. In a small village pins will be vastly more expensive than they would be in a big city where a pin manufacturer could reasonably hope to sell 48 000 pins a day. Of course there is nothing *special* about pins in this — it will be true of any manufactured item, the production of which will be cheapened by the division of labour. However, the division of labour will only be appropriate when there is a sufficient population. So, rather paradoxically, Smith concluded, *an increase in population will bring about an increase in welfare*, since it will make possible the division of labour, which produces a vast increase in the cheapness of goods.

Let us consider further the position of the pin maker considering setting up in the village. It *seems* there are two alternatives: either division of labour is used to supply cheap pins to the village (but then there will be a massive oversupply of pins) *or* a much smaller pin making operation is set up, which will result in vastly more expensive pins. But there is a third alternative. The pin manufacturer could set up the larger pin making factory in the village (which uses division of labour) and export his pins to other regions. By transporting the pins to other villages and towns throughout the countryside, the pin manufacturer may be able to reach enough people to sell all the pins. In this way the pin manufacturer would obtain much more profit than with a smaller pin making operation and the whole countryside (not just one village) gains the advantage of cheaper pins. The total welfare of the community (both the pin manufacturer and people in the surrounding countryside) is increased by the pin manufacturer 'exporting' his pins to other villages. It hardly needs to be said that this principle applies not just to pins, but to anything which, for one reason or another, can be produced more cheaply or of a higher quality in one region than in others. If each region concentrates on producing and exporting to other regions what, for one reason or another, they are best at producing, *not only do they maximise their own profits, they also maximise the benefits to those other regions*.

Obviously enough, one factor that will be necessary to facilitate trade between different regions is cheap and reliable transport. In Smith's day, the chief forms of transport were overland, by horse or ox, and by sea — Smith argued that sea travel was far cheaper.[10] Since cheap forms of transport are necessary for trade to take place between different regions, and since such trade is for the mutual benefit of all such regions, he argued that it is only to be expected that the wealthier regions of the world will be those which have easy access to sea travel. He pointed out that the wealthiest regions of the world — contemporary Europe and the cultures of Ancient Egypt, India and China, were for the most part coastal, or close to navigable rivers.[11] He also noted that the poorest parts of the then known world, such as Central Asia and Africa, did not have access to the sea or great rivers — in both those regions the great rivers were too far from each other to facilitate trade.[12] Smith saw trade as an important means of increasing wealth.

For Smith, the more people who were engaged in trade with each other, the better for all concerned. There are two main reasons for this. First, the larger the number of people available as potential customers, the more worthwhile it will be for a manufacturer to introduce the division of labour which makes products much cheaper. Secondly, the larger the number of people, and regions, that engage in trade with each other, the more skills and resources everybody will be in a position to benefit from. For example, suppose that because of the soil or climate of the village, it is almost impossible to grow fruit there. However, by trading with some distant region which is able to grow fruit well — by, for example, trading their cheap pins or good potatoes for fruit — they are able to add fruit to their diet. Or again, suppose that the only metal ore in the region of the village is iron, so that all their pots and pans must be made with iron, which is prone to rust. Copper makes much better pots and pans, but there is no copper ore in the region around the village. By trading with some distant region that does have copper, both regions benefit. The region with plentiful copper gains the benefit of say, high quality potatoes, while our village gains the benefit of copper pots and pans. Since voluntary exchange is a win–win situation, both regions are better off.

This leads to an important idea in Smith's work. Since free trade or voluntary exchange is a win–win situation, the more *other* regions that each region trades with, the more win–win situations each region will get into. Hence, the *more* other regions that each region trades with, the better off each region will be. The village will be better off if it trades with other villages in the region, the region will be better off if it trades with other regions in the country, and the country will be better off if it trades with other countries. The best situation, on Smith's view, is when everyone in the world is able to trade with anyone else. This will maximise the number of win–win situations everyone gets into, and so will maximise everyone's welfare.

SMITH ON TARIFFS AND 'PROTECTION'

There is one more aspect of Smith's thought that we need to consider. In Smith's day, and in our own, many people wanted tariffs to be placed on imports. The idea is simple and, according to its advocates, attractive. Suppose some other country can produce some thing (corn, for example) a lot more cheaply than we can. Should we import corn from this other country? If we do, then our own corn growers will be unable to sell their own corn; since the imported corn will be much cheaper everyone will choose to buy it instead of the locally grown sort. But it seems we should, if possible, avoid putting our own corn growers out of work. So what are we to do? Are we to import cheap corn and put local growers out of work, or should we get everybody to buy (expensive) local corn? There is, however, another option, and that is for the government to impose a tariff on the importation of corn. Let us suppose that Yland — the country that can grow corn very cheaply — can afford to sell corn to Xland for $1 per bag, but the growers in Xland can only grow corn for $1.50 per bag. So, the government of Xland says that Yland can sell its corn in Xland but that it will add an additional 50c to the price of each bag of corn — so that by the time it goes to sale in Xland it costs $1.50. This will mean that the corn growers will not be put out of a job — they will be able to 'compete' with the corn growers in Yland. Moreover, the government of Xland pockets for itself the 50c on each bag of corn sold in Xland — which of course, it is able to spend on the people in Xland to make up for the extra 50c they now pay on corn. So, not only are the jobs of the corn growers in Xland preserved, the government has more money to spend on the welfare of its people. So, on the face of it, it looks as though it is a good idea to impose 'tariffs' on the importation of goods that can be made much more cheaply. Yet Smith opposed it.[13] Here we will briefly look at Smith's reasons.

Smith's first reason is the fairly commonsense one that imposed tariffs also have an obvious bad effect for the people of Xland: corn becomes more expensive for them. Instead of being able to buy corn for $1 per bag, they now have to pay $1.50. In this respect the whole country is made (at least slightly) worse off so the corn growers can keep growing corn. But what about the argument that, by imposing tariffs, the corn growers can keep their jobs? Here Smith would say there are two alternatives open to Xland:

either (i) they can keep growing corn even though Yland can grow it considerably more cheaply;

or (ii) they can stop growing corn, and *switch to doing something else that they can do better* than Yland.

Smith would recommend that they adopt the second course of action. Suppose, for the sake of the argument, Xland can, because of its climate, grow *cotton* better than Yland. In Smith's own terminology, it has a 'natural advantage' in growing cotton. If the Xlanders who were previously growing corn switch to cotton, they can remain employed. Moreover, because Xland can grow cotton better than Yland, they can export their cotton to Yland and sell it at a profit. In this way wealth is brought back into Xland. Also, if the growers in Xland grow cotton better than they grow corn, the people in countries Xland *and* Yland now have the benefits of cheaper cotton. Finally, because there are no tariffs imposed on the importation of corn from Yland, the people in Xland will have cheaper corn, too. So, Smith believes option (ii) will have all the advantages of imposing tariffs yet none of the disadvantages, and so he believes it is the option that ought to be adopted.

This brings us to the end of our brief outline of Smith's views as explained in *The Wealth of Nations*. The reader is reminded that this is *only* the barest of outlines of a *very* long book.

SMITH'S IDEAS AND MODERN ECONOMIC RATIONALISM

One thing that will have struck the reader is how much of what Smith says has a bearing on recent and contemporary issues. Perhaps the most surprising point of similarity between what Smith says and some recent 'views' is that there is a sense in which he agrees 'greed is good'. It is, however, important to understand that Smith is not saying that greed — or to use his own term, 'self-interest' — is intrinsically good. Smith's own conception of moral right and wrong is pretty much the same as that held by the rest of us: he does *not* hold some inverted conception of morality (as did, perhaps, Friedrich Nietzsche) according to which what we normally regard as good should be seen as bad, and what we normally regard as bad should be seen as good.[14] It would be a mistake to think Smith adopted a Nietzschean view of morality. On the contrary, Smith saw sympathy, or fellow-feeling as the basis of morality. For Smith, self-interest is not *intrinsically* good, rather, it brings about the unintended good effect of the welfare of society. He says it is the *self-interest* of the butcher, baker and brewer that puts our dinner on the table. Self-interest, for Smith, is only 'good' in so far as, and because, it brings welfare to the whole community.

Another feature of Smith's work, which still has relevance today, is the importance of *competition*. If businesses are to be motivated to provide people with the best products they can, there must be other companies, selling similar products, with whom they are in competition. The existence of competition is necessary if the 'invisible hand' is to bring about an increase in the welfare of the general population. If the 'invisible hand' is to 'work', there must be, for any product, a *number* of companies making that product and competing with each other to make it as cheaply, and as well, as they can. The maintenance of competition, and the prevention of the formation of monopolies, is still a priority today.

A notion which is in common use today, and which had its origins in Smith, is that of 'natural advantage'. Smith said each producer, each village, each region, each country should search around for what it can produce better than anyone else. It may be better at producing something because of its climate, its soil, the minerals in the earth around it, or the skills and aptitudes of its people. If a region produces something better than any other region, it will be able to export that product to other regions, and so maximise its own profits, and the other regions have the benefit of getting access to the best product of that type. So everyone is better off.

For Smith, wealth is produced by trade. The more different villages, regions, and countries all trade with each other, the more wealth is produced for all who engage in that trade. Trade between different regions is to be encouraged: it is the mechanism that brings about an increase in everyone's welfare. An important consequence of this is that a natural measure of how much everyone's welfare is being increased is how much trade is going on. The more trade is going on, the more everyone's welfare is being increased; the less trade is going on, the less their welfare is being increased. That is, a natural measure of how much everyone's welfare in a country is being increased is *how much buying and selling is going on in that country*. (This is, of course, roughly what we now call gross domestic product, which is taken as a standard measure of the 'health of the economy'.[15])

Smith says the wealth of a community is enhanced by trade. The more *other* regions that each region trades with, the better each region would be. The situation that would most improve everyone's welfare, therefore, would be that in which each region in the world was able to engage in free exchange with every other region in the world. This is, of course, what we now call the 'global economy'. For Smith, like many modern day advocates of the free market, the global economy is a good thing, that will benefit everyone, and which should be welcomed and encouraged.

Finally, like modern economic rationalists and free market advocates, Smith was opposed to 'protectionism' by means of tariffs. Smith, and the modern advocates of the free market, both say that local industries should be forced to compete with rival industries in other countries. If they are unable to successfully compete, they should switch to some other activity, in which they have some 'natural advantage', and in which they are able to successfully compete.

THE CREATION AND MAXIMISATION OF WEALTH

Imagine two ponds of water side by side. We can increase the amount of water in one of the ponds by pumping it from the other pond, but this will of course have the effect of decreasing the amount of water in the other pond. We can't increase the amount of water in one pond without bringing about a corresponding decrease in the other. Of course, we can bring in water from some other source, but that will cause a decrease in the other source. The *total* amount of water will remain the same. Now it is tempting to think that *wealth* must behave similarly: that if one person becomes better off, it must be because someone else, or a number of other people, have become worse off. But Smith saw that this is not so. Unlike water, the total amount of wealth in the world can increase. This is made plain by our discussion of the small village in the previous section. Imagine two families, one of which specialises in the production of potatoes, and the other of which specialises in the production of cotton. The first has more than enough potatoes than it can eat by itself, but nothing with which to make clothes, blankets, and so on; the second has more than enough cotton, but no food. So, they voluntarily exchange a quantity of potatoes for a quantity of cotton. Obviously, both are better off as a result of this transaction: the welfare of both of them is increased. The total amount of cotton and potatoes in the world remains the same in the transaction, but the welfare of both groups is increased by the transaction. So, clearly enough, it is *not* the case that in any transaction in which one person becomes better off, another must become worse off.

Someone once defined dirt as matter in the wrong place. Whether or not this is a satisfactory definition of dirt, we can say it is *partly* (but not wholly) correct to define wealth as matter in the *right* place. Consider a body of fresh water deep in the Earth's crust, way down beyond the reach of our deepest wells, owned by nobody and accessible to nobody. It would be rather odd to describe this body of water as wealth. Yet if this water is somehow able to be transferred from deep in the Earth to a farmer's dam, we would now be quite happy to say it *is* wealth. No water has been created in this process: a body of water has just been transferred from one location to another. In this process some wealth has been created. In at least some cases it *is* true to say wealth is matter in the right place. (This is not necessarily true in all cases. Wealth can also be matter that has been transformed so that it becomes more useful in meeting human needs.)

Free exchange between individuals moves matter around: potatoes are exchanged for cotton, wool is exchanged for bricks and so on. In this process, all involved in the exchanges become better off, each individual person or group or country has its lot improved. Let us suppose this process of voluntary exchange were to go on indefinitely. It is tempting to think that eventually it would reach some ideal state, where everyone would be as well off as they could be. They would not, of course, be infinitely wealthy, but they would be as well off as they could be *given the initial resources present in nature*. If, for example, the soil had been more fertile, or contained more minerals, or there had been more rain and so on, they could have been better off. However, it seems plausible to think that if the system of free exchange is allowed to run its course then, given time, it will eventually produce the situation where things are arranged so that everyone is as well off as they can be with the 'initial' set of resources they have to go on. Similar remarks apply to *uses* to which resources are put in a society. Over time, we would expect the free market to gradually lead to that use of resources which maximises the profit to the user, and therefore also the welfare of the general population.

Finally, these same points also apply to people's talents and abilities. We previously considered the bootmaker who found he was better at being a blacksmith. In the free market, people come to use those of the skills and abilities they have which maximise their own profits, and so maximise the welfare they bring to society.

So, in summary, it appears as though we might expect the free market to lead us towards a state where the welfare of a country is maximised: resources will be used in the way most beneficial to society, and so will skills and abilities. So it seems as though, given time, *the operation of the free market should lead to a state of society in which everyone is as well off as they can be*. In the next chapter we will see that in neo-classical economics there is a mathematical proof that in certain circumstances this ideal state of affairs will in fact come about.

THE ROLE OF GOVERNMENT AND THE FREE MARKET

We have seen that, according to Smith, the free market, or the system of voluntary exchange between individuals, generates wealth. It is the mechanism which is responsible for 'the wealth of nations'. In the free market everyone goes about their business trying to make a profit. In doing so they bring about an increase in the welfare of society as a whole. What role is there in this for government? In this section we will look briefly at how Smith answered this question. The answer given by economic rationalists will be considered in the next chapter.

Smith himself, as we have already noted, believed that, in pursuing self-interest, a businessperson would often further the interests of society more effectively than when they really did intend to improve the welfare of society. He thought the welfare of society would be effectively advanced by letting the free market run and also opposed tariffs and protectionism. But Smith was not an opponent of all government activity. It is worth quoting what Smith said about the role of government or, as he called it, 'the sovereign'.

> [T]he sovereign has only three duties to attend to; three duties of great importance, indeed, but plain and intelligible to common understandings: first, the duty of protecting the society from the violence and invasion of other independent societies; secondly, the duty of protecting, as far as possible, every member of the society from the injustice or oppression of every other member of it, or the duty of establishing an exact administration of justice; and, thirdly, the duty of erecting and maintaining certain public works and certain public institutions, which it can never be for the interest of any individual, or small number of individuals, to erect and maintain; because the profit could never repay the expence [sic] to any individual or small number of individuals, though it may frequently do much more than repay it to a great society.[16]

The meaning of the first duty that Smith attributes to the government (or 'sovereign') is quite straightforward: it is to provide an army which protects the country from outside invasion. As we noted in the first chapter, this is something that *must* be provided by a government, if it is to be provided at all, since it would not be possible for a privately owned company to make a profit by running an army the object of which was to defend the country from attack. It is also clear what Smith had in mind by the second duty of government: it is to provide those institutions which protect people from crime and which punish criminals. These institutions include the police, the law courts and the prisons. We noted in the first chapter that it would be very difficult to make a profit from running a police force. The same could surely be said of law courts. So, these institutions must be run by governments, if we are to have them at all. The case of prisons, however, is a little different as the idea of a profit making prison is one that has some popularity nowadays.

What Smith had in mind with his third duty of government is less clear. The general idea seems to be the construction of those things which provide benefit to society as a whole, but which cannot be maintained by private individuals as profit making enterprises. Presumably, Smith would include in this category the example with which we began our discussion in the first chapter, the construction of lighthouses. He would also include the construction of drains, street lighting, sewage systems and bridges. More generally, Smith believed that governments should spend money on public works, particularly those which facilitated transport.[17]

It seems very reasonable to say that governments should concern themselves with the three duties described above. The three activities undoubtedly bring benefit to society, and, it seems, it is *only* governments that can provide those benefits. However, Smith also held that governments should *restrict* themselves to those three duties. More specifically, he held that governments should *refrain* from trying to control, or dictate to people, how they should use their skills and resources. In a brief but dense passage in *The Wealth of Nations*, he says:

> The statesman, who should attempt to direct private people in what manner they ought to employ their capital, would not only load himself with a most unnecessary attention, but assume an authority which could safely be trusted, not only to no single person, but to no council or senate whatever, and which would no-where be so dangerous as in the hands of a man who had folly and presumption enough to fancy himself fit to exercise it.[18]

Smith is saying at least five things in this brief passage.

1   It is not necessary for a 'statesman' to attempt to direct how the skills and resources of a society are to be used, since the free market will perform this task anyhow.

2   Any society which handed over to an individual statesman or ruler, or to a government, the role of doing this would be handing over a tremendous amount of power to that ruler.

3   It is beyond the capacities of any ruler or government to work out the best uses for the skills and abilities of an entire nation.

4   Any ruler or government which believed themselves to have the capacity to work out the best uses for the skills and abilities for an entire nation would be seriously deluded.

5   It would be especially dangerous for any nation to hand over such a tremendous degree of power to someone who was so seriously deluded. The conclusion Smith evidently draws is that nations should not hand over this power.

Claims 1 and 2 are surely uncontroversial.[19] The crucial claim implicit in the passage is claim 3, and it is worth saying a little more about it. Why should Smith believe it would be beyond the capacity of a ruler or government to work out the best uses for the resources of a society? Briefly, his reasons are as follows. In the free market resources and skills are used in the way that most benefits the general public. This happens 'automatically' in the free market: it is a consequence of the fact that in the free market exchanges are voluntary, and hence they are win–win exchanges in which all parties benefit. Yet could this outcome be ensured if there were, say, a group of public servants in Canberra who tried to get the same result? What would they have to do to get this result? They would have to look at each person and say, 'Well, Fred can contribute to the public good most by using his skills as a welder — so he should be a welder. The soil around Smithville can bring in more profit to its inhabitants, and more benefit to others, from growing rye than it can from growing anything else — so it should grow rye. The particular skills, abilities and resources available to the people of Brownsville mean that they should manufacture pottery ...' and so on and so forth. Would a group of bureaucrats in Canberra be able to do this? Almost certainly not. Just think of the amount of information they would need to do it. A lot more information would be needed than is gathered in a census. Presumably, you would need to know what subjects each person studied at school, what their IQ is, what their energy levels and interests are, and so on. It would also need to be supplemented with information about the resources available in each region. Moreover, it would need to be continually updated as people's needs changed.

Obviously, the expense of gathering all this information would be enormous. Moreover, all this information would need to be put together, and instructions given out from Canberra which ensured that every region in Australia had enough eggs, no region had too many tomatoes, everybody had enough access to garden furniture, and so on. Is it very likely that the bureaucrats in Canberra would be able to do a good job on this? Smith — and I suspect, most of us — would rather doubt that they could. However, the free market does seem to ensure that each region gets enough eggs, tomatoes and garden furniture. Smith believes the free market is likely to do a better job of ensuring the right goods are made and delivered to the right places than a government would. In fact, it seems likely that it would be quite beyond the capacities of a group of public servants in Canberra to do this — not because they are incompetent — but simply because the task is so *enormously* complicated. It is this line of thought which led Smith to believe that it is beyond the capacities of any ruler to work out the best uses for the skills and resources of a nation.

If we grant this claim, then claim 4, implicit in the passage quoted, plausibly follows. Since the task is so complicated, any ruler who thought they could do that job better than the free market would seriously over-estimate their own capacities. They would not have a realistic conception of what they could do. This in turn supports Smith's final claim: that we should be extremely reluctant to hand over to such a misguided person the enormous amount of power involved in telling everyone how they are to use their skills and resources. Governments should not, Smith concludes, try to take over from the free market this incredibly complex task. They should restrict themselves to providing an army, a set of institutions for implementing justice, and constructing those public works which benefit the community as a whole but which would not make a profit for a private company.

We can pursue this element in Smith's thought a little further. Suppose some society *did* hand over to its government the task of work-ing out the best uses for its skills and resources. Then, on Smith's view, two consequences would follow. First, the society would be handing over to the government a great deal of power. This power had previously been distributed throughout the whole of society, but now it would all be concentrated in the government. Second, the government would not be able to do the job of finding the best uses for the skills and resources any-where near as well as the free market. But, in Smith's view, it is just this operation, carried out by the free market, that is responsible for generat-ing 'the wealth of nations'. Since this job would be carried out badly by a government, the nation would become poorer.

In summary, the two consequences of a nation handing over to the government the job of finding the best uses for its skills and resources would be that the general population would lose a lot of the power it for-mally had, and it would become poorer. To go down that path is to go down a path towards poverty and powerlessness. This strand of thought in Smith was developed into one of the most influential defences of the free market written in the 20th century: *The Road to Serfdom* by Friedrich von Hayek.[20] The ideas of von Hayek are often claimed by eco-nomic rationalists to give support to their claim that governments ought to reduce their own activities as much as possible, and leave as much as they can up to the free market. We consider the question of whether von Hayek's ideas really do support economic rationalism in chapter ten.

CONCLUDING REMARKS

In this chapter we have looked at a line of thought, developed by Adam Smith, which says that free exchange, or individuals and companies operating in the free market, is the mechanism which generates 'the

wealth of nations'. This is a much more effective and efficient mechanism for generating wealth than could be provided by governments.
Smith's ideas are an early statement of the core of the case for economic rationalism. The reader may or may not consider his arguments plausible, but even the most enthusiastic advocate of the free market would
probably not wish to maintain that the arguments presented in this
chapter amount to a *proof* of the superior efficiency of the free market.
One feature of neo-classical economics is that it does produce a mathematical proof that under certain, clearly defined conditions the free
market *will* maximise the welfare of a country. We now turn to a
non-mathematical, non-technical presentation of these key ideas of
neo-classical economics.

3

ECONOMIC RATIONALISM, EFFICIENCY AND THE FREE MARKET

In chapter one we defined economic rationalism as the doctrine that the primary role of government should be to maximise economic efficiency. In chapter two we briefly surveyed the main ideas of Adam Smith's *The Wealth of Nations*. For Smith, the operation of the free market leads, via the 'invisible hand', to an increase in general welfare. On the face of it, it is not clear how these two chapters tie up with each other, but the answer to this is quite simple. It can be shown that, under certain circumstances, the free market maximises economic efficiency. So, an economic rationalist who wishes to maximise economic efficiency will also advocate the free market; or more precisely, an economic rationalist will say *free markets should be maintained in those conditions which maximise economic efficiency*. This, of course, raises the question: just what are these special conditions that maximise economic efficiency? These special conditions are rather complicated, and one of the aims of this chapter is to spell out just what they are.

This chapter will consider the modern, or neo-classical, case for the thesis that the free market maximises economic efficiency. As it can be very difficult to keep track of just where the economic rationalists and their opponents agree and disagree, it will be useful to give an overall summary of the argument of this chapter before we plunge into the details.

THE FIRST FUNDAMENTAL THEOREM OF WELFARE ECONOMICS

At the core of the economic rationalist case for the free market is a theorem of economics. This theorem is known as the First Fundamental Theorem of Welfare Economics.[1] (The term 'welfare' here does not refer to social security benefits — it means, rather, well-being or wealth, in the sense in which, according to Smith, the *welfare* of both participants in a voluntary exchange is increased.) The *First Fundamental Theorem of Welfare Economics* says:

> Under certain special conditions, specifically conditions of *an ideal market*, the economic efficiency of a society is maximised.

From now on, we will refer to the First Fundamental Theorem of Welfare Economics simply as the *First Theorem*. We should observe here that to say that some thing is a theorem is to say it has been mathematically proved to be true; it does *not* mean more or less the same as 'theory'.[2] So, the First Theorem is something that has been *mathematically proved*. Therefore, it is something that is accepted by both economic rationalists and opponents of economic rationalism.

The First Theorem tells us that *if* the free market in a society is ideal, then the economic efficiency of the society will be maximised. Since economic rationalists say that maximising efficiency is what we should aim at, it might be thought that what economic rationalists say is that governments should ensure that the free market in a society is ideal. This is only true as a rough first approximation. The complicating factor here is that everybody, whether they oppose economic rationalism or accept it, agrees that it is not possible to get any free market to be 'ideal', in the sense we are concerned with here. So we can say both the advocates and opponents of economic rationalism agree that:

(1) if a free market were to be an 'ideal' state, then its economic efficiency would be maximised; but,

(2) it is not possible to ever achieve a perfectly ideal market.

If everyone accepts both (1) and (2), then where do their disagreements lie? One answer is this. Although economic rationalists concede it is not possible for a perfectly ideal market to exist, they nevertheless say it is possible for a society — perhaps with help from the government — to get *close to* an ideal market. Real economies can (or with government help can be made to) approximate ideal markets, say the rationalists. One reason for rejecting economic rationalism is scepticism about the idea that real economies do, or can be made to, approximate ideal markets; however, it is not the only possible reason. A person could accept that real economies can be made to approximate to ideal markets and also agree that this will maximise economic efficiency, and yet still reject economic rationalism for the simple reason that they may reject the idea that the primary role of government should be the maximisation of economic efficiency.

In this chapter we will start by looking at how the 'core' of the ideas of the First Theorem are already implicit in the ideas expounded by Adam Smith. We spend considerable time looking at the notions of *ideal markets* and *economic efficiency*. We do *not*, however, go through an actual proof of the First Theorem — it requires a detailed mathematical argument to do that. We will also very briefly consider the question of whether actual economies do, or can be made to, approximate ideal markets. However, our discussion of this question will be far from complete: this is very much a question for the experts and all we can hope to do is briefly survey some of the main issues.

However, one question we will not look at in this chapter is whether governments *ought* to be primarily concerned with maximising economic efficiency. This question is a moral question, or, at least, it is a question with a moral dimension. It is with this moral question that we will be concerned in the second part of this book.

THE BASIC IDEA OF THE FIRST THEOREM

Let us begin by considering the key ideas of the previous chapter. We imagined a village in which some people grew potatoes, some grew wheat, others were blacksmiths and so on. One family might start off growing oats but discover the soil is better suited for growing potatoes, so they switch to growing potatoes. This benefits the family because they maximise their own profits if they grow potatoes. It also benefits the public because they are now able to buy good potatoes instead of bad oats. One person may start off as a bootmaker but switch to being a blacksmith when he discovers his own skills are better suited to that occupation. This benefits both himself and his customers. We can imagine the village being in an ongoing process of finding out to which uses the soil and other resources around the village, as well as the abilities and skills of the people in the village, are best put. It is tempting to think that if this process were continued long enough the village would *eventually* find the way of using its resources and skills that was best. This best way of using the resources and skills would be best for each owner of those resources and for each possessor of skills, since it would enable them to maximise their own profits. It would also be best for people who *buy* those goods and services. This 'best way' of using the village's resources and skills would maximise the welfare of the possessors of the goods and services, and, by the 'invisible hand', it would maximise the welfare of their customers too. What the First Theorem basically says is that if it is an 'ideal market' the village will indeed arrive at this best way of using its resources and skills, and so maximise its own welfare. So, let us now examine this notion of an ideal market.

THE IDEAL MARKET

Ideal markets maximise welfare by ensuring that each producer makes the best products possible, as cheaply as they can. Obviously enough, one condition that must be met if our imaginary village is to be an ideal market is that there must be *competition*. Consider, for example, a bootmaker in the village. If he is the only bootmaker for many miles around, he may not be motivated to offer footwear for sale cheaply. If he knows people *must* come to him, he may feel free to charge excessive amounts for his boots. Neither will he be motivated to make boots as well as he can — he may feel he can get away with selling shoddy boots. Perhaps his own welfare would be maximised if he had no competition, but the welfare of his customers would not. So, there must be other bootmakers with whom he is in competition. The same applies, of course, to all other business activities: no one must have a *monopoly* in any area of production. Suppose the bootmaker were the only bootmaker in the district. Then he would have a degree of control over the price of his boots. He (probably) would sell the boots at a higher price than he would if he were in competition with other bootmakers and had to get the buying public to buy *his* boots rather than those of his competitors. He would be able, at least to some extent, to control the price of his boots.

In economic textbooks on perfect competition, the requirement that there be no monopolies is supplemented with the additional requirement that there be no oligopolies capable of controlling the price of what they make. A monopoly exists in some area of production if there is just one producer in that area. An *oligopoly* exists if there are only a few such producers. One concern is this. Suppose there were just two bootmakers in the village. Although both of them might be able to make a comfortable living each charging $50 for a pair of boots, they might form an agreement with each other to sell their boots for $150 a pair. That way they would both become much richer. There may, indeed, not even be an explicit agreement between the two bootmakers — they may both know it is in both their interests to keep boot prices at $150, and both do so without actually talking to each other about the matter. Again, although this would be good for the welfare of the bootmakers themselves, it would *not* be good for their customers. So, for there to be an ideal market, there must be no monopolies or oligopolies capable of controlling the price of what they sell. In the language of economists, there must not be any 'distortions' of price due to monopoly or oligopoly.[3] This enables us to state the first condition that must be met for an ideal market.

I There must be no distortions of price due to monopoly or oligopoly.

When we hear the word 'monopoly' we usually think of some large company or corporation — but monopolies do not have to be companies or corporations. Trade unions are a form of monopoly. A trade union, in effect, says to employers in a particular field, 'You must employ *our* members (and only our members), under certain conditions, or the whole union will go out on strike and you won't be able to run your business.' This means that a particular trade union — for example, a steel workers' trade union — is the only supplier of *labour* in the steel working industry. In effect, it has a monopoly on the supply of labour in the steel working industry. What this means, of course, is that the first requirement for an ideal market — that there be no monopolies — also means that there will be no trade unions. In an ideal market, trade unions would not exist.

Let us now move on to the second condition that must exist for an ideal market. Consider a family which grows corn. Suppose that, for some reason, a new method of growing corn becomes more economically viable than the old, traditional way. There is no guarantee that the family will switch to this new way of growing corn. They might not be bothered changing to the new way, or they might keep growing corn in the old way because it is a family tradition to do so. Or it may be that growing and harvesting corn in the old way is connected with many traditions and festivals in the area, and they do not wish to discard these traditions, or wish to preserve the connection they have with the way they actually grow corn. For a variety of reasons, they may be reluctant to give up the old methods even though they are less profitable than the new ones. (Of course, at least some of these reasons for sticking with the old methods need not be irrational, and in fact the connection that forms of work may traditionally have with other aspects of life is emphasised by some conservative critics of economic rationalism. We return to this in chapter ten.)

Whatever reasons the family may have for persevering with the traditional farming methods, it is clear that if people *are* to switch to the most efficient method of production, they must be *adaptable* or *flexible*. The welfare of society as a whole is maximised only if each producer makes that which they are able to make most efficiently. But this will require each producer to be flexible or adaptable enough to switch to whatever it is they can produce most efficiently. The more flexible or adaptable people are, the better are the chances that the welfare of society will be maximised. How adaptable must producers be in an ideal market? The answer is that they must be *infinitely adaptable*; that is, in an ideal market producers instantly switch to the most efficient way of making a given product. Of course in real life, no one can switch instantly to the most efficient mode of production — but recall, even the most enthusiastic advocates of economic rationalism agree that ideal markets are not possible in real societies. The most that they claim is that real societies either do, or can be made to, approximate them. So, the most that economic rationalists would say is that real economies can be *highly adaptable*. Nevertheless, it is a condition of ideal markets that economies be infinitely adaptable. So, we can state the second condition that must be met for an ideal market.

2   The market must be infinitely adaptable; that is, producers must instantly switch to the most efficient way of producing a given product.

We now move to the third condition necessary for an ideal market. Let's suppose there are two bootmakers in our village, making boots of identical quality. One bootmaker has a shop which is clearly visible, but he sells his boots at high price. The other bootmaker offers his boots for sale at a lower price, but since his shop is stuck out the back of another building, people do not know about his cheaper boots and so do not buy them from him. Obviously, the general population would be better off if they did buy their boots from the second boot-maker, but in order to do this they need to *know* that his boots are available at a cheaper price. More generally, the welfare of the population will be maximised only if people have full knowledge of the prices at which various goods are available. This enables us to state the third condition for an ideal market.

3   Knowledge of price must be freely accessible.

In considering the fourth condition that must be met for an ideal market, we need to look more closely at just how the 'invisible hand' brings about an increase in the general welfare. Consider our bootmaker selling footwear to the public. The bootmaker is motivated to make a profit for himself and in order to do this he must get people to buy his boots. One way he can get people to buy his boots is by supplying them with the type of boots that *they* want. But this is not the only possible way. Imagine a smooth and fast-talking salesman who was able to persuade people to buy the shoes that he (the salesman) wanted them to buy. A farmer might go into the bootmaker's shop intending to buy, say, waterproof boots, but the salesman manages to get the farmer to buy boots that really do not serve the farmer's interest at all. This obviously increases the bootmaker's welfare, but it does not increase the customer's welfare. If the 'invisible hand' is to increase the welfare of the general population, producers must sell to them what the public wants to buy, *not* what the producers would like them to buy: it must be *customer preferences* which determine what gets made and sold. This enables us to state the fourth condition that must be met for an ideal market.

4   The consumer is sovereign: that is, what gets made and sold is determined by consumer preferences.

Let us now consider the fifth condition for an ideal market. Our bootmaker will obviously require leather to do his job. Assuming he does not own his own animals, he will need someone to supply the leather to him. In order to be assured of a reliable supply of leather, he enters into a contract with, say, Farmer Brown, who agrees to supply him with one hide per week for the next five years. When the bootmaker first enters into this agreement Farmer Brown supplies high quality hides, but over the years, the quality of the hides Farmer Brown supplies decreases. The bootmaker would be able to make better boots, more profit for himself, and improve the welfare of his customers if he switched to another leather supplier. However, he is prevented from doing so by the *contract*. Here the existence of a contract is preventing the general welfare from being maximised. The effect, of course, would be the same if it was, say, government legislation that forced the bootmaker to get his leather from Farmer Brown, rather than the contract that the blacksmith and Farmer Brown had arranged between themselves. The fifth condition for an ideal market is, therefore:

5   There are no inefficiencies due to either contractual obligations or legislation.

If a number of bootmakers are competing against each other to sell their boots to the public, there will be pressure on them to make available to the public boots that are as good, and as cheap, as they can. The same applies for blacksmiths, wheat growers and others. So, if the 'invisible hand' is to ensure everything is made as cheaply and as well as possible, the production of *every* good and *every* service must be carried out by a company (or an individual) operating in the free market and competing against producers of similar products. Yet, of course, in our society, this is not so. In the first chapter we noted that there are some goods which, by their very nature, could not be provided by private companies trying to make a profit in the free market. These are the goods that have the properties of being non-excludible (that is, it is not possible to exclude people from using them) and non-rival (that is, one person's using the good does not prevent another from using the very same good). We noted that goods that have these properties are called *public goods*. Examples of public goods are lighthouses, footpaths, drains, roads and so on.

Since a private company could not make a profit supplying these goods, if we are to have them at all they must be supplied by governments. The money for these services does not come from customers who choose to pay for the government service rather than that offered by its rivals, rather, it comes from taxes, which people are compelled to pay, and will pay no matter what the quality of the service delivered. Therefore, the motivation to offer the service as cheaply and well as possible, which would be present if the service were offered by a private company, is absent when offered by a government organisation which will get its funding whether it offers a good service or not. Of course, this does not necessarily mean that government organisations *won't* offer a good service, but if they will get their funding whether they offer a good service or not, there is at least the possibility that they will be less motivated to provide a good service than those who depend for their money on successfully competing against others. The ideal market is, by definition, something which *assures* or *guarantees* that things are produced as cheaply and as well as possible. So, we must define an ideal market in such a way that it ensures that everything — all goods and all services — is provided by private companies competing against each other in the free market. In an ideal market there are no 'public goods' which must derive their funding from taxes. This is our sixth condition:

6   There are no public goods.

Like many of the conditions that must hold for there to be an ideal market, there is no question of the condition actually being met in reality. To remove all public goods would mean removing all roads (except tollways), drains, footpaths, public lighting and so on. No-one regards this as a serious possibility. Like many of the other conditions, economic rationalists see this as an ideal which may be approached, but which cannot be reached.

We now come to the seventh and last condition that must be met for an ideal market. This last condition is somewhat more complicated than the others and like many of the others it is not possible to achieve in practice. It probably also has less connection to 'common-sense' than any of the other conditions. This final condition is as follows:

7   There are no externalities.

An 'externality' has the following features.

1   It is a by-product — possibly quite unintended — of economic activity.
2   It is *either* good or bad: an externality is not a *neutral* thing.

3   Externalities, even the good externalities, are not bought and sold. If a person is the recipient of a good externality, that is their good luck; if they are the recipient of a bad externality, that is their bad luck.

When people talk about externalities, what they usually have in mind are negative or bad externalities. The most obvious bad externality is pollution. Suppose you live next to a tyre factory that pumps out a lot of smelly black soot. The black soot is a by-product of the tyre making process; it is a bad or negative thing and (obviously enough) it is not bought or sold — if the wind happens to be blowing in the wrong direction you will just get it dumped in your backyard. So the black soot is an externality. But not all externalities are bad: if you live next to a perfume factory pleasant odours might waft over from the factory and could be regarded as a positive externality.

Almost any industry will have a myriad of both positive and negative externalities associated with it. If I live next to a horse farm I may enjoy watching the horses running around in the paddock, but their whinnying in the early morning may wake me up. The sight of a wheat field waving in the wind may be beautiful, but the little bits of dust and hay that fly around in the air at harvest time may cause me to itch and sneeze. It may be very difficult to work out all the positive and negative externalities associated with an industry and in at least some cases, very difficult indeed to work out whether there are, on balance, more positive or negative ones.

As we observed above, the seventh condition for an ideal market is that there be no externalities. What is the point of including such an obviously false condition? It must be remembered here that the purpose of defining the notion of an ideal market is *not* to describe how actual economies really behave; it is to specify *the conditions which must be obtained if different companies, competing against each other and each adopting the most efficient means of making their own product, will result in a maximisation of general welfare*. It is not too difficult to see that if there *are* externalities, then this process might not result in the maximisation of general welfare. Consider a tyre factory competing against other tyre factories. There will be pressure on it to adopt the most efficient way of making tyres — that is, the way of making tyres that is cheapest and results in the best quality tyres. Now, it might be that the most efficient way of making tyres also is very polluting. If the company adopts this way of making tyres, then the general population will have the benefit of tyres that are cheap and good, but they will also suffer from severe pollution. Now, let us suppose that the second most efficient way of producing tyres is not polluting or only produces an inoffensive odour in small quantities. If the company were to adopt this second most efficient way of producing tyres, the public would have the disadvantage of having to pay more for their tyres (or they would be of lower quality), but they would have unpolluted air.

The important point is that if the pollution produced by the most efficient way of making tyres was very severe, or if the tyres were only slightly more expensive under the second most efficient way, then people might be better off with the slightly more expensive tyres and fresh air than they would be with cheap tyres and pollution. So, if there are negative externalities such as pollution, it cannot automatically be assumed that the community will be best off with the most efficient way of making tyres. There can only be an assurance that the most efficient way of making tyres — or any product — will also result in the maximisation of the welfare of the community as a whole if it is assumed that there are no negative externalities.

Parallel remarks apply for positive externalities. Let us now assume that the *most* efficient way of making tyres does not produce any pollution: it produces no negative externalities, but neither does it produce any positive externalities. But suppose — rather fancifully — that the second most efficient way of producing tyres also produced a sweet smell that was pleasant to those living around the factory. It is conceivable, although of course rather improbable, that the total welfare of the community might be greater with the less efficient way of producing tyres together with the pleasant odour than it is with the most efficient way and no odour. So again we can only be sure that the most efficient way of producing tyres will result in the maximisation of community welfare if it is assumed that there are *no* positive externalities.

Whilst the idea that there should be a way of making tyres that is associated with a pleasant aroma is *not* very likely, it would be a mistake to think it is never the case that some less than maximally efficient means of production has so many positive externalities that the community is better of with it. Consider traditional farming techniques versus modern battery farms. Traditional 'mixed' farms were pleasant and picturesque places when compared to noisy, smelly battery farms which, of course, place animals under sometimes horrific conditions. The modern battery farms are more efficient producers of eggs, veal, bacon and so on, however, it is perhaps debatable whether the benefits to the community that come from having cheaper eggs and meat really do outweigh the benefits that come from a more pleasant rural environment with more expensive farm produce. (It should also be noted that, for example, in France it has been decided to preserve the traditional rural environment even though this means more expensive rural produce. A similar decision has been made in parts of Japan.) The more general point, though, is that so long as there are positive externalities, it cannot be assumed that the most efficient way of making a product will necessarily be the way that most benefits the community. Having different companies competing against each other, trying to maximise their own profits by adopting the most efficient way of making a product, will *necessarily* result in the maximisation of the general welfare *only* if there are no (positive or negative) externalities.

As we noted above, the idea that there might be no positive or negative externalities seems to be clearly false. But it has been suggested that it might be possible to remove the negative externalities by extending people's *property rights*.[4] The idea is this. Suppose the government gives Smith 'property rights' over the air in his backyard. This means Smith owns the quantity of air in his backyard while it is in his backyard, but when it flows over into Brown's yard it then becomes Brown's property. Now, suppose the tyre factory makes its tyres by a method that emits smelly, dirty soot, which fouls the air. If this soot flows into Smith's yard, then Smith can claim the tyre factory has violated his property rights by fouling *his* air. Smith would then be able to sue the tyre company for violating his property rights. What is the sensible thing for the tyre company to do in these conditions? If it wishes to avoid having to pay fines for violating Smith's property rights, and for violating the property rights of everyone else affected by the soot, it will stop making tyres by the method that produces the soot, switching instead to some non-polluting method which does not involve violating the property rights of others. So, by introducing certain property rights, it seems to be possible to remove negative externalities. Of course, the non-polluting method of making tyres might be more expensive, and so might result in more expensive tyres. But this need not mean that the welfare of society won't maximised with the more expensive way of making tyres: people might be better off with more expensive tyres and clean air.

In summary, it might be possible to remove negative externalities by introducing appropriate property rights.[5] Trying to achieve an ideal market can be, it seems, like trying to get a rug that is too big for its floor space to lie down flat: if we push down one bump, another comes up in a different spot. This completes our account of conditions that must be met for an ideal market. To summarise, we have mentioned seven conditions that must be met.[6]

1 There must be no distortions of price due to monopoly or oligopoly.
2 The market must be infinitely adaptable.
3 Knowledge of price must be freely accessible.
4 The consumer must be sovereign.

5 There must be no inefficiencies due to either contractual obligations or legislation.

6 There must be no public goods.

7 There must be no externalities.

Note that all seven of these conditions must be obtained for there to be an ideal market; if just one of them fails to be obtained, we do not have an ideal market. So, quite clearly, ideal markets are not possible, and as we noted at the start of this chapter, even the advocates of economic rationalism agree that they are not possible. What they do say, however, is that it is possible to get society *close* to an ideal market. We briefly look at whether it *is* possible to do this in a later section.

HOW IDEAL MARKETS MAXIMISE WELFARE (LEADING TO PARETO-OPTIMALITY)

The First Theorem says that if the markets of a society are ideal, then the welfare of that society will be at a maximum. We have just looked closely at the notion of an ideal market; now let us examine the idea of the maximisation of the welfare of a society. To say that the welfare of a society is maximised is not to say that everyone is infinitely wealthy. Rather, the idea is this: we can regard the amount of wealth a society is capable of creating as ultimately limited by what resources nature has provided. A society with access to abundant natural resources will, generally, be able to become wealthier than one that does not. It will also be limited by science and technology: a society with access to highly sophisticated science and technology will, generally, be able to create more wealth from its resources than one that does not. Roughly speaking, what the First Theorem tells us is that ideal markets will maximise the total amount of wealth it is possible to make from a given quantity of natural resources.

Why should this be so? The key idea here is one we have already encountered before: that voluntary exchanges between individuals are win–win situations. We now come to the core of the case for economic rationalism. It must be emphasised that the following is not a proof of the First Theorem. It is merely a highly informal exposition of the key idea of the proof.[7]

Imagine two companies, A and B. Company A builds houses, company B makes furniture. Initially, let us suppose, A makes houses out of pine wood and B makes furniture out of hardwood. But, let us suppose, pine is not very good for making houses. It is weak and so a lot of wood must be used. This makes the houses expensive. Moreover, they do not stand up well in storms. Company A would do better if it switched to making its houses out of hardwood.

Company B does make its furniture out of hardwood, but since it is very hard, it requires a lot of work to do all the carving and decoration that goes into making the furniture. Moreover, for the most part, it is not necessary to make furniture out of such strong wood. In the light of this, it might be thought sensible for A and B to simply exchange the wood they have: perhaps A should give B its pine and in exchange B gives A its hardwood. However, let us suppose things are not quite that simple and that the very best thing for A to do would be to use hardwood to make the main parts of their houses, but to use pine in a few special areas, such as those areas that do not need to be strong but need a lot of intricate carving. Similarly, let us suppose, the very best thing for B to do is to use mostly pine to make furniture, but also to use hardwood to do some special jobs, such as making the frames of couches.

So, let assume the two companies start to exchange wood. Company A gives some of its pine to B, and B gives some of its hardwood to A. We need not here concern ourselves with how they work out a rate of exchange: let us simply suppose they come to some mutually satisfactory arrangement whereby A gives X tonnes of pine and B gives Y tonnes of hardwood.

Initially, both companies will receive great benefit from these mutual exchanges. If A had just previously only been using pine to construct its houses, it will gain much from giving B a quantity of pine and receiving some hardwood in return. Likewise, B will benefit a great deal from getting the pine. How long will this process of exchange go on? It might be thought that it will go on until A has given all its pine to B and B has given all its hardwood to A, so that A is making its houses entirely out of hardwood and B is making its furniture entirely out of pine. But a moment's reflection is enough to assure us that this probably won't happen. Remember, the very best houses are those made mostly from hardwood, but with some pine, while the very best furniture is made mostly with pine but includes some hardwood. So, neither company will voluntarily go on making exchanges until they end up with just one type of wood. If the companies are making these exchanges voluntarily — and we are assuming they are — the exchanges will stop sometime before that point is reached. So the question arises, at precisely *which* point will the exchanges stop?

Here we need to go back to the fundamental point noted by Adam Smith: that voluntary exchanges are win–win situations. If they were not win–win situations then they would *not take place at all*. If one or both participants in a possible exchange were made worse off by that exchange then, provided it is purely voluntary, the exchange will simply not take place. (In voluntary exchanges we find 'it takes two to tango'.)

So, we have our two companies exchanging wood, but at what point will the exchanges stop? Plainly, *when one, or both, of the companies would be disadvantaged by any further exchanges.*

Let us summarise the situation between our two companies. Initially company A had only pine wood while company B had only hardwood. They then started to exchange wood. For vividness, let us suppose A sent a truck load to pine wood to B while B sent a truck load of hardwood to A. After this exchange had taken place, both companies were better off. They then exchanged another truck load. After this second exchange both companies were, again, better off. They kept exchanging truck loads, each time both companies becoming better off. This process of voluntary exchange will go on until at least one of the companies would have been made worse off by any further exchanges. At that point the exchanges will cease. In the jargon of economists, this point at which voluntary exchanges will cease is known as an 'equilibrium' point.

We now come to the core of this (informal) presentation of the argument for the First Theorem. The key idea is that when the two companies reach this equilibrium point, there is a sense in which the welfare of the two companies will be at a maximum. Suppose our two companies have reached the 'equilibrium' point. At this point, both A and B will have a certain quantity of pine, and a certain quantity of hardwood. There are only two ways it is possible to change this particular distribution: going back towards the initial situation where A had only pine and B had only hardwood, or 'forwards' towards the point where A would have only hardwood and B would have only pine. Clearly, if we went any distance at all in the 'backwards' direction, we would make both A and B worse off. This is a direct consequence of the fact that A and B got to the equilibrium position from the initial position by voluntary exchanges that made both of them better off. Therefore, going back in that direction would make both of them worse off. Could we, perhaps, make both of them better off by going 'forward' from the equilibrium position towards the situation where A only has hardwood and B only has pine? No, we could not. Remember that they stop at the equilibrium position *because* any further exchanges would start to make at least one of them worse off, and so we would not get both parties voluntarily agreeing to the exchange. Going further forward, therefore, might make *one* of the parties better off but it would have to make the other worse off. In summary, we can therefore say, once the two parties have reached the equilibrium position, any alteration to the distribution of wood that made one of the parties better off would make the other worse off. It is in this sense — that any alternative distribution that made one of them better off would make the other worse off — that the equilibrium point maximises the welfare of both companies. This is the core of the idea behind the proof of the First Theorem.

It is now appropriate to introduce some terminology. We have just seen that there is a sense in which free exchange between two companies will maximise the welfare of both of them. It will lead to an allocation of the resources between them that is in a sense 'optimal'. Economists have a special name for this particular type of optimality. It is called 'Pareto-optimality' because it was first formulated by the Italian economist Vilfredo Pareto (1848–1923). We can define Pareto-optimality as follows:

An allocation of the resources of a society is *Pareto-optimal* if and only if any alternative distribution that makes someone better off would make at least one other person worse off.

It seems reasonable to say that if the allocation of resources in a society is Pareto-optimal, then there is a sense in which the welfare of that society is at a maximum. Sometimes economics textbooks do not refer to this as a definition of maximum welfare, but as a definition of *efficiency*. This might seem puzzling, but it is actually quite easy to see why it can also be seen as a definition of efficiency. Imagine two cars: one can go 50 kilometres on 5 litres of petrol, the other can go 200 kilometres. We would have no hesitation in saying the second car was more efficient: it gives us more of what we want from a set quantity of petrol. Similarly, a Pareto-optimal allocation produces more welfare for society from a given quantity of resources than one that is not Pareto-optimal; it is a more efficient arrangement for producing wealth from a set quantity of resources. The definition of the maximisation of welfare we have just given can therefore be seen — and usually is seen — as a definition of the most *efficient* way of producing wealth from a set quantity of resources. It is normally seen as a definition of efficiency.

It is *Paretan efficiency*, or Pareto-optimality, that is maximised by the ideal markets. As we saw in our discussion of Company A and Company B, the voluntary exchanges between them will lead to an equilibrium point that is Pareto-optimal. We may therefore state the First Theorem quite succinctly as follows:

Ideal markets ensure Pareto-optimality.

We will not here give a mathematical proof of the correctness of this theorem. (That is something that is done in economics textbooks.) But we can persuade ourselves that, in the light of our discussion so far, the theorem seems plausible. In ideal markets, the producers of *all* goods and services are striving to find the most efficient way of making that which they sell to the public. All are subject to this pressure: there are no monopolies and there are no tax funded public goods. They are all technically capable of instantly switching to this most efficient means of production, and neither are they prevented by contracts or government regulations from doing so. Any information about price they require to switch to the most efficient means of production is readily available. So, in an ideal market, the type of change in the allocation of resources that occurred between companies A and B, and which resulted in everyone benefiting, will occur for the producers of *all* goods and services. So, it does seem fairly plausible that ideal markets should maximise the welfare of society — at least in the special sense of leading to Pareto-optimality.

ECONOMIC RATIONALISTS AND IDEAL MARKETS

As we have already noted, even the most enthusiastic advocate of economic rationalism agrees it is not possible for any actual society to achieve an ideal market. Instead, economic rationalists say we should move society *closer* to an ideal market. And in fact, almost all major economic policies of both the Howard Liberal government and the Keating Labour government were designed to do that. One condition that must be met for an ideal market is that there be no public goods — and therefore there must be no institutions offering some service to the public that are funded by taxpayers. So, one important economic rationalist strategy, to get society close to an ideal market, is to remove as many public goods as possible. An important means for doing this is *privatisation,* or the selling of publicly owned institutions to private individuals and privately owned companies. The idea, of course, is that by forcing such an institution to compete in the free market it will become more efficient. *Corporatisation* is the process whereby a government funded institution comes to be run more like a private, profit seeking company even though it may continue to gain some or even all of its funds from the government. The idea is that since private companies have been forced to be efficient in order to survive, they will have developed the most efficient way of doing things. When a publicly owned institution is corporatised, it adopts the efficient methods that were developed by private companies. In this way — so the theory goes — we can bring society closer to the maximum efficiency that would exist if there were *no* public goods, even while retaining some public goods.

Of course, not everything can be done by companies in the free market: in the first chapter we noted that, because of the assurance and free rider problems some jobs can only be done by governments. Yet even in those areas that *must* gain their funds from governments, it is still possible to partly move those activities closer to activities in the free market by 'outsourcing'. When a government funded organisation outsources, it pays a private company to do some job normally done by the government. In this way jobs can get done which could not be done without government funding, but the jobs are done by private companies who have learned how to do things more efficiently in the free market.

The first condition that must be met for an ideal market is that there be no monopolies or oligopolies. In Australia, we have an organisation — the Australian Competition and Consumer Commission (ACCC) — one aim of which is to ensure there are no monopolies. There are also laws designed to prevent monopolies from conducting 'predatory pricing', whereby a large, well established company temporarily lowers the price of its own products to such a point that a newcomer to the field cannot possibly compete and so goes out of business. Predatory pricing can maintain an existing monopoly and may enable the established company to charge a much higher price for its product in the long term.

We also noted that unions can be regarded as a type of monopoly on the provision of labour. So an economic rationalist government would tend to discourage unions. One radical way of moving society closer to an ideal market would be to outlaw trade unions, but another way, which can have something of the same effect, is to remove *compulsory* trade unionism. If it is not compulsory to be a member of a trade union, then individuals who are not members will be free to lower the wage at which they will work (to lower the 'price of their labour') in order to get a job. However, abolishing compulsory trade unionism does not enable maximum efficiency to be achieved if there is also a minimum wage. Consequently, a strict economic rationalist government would discourage minimum wages.

The second condition for an ideal market is that the market be infinitely adaptable: that is, that companies instantly switch to the most efficient means of production. One important way in which the adaptability of companies can be increased is *deregulation*, or the removal of government restrictions on what companies can and cannot do, and how they can do it. The idea is that by 'freeing up' companies from government rules and regulations they will be able to go directly to the most efficient way of producing their goods and services, rather than being held back by government rules determining what they do and how they do it. So deregulation enables society to come closer to meeting the requirement of infinite adaptability. It is obvious that deregulation also helps the fifth requirement — that there must be no inefficiencies due to contractual obligations or government legislation — to be met.

So, in summary, privatisation, corporatisation, acting against the formation of monopolies, outsourcing and deregulation are all strategies by means of which society is brought closer to an ideal market. And the First Theorem tells us that if a society becomes an ideal market, its welfare will be maximised, in the special sense of being Pareto-optimal. So, according to economic rationalists, by bringing society closer to an ideal market we are bringing society closer to the maximisation of its welfare.

EVALUATING THE CASE FOR ECONOMIC RATIONALISM

This completes our account of the *economic* case for economic rationalism. Does it establish that we ought to accept economic rationalism? There are, broadly speaking, two ways in which we might answer this question. One way is by looking at the economic side of the question. The First Theorem said that if a society is an ideal market then its welfare will be maximised. We have also noted that everyone, whether they are an economic rationalist or not, agrees it is not possible for society to be an ideal market. Where the economic rationalists disagree with the others is over the question of whether it is possible to get society *at least fairly close to* an ideal market. That is an *economic* issue. However, the question of whether a country ought to adopt economic rationalism also has a *non-economic* dimension. This can be brought out by observing that a person could agree with the economic rationalists that it is possible to get society close to an ideal market, and yet still maintain that we *should not* adopt economic rationalism. They may do this for a variety of reasons: they may believe that economic rationalism gives rise to a gap between the rich and the poor which they believe to be morally unacceptable; or they may believe that although economic rationalism leads to a maximisation of wealth, it does not lead to a 'balanced' life, but rather to a life in which there is too much emphasis on material possessions, or on work and 'getting on' to the detriment of other important aspects of life. They may be concerned that by itself it does not ensure each person in a society has a fair degree of access to medical or legal services, or to education, or they may believe that it will, in the long run, lead to the destruction of the natural environment. The point to note here is these are non-economic reasons for doubting the wisdom of going down the path of economic rationalism. We need not decide here and now if they are *good* reasons; all we need to observe is that there are also (possible) non-economic ways of criticising economic rationalism. The simple point is that it is possible to critically evaluate economic rationalism from either an economic or a non-economic perspective. Whilst the bulk of this book is concerned with non-economic critical evaluation, in the remainder of this chapter we will briefly look at some possible economic criticisms. It should be noted, however, that these economic questions are ones that are very much for the experts. We will only look very briefly at some of the main issues.

A BRIEF SURVEY OF THE ECONOMIC ASSUMPTIONS UNDERLYING ECONOMIC RATIONALISM

In our account of the First Theorem, we noted there are seven conditions that must be met if a market is to be ideal. Yet we also noted that there is good reason to believe that several of these conditions could never be met in actual markets. Here we will look in a little more detail at just why some of those conditions will not be met. In particular, we will focus on the first of these conditions, that there be no monopolies or oligopolies, and the fourth, that the consumer must be sovereign. We begin by discussing the requirement of no monopolies.

If you were a shopkeeper, would you welcome competition? Would you be pleased if someone opened up a shop near to yours, selling the very same type of thing that you did? Of course, you *might*. You could be the type of person who enjoys the 'battle' of competition. But there are also, obviously enough, reasons why you might not welcome competition. Perhaps the new person is very determined to get as many customers as possible and is prepared to work extremely long hours, paying themselves almost no money, in order to be able to offer goods for sale as cheaply as possible. At first you might say, 'Well, if this person is prepared to live very cheaply just to get a few more customers, good luck to them.' But suppose your rival is able to undercut your prices to such an extent that nearly everyone starts buying their goods at that shop. You would be faced with two choices: *either* start to live extremely modestly yourself, so you can offer prices as low as your rival, *or else* go out of business. Neither option is attractive, so not surprisingly, many companies do *not* welcome competition and will do their best to avoid getting into a state of competition.

A company is operating in an ideal market only if pressures from other companies compel it to sell its products as cheaply as possible. However, it is in the interests of a company to remove itself from this condition. By making a product even a little bit different from that of its competitors the absence of direct competition may enable the producer to charge a slightly higher price and to make slightly more profit. Consider toothpaste companies. There is perfect competition in the toothpaste industry if and only if there are many producers making exactly the same type of toothpaste. If they are all making the *same* type of toothpaste then the company that will do best will be the one that can supply it most cheaply to the buying populace. Of course, a toothpaste manufacturer may reason they can do better if they make their toothpaste a little different from their rivals' toothpaste. They might put 'special brighteners' in their toothpaste, or they might make some change that has nothing to do with the cleaning powers of the toothpaste, such as making it in bright colours, or putting glitter in it, believing that it will thereby make it more attractive to parents trying to get their children to brush their teeth. If a company is the only one making toothpaste with glitter in it, they will have a little more control over its price. At least until some other company starts putting glitter in *their* toothpaste, there will not exist the same degree of pressure to produce the glitter toothpaste as cheaply as possible. A tiny move away from an ideal market has been effected. However, this is not an important departure from an ideal market. It is fairly easy for other companies to put glitter in their toothpaste, too. Moreover, they will put glitter in their toothpaste if they see the other company is making a lot of money. In this particular case, the operation of competition between the rival toothpaste manufacturers will naturally tend to remove this departure from an ideal market. The market will, of its own accord, tend to return to its ideal state.

However, not all these departures from an ideal market will be of this character. With the glitter toothpaste, the departure from the ideal market set in train a course of events which ended up with the market returning to its ideal state — but this does not always happen. Sometimes an (initially quite tiny) departure from the ideal market might set in train a course of events which will have the effect of making that departure from the ideal market get bigger and bigger. One way such a change can occur is as follows. Suppose initially there are a number of manufacturers making more or less identical products. They might be, to stay with our previous example, toothpaste manufacturers all making more or less identical brands of toothpaste. All these different brands of toothpaste are, we will suppose, identical both in the sense that each one cleans teeth as well as the other and each one costs as much to buy as the other. Let us suppose, however, that for some reason or another, one of these brands sells slightly more than the others. This slight increase in sales might not have anything to do with the merits of that particular toothpaste; it *may* be because that brand is just a little bit better than the others, it may be due to clever advertising, or it may just be good luck. For our purpose it does not matter what causes this initial slight advantage.

Now let us suppose that this slight increase in sales enables this particular brand of toothpaste to employ a few more people, which in turn enables them to introduce some economies of scale, or other means of increasing their output that is not available to their competitors. Having done this, they are now able to offer their own toothpaste for sale at a lower price than their competitors. This in turn enables them to sell even more toothpaste than their competitors which in turn enables them to introduce still more economies of scale, to pay for research which enables them to improve the quality of their toothpaste, pay for more advertising, and so on. These things would enable them to get even further ahead of their competitors, which would enable them to introduce even more economies of scale, even more research, and so it continues. In this case, the tiny initial advantage set in train a course of events which caused that advantage to get bigger and bigger.

So, suppose that one company has a tiny advantage over its rivals in some way. What will happen as a result of this? Will the other companies tend to catch up so that an ideal market is restored, or will the first company tend to get further and further ahead? Economists disagree on what will generally happen. Some say the ideal market will tend to be restored, while others say the leading company will tend to get further and further ahead. There is some evidence to suggest that what will happen will depend on the nature of the industry involved. In the toothpaste industry it appears that what happens is that something *reasonably close* to an ideal market does seem to be maintained. The same is perhaps true in some agricultural industries. But in, for example, some aspects of the computer industry it does seem to be possible for a single company (such as Microsoft) to keep getting further and further ahead of its rivals. The point is: there is controversy amongst economists about whether a real society will exhibit a natural tendency to 'approximate to' an ideal market, or whether they will exhibit a natural tendency to move further and further away from it.

We noted before that there were good reasons why companies would want to avoid competition. One possible way of doing this is by simply growing so big that your rivals cannot compete with you; but this is not the only way. Two other ways are by 'taking over' your rivals, or by 'merging' with them. In recent years, both strategies have been used by some of the world's largest companies.

The above remarks show an interesting point about 'economic rationalism'. It seems to often be assumed by non-economists that an economic rationalist government would be the natural ally of big business. This is to some extent true: under economic rationalism money will tend to be directed away from wage and salary earners towards the already very wealthy, and for a variety of complex reasons intense competition itself tends to lead to the vast majority working harder for less, while a very small minority become astronomically wealthy. (We discuss these features of economic rationalism in more detail in a later chapter.) But despite all this, there is one respect in which an economic rationalist government will be a natural enemy of big business. We have just seen that companies will try to move away from the ideal market, towards a state in which they have at least some control over the price of their products. They will try to move from the 'ideal market' end of the spectrum in the direction of the 'monopoly' end of the spectrum. If a company does enjoy a monopoly, or is in an oligopoly, it will naturally resist any attempt to move it closer to the ideal market end of the spectrum. However, economic rationalists see ideal markets as best, so there will inevitably arise a tension between big business and an economic rationalist government, with big business trying to maintain any position of monopoly or oligopoly, while the government pushes in the opposite direction, towards the ideal market.

The fourth condition that must be met for an ideal market is that *the consumer be sovereign*. Roughly, this means the market must always be trying to give the consumer whatever the consumer wants. For example, the consumer might want clothes in a particular style. The role of clothing companies, then, would be to try to give the consumer whatever it is that he or she wants, such as clothes in a particular style. If the consumer is sovereign, then all that companies do is merely provide consumers with whatever it is that they want. They can't 'persuade' consumers to buy things they don't really want. So, if the consumer is sovereign, then the 'sequence' shown in Figure 3.1 holds.

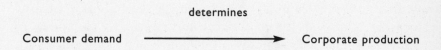

determines

Consumer demand ⟶ Corporate production

Figure 3.1

Just how sovereign is the consumer? This is controversial. In the 1960s, the noted economist John Galbraith argued that, far from consumer demand determining what corporations provide, things often happen the other way around.[8] That is, Galbraith claims that often what you get is the situation shown in Figure 3.2.

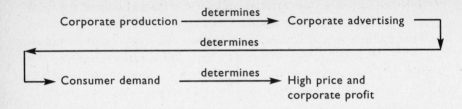

Figure 3.2

Galbraith calls this 'the revised sequence'. Essentially, what Galbraith says is this: suppose a big company like Ford or General Motors decides to bring out a new model of car. This will require the investment of many millions or even billions of dollars in research and development, the construction of new machinery, training of personnel and so on. The company will wish that the large amount of money it spends in this way is not wasted. So it engages in a very active advertising campaign to persuade people to buy the new car. Galbraith claims that big companies persuade people to buy their products; they *create* a demand for their products. This is quite different from the 'consumer is sovereign' view which sees companies merely giving people what they 'already want'.

Although many economists feel that Galbraith may have overestimated the extent to which big companies can create a demand for their products, or underestimated the extent to which new products may be based on 'market research', it seems to be generally acknowledged that there is at least some truth in what he says. How serious a departure from an ideal market is this? It should be noted that, according to Galbraith, it is *large* companies that are able to create a demand for their own products. So, if goods and services are mostly provided by large companies, then perhaps the phenomenon to which he draws our attention does constitute a tendency for markets to seriously depart from the ideal state. Yet as we have just noted, economists are divided on the question of whether the market will naturally tend to preserve many companies of more or less equal size, competing against each other, or whether it will naturally tend towards oligopoly and monopoly. So it is perhaps uncertain to what extent markets will produce a situation of the type envisioned by Galbraith in which demand is *created*.

SUMMARY

Let us now summarise the main points of this chapter. In this chapter we have used two technical notions: the notions of Pareto-optimality and the ideal market. Pareto-optimality is a precise concept, which describes the state of a society in which, in one sense, everyone is as well off as can be. A society is in a Pareto-optimal state if and only if it is not possible to make a member of that society better off without making at least one other member worse off. There is, therefore, a sense in which a Pareto-optimal state cannot be improved upon. We have also used the First Fundamental Theorem of Welfare Economics, which states that:

Ideal markets ensure Pareto-optimality.

More informally, the First Theorem states that if the markets in a society are ideal, then society as a whole will be as well off as it can be. It is important to understand that this is a *theorem* (something that can be proved mathematically), not a *theory* (a 'conjecture').

Everyone, whether they advocate economic rationalism or not, agrees that it is never possible to get the markets in any actual society to be ideal. It can't be done. But economic rationalists think it is possible to get society *so close* to an ideal market that the society will therefore be brought close to the state of Pareto-optimality. Economic rationalist policies — such as deregulation, privatisation, outsourcing, elimination (or minimisation) of public goods, corporatisation, and the abolition of both the minimum wage and compulsory trade unionism — are all intended to have the effect of bringing society closer to that state of being an ideal market and hence closer to Pareto-optimality.

Should we adopt economic rationalism? We noted that there are, broadly speaking, two aspects to this question. These are the *economic* aspect and the *non-economic* aspect. The *economic* aspect of the question is: to what extent is it possible to get an actual economy to approximate an ideal market? This question is for the expert economists; in this chapter we only very briefly looked at some of the main issues involved. Even if it is decided that the economic rationalists are right and that it is possible for real economies to approximate ideal markets, other questions may still remain. It is entirely possible for a person to agree that society can get very close to an ideal market and also agree that this would lead to society being in a Pareto-optimal state, yet *disagree* that this is what society should aim for. They may do this for a variety of reasons, some of which we have already mentioned. They may agree that there is a sense in which Pareto-optimality maximises the *total* welfare of a society, but be concerned about the unequal way in which that wealth would be distributed, or they may be concerned about 'quality of life' issues, the 'stress levels' people may experience in a market as close as possible to ideal, the lack of job security, or the environmental effects of intense competition. These questions are not *purely* economic questions, although they may have an economic component. These *non-economic* aspects of the question: should we follow the path of economic rationalism? form the subject of the second part of this book. We will, in particular, focus on the ethical, or moral, aspects of the question. But first we must consider some fundamental questions concerning the nature of the relationship between the 'rational' and the 'ethical' or 'moral'.

PART TWO

THE ETHICAL CASE FOR ECONOMIC RATIONALISM

4

RATIONALITY AND MORALITY

Many commentators have noted that the very name 'economic rationalism' seems to imply that its advocates are being rational about economic matters. It suggests that an 'economic rationalist' is simply a person who is advocating that we be rational when it comes to economics. Of course this in turn suggests that people who reject economic rationalism are saying we should not be rational: that we should, perhaps, be 'irrational' in the economic realm. But it is obvious that opponents of economic rationalism will not accept this way of describing things. I do not know of a single opponent of economic rationalism who has said, 'I think we ought to be irrational about economics.' The disagreement between economic rationalism and its opponents is not a disagreement between one group who wants to be rational and another group who wants to be irrational. Evidently, both sides think they are being rational. So, it is at best rather misleading for just one side of the debate to be called 'the rationalists'.[1] But more importantly, it is a substantive and important question whether those who call themselves economic rationalists really are the only ones being rational. One aim of this book is to consider whether or not they are. A place to begin this investigation is with an examination of the notion of rationality.

THE NOTION OF RATIONALITY

I once saw an expert on financial matters being interviewed on television. He was giving advice to young people. He said, among other things, that the *rational* thing for young people to do was to live at home with their parents for as long as possible. Living rent free, they could save up as much as possible for a house. This would minimise the amount of money they would have to borrow when buying a house, and therefore minimise the amount they would have to pay back to the bank. Now, I assume that not many would quarrel with the claim that the recommended course of action (living with one's parents for as long as possible) would result in a minimisation of the amount of money to be paid back. But does it necessarily follow that this is the *rational* thing for a young person to do? I think we would say, 'It depends.' Perhaps for some young people it is rational, whilst for others it is not. For some young people the benefits of, say, renting a flat with their girlfriend or boyfriend would outweigh the benefits of minimising the size of the loan that had to be repaid when they got around to buying a house of their own. These benefits may not necessarily be purely financial: they may simply find, all things considered, that their life is better living with their friend and for them this outweighs the benefit, that would come later in life, in paying off their home loan sooner. Such a course of action need not be 'irrational'.

Which course of action is rational for an individual to take will depend, in part, on what that individual *wants to achieve* and on *what they value*.[2] Suppose you are going on a holiday. Is it rational to take a longer, although more scenic and pleasant drive to your destination, or is it rational to take the shorter but less pleasant route? There is no 'right' answer to this question that is independent of the aims, values and preferences of individual holiday makers. If you like to look at scenery as you drive, and are not particularly concerned about having a little less time at your destination, then it may be rational to choose the scenic but longer route. But if you could not care less about scenery, and want above all to maximise the amount of time spent at your destination, it may be rational to choose the shorter but less pleasant route. *What is rational for you to choose will depend upon your aims, your values, or your desires.*

Although the above point is quite elementary it is often resisted.[3] Sometimes people think that the notion of rationality is somehow being 'degraded' if it is said that values and desires enter into rationality. It is important here to distinguish between rationality of action and rationality of belief. When we are concerned with *rationality of action*, we ask: what is the rational thing *to do*? What is the rational course of action to adopt? The course of action that is rational to take will depend on our aims, and on our values and desires. (The rational course of action for me to adopt may be to go by the long route if I value beautiful scenery, but to go by the short route if I do not.) If we are concerned with *rationality of belief*, we are concerned with the question: what is the rational thing for me to believe? It is much less clear whether the rational thing to believe depends on your aims, values and desires. Indeed, many thinkers (although not all) say that what is rational to believe is quite independent of a person's aims, values and desires.[4] What they mean is this. Suppose a person fervently wishes that the weather will be fine tomorrow — they may be holding a picnic, and rainy weather would ruin the picnic. We can say they want or desire fine weather tomorrow, but this has no bearing at all on whether it is rational for them to believe it will not rain tomorrow. It is rational for them to believe it will rain tomorrow if the *evidence* indicates it will rain tomorrow. This evidence might include, for example, the forecast from the bureau of meteorology, satellite photographs of the region and so on. Rationality of belief depends upon evidence, and generally it is thought that what you value, aim for, or desire is independent of what is rational to believe is so. (It might, unfortunately, be that what is rational for you to believe is the case is the precise opposite of what you would wish to be the case.)

So, in summary, it is important to distinguish between rationality of belief and rationality of action. The *course of action* that is rational for a person to take will depend on what they want or value. But what *belief* is rational for a person to adopt will not, at least in general, depend upon what they want or value; rather, it will depend upon what the evidence available to them indicates is true.

RATIONALITY OF ACTION

Let us look more closely at the notion of rationality of action. This notion comes into play when we ask ourselves: what is the rational *thing to do*? Consider, for example, a woman buying a car with $20 000 to spend. She will, ideally, want a car that can do a wide variety of things: tow her caravan, go 'off road', be reasonably cheap to run, not be prone to rusting, look good and so on. As we observed in the first chapter, the rational course of action for her to take will be to buy that car which gives her the maximum number of the good things she wants in a car (or, if some things are more important than others, the maximum number of important things). More generally, we can say it is rational for a person to adopt that course of action which will maximise the quantity of things that they want, or are of value to that person. Let's now apply this idea to economic rationalism. It is easy to see that it certainly *appears* to be rational in this sense. Economic rationalists say that we should get society as close as we can to an ideal market because in that way *the total welfare that can be generated from the set quantity of resources available to society will be maximised*. Obviously enough, wealth is something that we want, so, by adopting economic rationalism we can maximise the amount we get of something we want. Economic rationalism therefore certainly appears to fulfil the definition of rationality. No wonder it is called 'economic rationalism'. It seems to be undeniable that it is rational.

RATIONALITY AND DECISIONS AFFECTING MANY PEOPLE

Unfortunately, things are not that simple, as shown by the following imaginary example. Let us suppose that some parents, who we will call Rob and Chris, have two children. Rob and Chris are not very well off and cannot afford to give their children any Christmas presents. At this point a rich but eccentric uncle makes them a rather unusual offer. 'I know that you cannot afford to give your children any Christmas presents. So *I* will supply them with presents. *But I will give you two, and only, two options.* The first option is that I give both of your children three presents each, so between them they get a total of six presents. The second option is that I give one of your children four presents and the other ten presents. That way they get a total of fourteen presents between them. Now, I know what you are thinking. "Let's take the second option of fourteen presents, that way we can divide the presents up evenly and give each one seven presents." But, believe me, if I find out that you have done that I will take all the presents away. Would the children like that? And I can assure you, I have my ways of finding out if you have divided them up evenly. So, you have only two options. Which one will it be?'

Rob and Chris decide to discuss the offer their rich uncle has made them. Since they are unable to provide their children with *any* presents themselves, they agree that they should accept *one* of their uncle's offers; but they disagree about which option they should accept. Here is what they said.

ROB   Well, I think it is clear that we should go for the second option. That way the two kids get between them fourteen presents. That's a lot more than six presents. Also, each one of them is better off with the second option. Let's just suppose, for the sake of the discussion, that if we go for the second option we will give Kim ten presents and Alex four. Both of them will be better off than they would have been if we had chosen the first option. Alex will have four presents instead of three, so Alex is better off in the second option, and Kim has ten presents instead off three, so Kim is better off, too. They are both better off with the second option. So, I think it's clear *that* is the option we should choose.

CHRIS I understand all that, but I'm not so sure we should accept the second option. Look at some of the consequences that would follow from that option. One of our children — Kim, for the sake of the argument — would then have a lot more toys than the other. That might create envy and cause fighting. Alex might want to know *why* Kim was given so many more presents. How would we explain it in a way that would make Alex feel better? Alex might even come to feel less loved than Kim. I'm sure you would not want that.

ROB No, of course not. But we can always make it clear that we love Alex just as much as we love Kim. We could make it up to Alex in other ways, perhaps. That should not be too difficult. I think it should be possible to do the right thing by our kids this Christmas — make sure they get the maximum number of toys that we can — and still ensure both of them are equally loved. That's what we should try to do.

CHRIS I'm not convinced. There is another aspect to this that you are not considering. It is simply *not fair* that one of our children should get a whole lot more presents than the other. If we accept the first option, they will each get the same number of presents — and that's *fair*. I think we should treat our children fairly, don't you?

ROB Well, I think it is important to do what is best for them, and I think the second option is what is best for them. But about fairness. Life isn't fair, and I don't think we do them any favours by bringing them up to believe that it is always fair. They have got to learn to live in the real world. I think that teaching them life isn't fair is a valuable lesson. If they go through life thinking it is, they'll just be steamrolled. We should make it clear that, although one of them got more presents than the other, we love both of them equally. We can just explain that our uncle made us this offer, and that if we give them an equal number of presents, then they won't have any presents, because our uncle said he would take them away. Our kids will understand that. How would *you* explain it to them if they later found out that they could have had fourteen toys instead of just six?

CHRIS Well, I would just explain to them that we thought it more important we should treat them both equally; we wanted to be sure that they both felt equally loved. Knowing you are loved is more important than having a lot of toys. And as for the lesson that life is not always fair, I think there are other ways of teaching them that without being unfair to them ourselves; and in any case, Christmas would be a very callous time to try to teach them that lesson.

We will leave our discussion between Rob and Chris there. Some people might find themselves more in sympathy with Chris, others with Rob. But here we are not concerned with the question: which one of them is *actually right*? Instead, let us ask the question: is one of them being clearly irrational? The answer to this question is, 'No'. Both parents are defending their point of view with reasoned arguments. Each one presents reasons for their own point of view, and responds with suitable arguments against the reasons provided by the other. Although we might disagree with one of them — or perhaps even with both of them — neither is being clearly irrational.

In the case we have imagined, the parents need to decide how the presents will be given to their two children. It is because *more than one* child is involved that the problems arise. Let us suppose that, instead of having two children, they had only one. Again, they were not able to buy any Christmas presents, and their rich uncle offered to help them out. He offered them two options: he would either supply them with *six* Christmas presents for their child, or with *fourteen*. It is natural to suppose that if they were offered such a strange choice there must be some kind of a catch — perhaps the six presents would be of a lot more value than the fourteen. But the uncle assures them there is no such 'catch'. All the presents are equally good, it's just that on the first option their child gets six of them and on the second they get fourteen. Of course, Rob and Chris *might* be worried that their child could be spoilt by receiving fourteen presents, but let us assume that actually they have no such worries. In such a case it seems perfectly clear that the rational thing to do is to choose the option of fourteen presents. If decisions are being made which involve the welfare of only one person, it seems very clear that the rational thing to do is to choose the option that results the maximisation of that person's welfare, or in the maximum number of their wants or desires being satisfied. However, if more than one person is involved, things become much less clear and it is much more controversial what the rational course of action is.

Earlier in this chapter we said that a course of action was rational for a person if it maximised the number of values, or desires, that could be satisfied by the outlay of a set quantity of resources. This definition of rationality is fine for an individual making decisions on their own behalf. (As when a person decides what car to buy.) It also works well enough if a person or group of people are making decisions on behalf of *one other person*. (As when Rob and Chris made a decision on behalf of just one child.) But it is much less clear that it is a satisfactory definition of rationality if a person or group is making a decision on *behalf of more than one person*.[5] When decisions affecting more than one person are being made, a whole new set of considerations comes into play which were simply irrelevant when the decision only concerned one person. Is a particular course of action fair to all affected by it? If some course of action is not fair, will it lead to conflict? Will it lead to resentment? Suppose the course of action that maximises the total welfare of those affected by the decision is also unfair: how are we to weigh up its unfairness against the fact that it does *maximise total welfare*? These questions simply do not arise when a course of action affects only a single individual, but they do arise if many people are affected by a decision. The important point is that the *concept of rationality*, which is perfectly acceptable for decisions affecting a single individual, is much less obviously satisfactory for decisions affecting groups.

RATIONALITY AND ECONOMIC RATIONALISM

These points clearly are relevant if we consider the question: is economic rationalism really rational? Economic rationalists recommend that we should try to get society as close as possible to an ideal market, because that way there is a sense in which the *total* welfare of the society will be maximised. (In this sense, economic efficiency is maximised.) We saw in the previous chapter that to what extent it is possible to get an actual society close to perfect competition is a controversial topic. Let us, for the sake of discussion, grant to the economic rationalist that it is possible to get society close to an ideal market, and therefore that it is also possible to get society (close to) maximum wealth. Does it follow that this is the rational thing to do? Obviously, the decision to adopt the path of economic rationalism is a decision which affects many people. It is said it will maximise the total wealth in the whole community (in something the same way the second option that the rich uncle offered to Rob and Chris maximised the total number of presents their children would receive), but even economic rationalists themselves agree that this wealth will not be equally distributed. It is an empirical fact that as societies get closer to ideal markets the gap between the rich and the poor tends to increase, even if the poor may become better off. So, as we saw in the imaginary case with Rob and Chris, a whole new set of considerations come into play when we want to know the rational decisions affecting a *number* of people. The conception of rationality which is perfectly appropriate for decisions affecting an *individual* (maximise the number of values or wants that can be satisfied from a set quantity of resources) is not so obviously satisfactory when considering whether or not to adopt economic rationalism.

It is appropriate at this point to discuss a possible misunderstanding that may come from our imaginary story about Rob and

Chris. As a matter of fact, nearly everyone to whom I have described this imaginary story has said that the right thing for Rob and Chris to do is to accept the offer in which both children get only three presents. It seems to be widely thought that not only is this the right option, but that it is *obviously* right and that any parent who did not choose it would be rather strange. Some people have concluded that this shows that it is similarly *obviously* right for governments to ensure that wealth is equally distributed throughout the community, even if this means that the total wealth is less, and even if everyone is worse off. But this does not follow, for the very simple reason that the nature of the obligations that parents have to their children may be very different from the obligations that a government has to its citizens. It may be, for example, that there is an obligation on parents to make decisions on behalf of their children because the children are not capable of making the best decisions for themselves, whereas the role of government is merely to maintain conditions which enable peaceable, law-abiding citizens to make their decisions and to be reasonably confident of the outcomes of those decisions. We cannot assume that the obligations of a government to its citizens are exactly the same as the obligations of parents to their children, and so we cannot assume it is *obviously* correct for governments to try to maximise equality.

However, this is not the point of the little story. The point of the story is that, when decisions are being made which affect a number of people, working out the right thing to do might not be a matter of just doing a few sums, but it can still be a rational process. When decisions affecting the welfare of a number of people are being made, issues arise which are not present when only a single person is involved. These issues involve fairness, justice, harmonious co-existence and the impact on the psychological conditions of those affected by the decision. Discussing *these* matters is not simply a matter of doing some maths and working out if there is some option that makes everyone better off, but neither does it mean that the discussion of the issues is irrational.

What the above observations show is that the idea that economic rationalists are simply being *rational* about economic matters is really very questionable. Economic rationalism *is* rational on a conception of rationality that applies to decisions affecting a single individual — or it would be rational if only one person were affected by economic rationalist policies. But, obviously enough, the decision to adopt economic rationalism is not a decision of that nature: it can affect millions. *So, it appears that economic rationalism may only be 'rational' according to an inappropriate conception of rationality.*

We noted in our discussion of Rob and Chris that when decisions are being made involving a number of people, issues arise that do not arise when only one person is affected. Several of the issues that arise concern the ethics or morality of the decisions. These issues concern notions such as fairness, equality, justice and 'deservingness'. A moral dimension arises when decisions are being made affecting a number of people. However, the notion of rationality suitable for making decisions affecting only a single individual (that of maximising the number of desires satisfied by a given quantity of resources) leaves out all of the issues in this moral dimension. It is not a *complete* conception of rationality *for decisions affecting groups*.

The aim of the second part of this book is to examine the moral dimension of the question: should we adopt economic rationalism? It should be noted that the book does not claim to be a *complete* discussion of the pros and cons of economic rationalism. In particular, it does not critically examine the economic claims of the rationalists. We must leave those discussions to the experts. But even if we agree, for the sake of the discussion, that the economic claims made by the rationalists are all correct, we can still appraise the ethical or moral aspects of the type of society that they are offering us.

It should be stressed that to introduce ethical or moral issues into the question: should we adopt economic rationalism? is *not* to be 'irrational'. It would be a mistake to think that a purely rational person asks only, 'Which course of action will result in the maximum number of desires being satisfied, or the maximum amount of wealth being created?' It would also be a mistake to think that a person who considers ethical issues is allowing 'emotion' or 'irrationality' to affect their thinking. Go back again to our discussion between Rob and Chris. Rob — who said they should choose the option of fourteen presents — has a belief about what would be best for their children. Rob's view might be right, but it may also be wrong. Chris had an alternative view which may also be right or wrong. Chris introduced certain considerations, and together Rob and Chris rationally discussed those considerations. What *would* have been irrational is if Rob had simply refused to discuss the considerations raised by Chris at all, and had simply said, 'We should go for the maximum number of presents, and that's that.' A similar situation exists in discussing economic rationalism. Ethical issues of fairness or justice arise when considering whether or not economic rationalism should be adopted. Now, some people might carefully consider these ethical and moral questions, and then decide that really they do not constitute a good argument against economic rationalism at all; they may decide that the best thing to do is to aim for ideal markets and Pareto-optimality.

Such a decision could be perfectly rational, but what would not be rational would be to simply ignore the ethical and moral arguments altogether, to not even think about them, but simply assert, 'We should go for ideal markets, and Pareto-optimality, and that's that.' It is not necessarily irrational to take the moral arguments into consideration, and to then reject them, but it is irrational to not take them into consideration at all.

5
UTILITARIANISM

Advocates of economic rationalism from neo-classical economics say we ought to do our best to get society as close as we can to an ideal market. They recommend that we do this because they believe that by doing so there is a sense in which the welfare of society will be maximised. Should we accept their advice? In the previous chapter we noted that there are many ways in which we can evaluate what the economic rationalist says. One way is by looking at the moral or ethical arguments for and against economic rationalism. We start that task in this chapter.

If ever there was a theory of the nature of moral right and wrong that seemed to be a 'natural supporter' of economic rationalism it would be the moral theory known as *utilitarianism*. The aim of this chapter is to look at an argument for economic rationalism from utilitarianism.

Briefly, utilitarianism is the theory that the morally best course of action is the one that brings about 'the greatest happiness for the greatest number'. The argument for the moral correctness of economic rationalism is that it (allegedly) brings about the greatest happiness for the greatest number. It is useful for our purposes to represent this argument as follows:

PREMISE 1   That course of action which brings about the greatest happiness for the greatest number is the action which is morally correct (the Principle of Utilitarianism).

PREMISE 2   Economic rationalism brings about the greatest happiness for the greatest number.

Therefore, economic rationalism is morally correct.

This argument is *valid*; that is, its conclusion follows logically from its premises. But, of course, that does not show that the conclusion is true. In order to show *that*, it is also necessary to show that the *premises* of the argument are true. Most of this chapter is taken up with a discussion of the arguments for and against the premises, but first we need to look briefly into the background of utilitarianism.

THE MORAL THEORY OF UTILITARIANISM

Although views of morality which exhibit some similarity to utilitarianism can be traced back to the Ancient Greeks (in particular, to the philosopher Epicurus (341–270BC))[1], the person who is generally considered to have first explicitly formulated this theory was the English philosopher Jeremy Bentham (1748–1832), who coined the term 'utilitarian' and also gave the formulation 'the greatest happiness for the greatest number'.[2] John Stuart Mill (1806–73) gained a wide audience for his development of utilitarian views.[3] Two prominent contemporary utilitarian philosophers are JJC Smart and Peter Singer.[4] (It should also be noted that none of these authors have given their approval to economic rationalism.)

Let us begin by considering the rough, intuitive case for utilitarianism. Suppose that you are serving on a local council and you have $300 000 of council money to spend. You want to know what the morally right thing to do is. Obviously, it would not be *morally* right to spend it on yourself, even if you could get away with it. You should spend it on the community. Let us suppose, for simplicity, there are two possible projects on which you could spend the money. You could spend it on a swimming pool or on a set of tennis courts, but there is not enough money to build both. Which one should you build? According to utilitarianism, the way to determine the answer to this question is to determine how much human happiness each of these courses of action will produce. Let us suppose surveys somehow show that if you build tennis courts, sixty people will be given 8 units of human happiness each, so the total amount of human happiness produced by building the tennis courts will be $60 \times 8 = 480$ units.[5] Suppose also that no-one will be made unhappy by building the tennis courts, so the *unhappiness* associated with the tennis courts is zero. The next thing for you to do would be to work out the happiness associated with the swimming pool. Suppose surveys show that one hundred people would be given 12 units of happiness each by the construction of the swimming pool. So the happiness associated with the construction of the pool would be $100 \times 12 = 1200$ units.

However, let us also suppose some people would be made unhappy by the existence of the pool. The sound of young children whooping and splashing and yelling would cause disturbance to nearby residents. Let us suppose eighty residents would each experience 5 units of unhappiness as a result of the construction of the pool. So the total unhappiness associated with the construction of the pool would be $80 \times 5 = 400$ units. Therefore, the *total* happiness that comes about with the pool (the happiness *minus* the unhappiness) is given by $1200 - 400 = 800$ units. So, even though the swimming pool has some unhappiness associated with it, the *total* happiness associated with it (800 units) is still greater than the total happiness associated with the tennis courts (480 units). So building the swimming pool brings about *the greatest happiness for the greatest number*, and so, from the point of view of the utilitarian, building the swimming pool is the morally right thing to do.[6]

The above paragraph illustrates what utilitarianism is; however, it is natural to protest that the utilitarian is making some rather unrealistic assumptions. In the above imaginary example, we assign *actual numbers* to the quantities of happiness and unhappiness associated with various courses of action, yet in real life we cannot do this; we cannot say, for example, that someone will be caused to experience five units of unhappiness as a result of the construction of a swimming pool. Doesn't this mean that, from a practical point of view, utilitarianism is quite useless as a means of deciding the morally right thing to do? Not necessarily. For the utilitarian, the morally right course of action is the one that produces the *greatest* happiness for the greatest number. We can perhaps know that a course of action produces the greatest happiness if it produces *more* happiness than the other options, and we may be able to know this without assigning actual numbers to the quantities of happiness or unhappiness. We may, for example, be quite confident that, on balance, more people will be made happier by the pool than the tennis courts even without being able to put exact numbers on it. If we are to say that one course of action clearly or obviously produces *more happiness* than the other then, for the utilitarian, that is enough to justify us in saying it is morally right. Assigning numbers to it, as we did in the example given above, helps us obtain a precise idea of just what the expression 'greatest happiness for the greatest number' actually means.

This completes our outline of utilitarianism. Is it a satisfactory theory of the nature of moral right and wrong? Often, when people first have it explained to them, they say something like, 'Well, it sounds reasonable enough to me.' Actually, there are some quite serious problems with utilitarianism, but we will postpone our discussion of these issues until the final section of the chapter. For the moment, however, let us assume that it is acceptable as a theory of morality. The question we will consider now is: assuming the correctness of utilitarianism, is economic rationalism morally right? That is, does economic rationalism lead to the greatest happiness for the greatest number?'

DOES ECONOMIC RATIONALISM PRODUCE THE GREATEST HAPPINESS FOR THE GREATEST NUMBER?

Let us begin this section by closely examining the argument *for* the claim that economic rationalism produces the greatest happiness for the greatest number. Economic rationalists, we recall, believe that the aim of government policy should be to maximise economic efficiency. They believe the free market is an especially important device for doing this. According to the *First Fundamental Theorem of Welfare Economics*, the free market — or strictly speaking, the free market under ideal conditions — will bring about a state of Pareto-optimality. There is a sense in which, if an economy is in a state of Pareto-optimality, then it is operating with maximum efficiency, but in a state of Pareto-optimality there seems to be a sense in which the welfare of the community is maximised. This is because a community is defined to be in a state of Pareto-optimality if it is not possible to make someone in that community better off without making at least one other person worse off. So, the argument goes, the total welfare of a community as a whole is maximised in a state of Pareto-optimality. However, if the total welfare of a community will also be maximised then (it is plausible to think) the total human happiness in that community will also be maximised, and according to utilitarianism, the maximisation of human happiness is what is morally good. It might be helpful if we represent this rather long chain of argument as shown in figure 5.1.

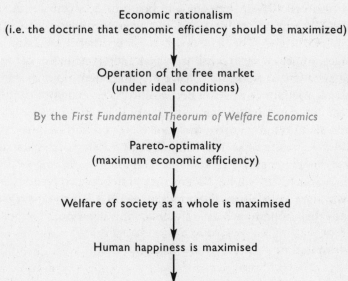

Economic rationalism
(i.e. the doctrine that economic efficiency should be maximized)

Operation of the free market
(under ideal conditions)

By the *First Fundamental Theorum of Welfare Economics*

Pareto-optimality
(maximum economic efficiency)

Welfare of society as a whole is maximised

Human happiness is maximised

Attainment of what is, according to utilitarianism, the morally best state of affairs

Figure 5.1

We are granting to the economic rationalist the claim that the markets in a society can be brought close to ideal, and therefore that the society can be brought close to a state of Pareto-optimality. The question we must consider is: will this result in the maximisation of human happiness? There is a very good reason to believe it will not, and the basic reason for this is simple. We have already noted that there is no reason to believe that a Pareto-optimal state will result in an equal distribution of the wealth in a society. Indeed, even the defenders of economic rationalism agree that it will tend to produce an *unequal* distribution. To say that a society is in a Pareto-optimal state is to say it is not possible to make one member of that society better off without making at least one other member worse off. Imagine a society that consists of billionaires and beggars. If any attempt to make a member of that society (such as a beggar) better off would necessarily make someone else (even a billionaire) worse off, *then the distribution of wealth in that society would be Pareto-optimal.* 'Pareto-optimality' can exist with great differences in wealth.

It might at this point be protested: surely it is *always* the case that making someone (such as a beggar) better off will make someone else (perhaps a billionaire) worse off; after all, the money for the beggar has got to come from *somewhere*. But this is not so. Remember Adam Smith's key idea: voluntary exchanges are win–win situations which improve the welfare of both participants. Both participants in a voluntary exchange are made better off. So, in a voluntary exchange one person is made better off *without* someone else being made worse off. A society gets into a Pareto-optimal state by, as it were, carrying out all possible win–win exchanges. The key point is: since there can be win–win exchanges, sometimes it *is* possible to make someone better off without making anyone else worse off. However, in a Pareto-optimal state, it is *not* possible to make one person better off without making someone else worse off. So, if in a society containing very rich and very poor people it is not possible to make any of the poor better off without making anyone else worse off, that society will *still be in a Pareto-optimal state.*

Now, let us imagine a very simple 'economy' consisting of just two people: A and B. (It will be evident that principles involved would still apply with larger economies.) Suppose that on a Pareto-optimal distribution in this economy we have the following situation:

A has $1 000 000

Distribution I

B has $100

So, the total wealth in this economy is $1 000 000 + $100 = $1 000 100. Since this is, by assumption, Pareto-optimal, any redistribution (say, from A to B) that makes B better off, will make A worse off. Let us consider such a possible redistribution:

A has $900 000

Distribution II

B has $100 000

Distribution II may or may not be Pareto-optimal. It is certainly *possible* for Distribution II to *not* be Pareto-optimal. The *total wealth* in the community in Distribution II is $900 000 + $100 000 = $1 000 000. Therefore, the total wealth in the community under Distribution II is *less* than the total wealth in Distribution I. But does it follow that the total amount of human happiness is greater under Distribution I? Plainly, it does not. There are a number of points that might be appropriate to make: that it is possible to be happier even if you have less money; that a poor person might be happier than a rich one, and so on. Even if it is granted that the more money a person has, the happier they will be, there is still good reason to believe that the *total happiness* will be greater under Distribution II than in Distribution I, even though there is less total wealth. To see this, let us consider the following: suppose that a billionaire and a battler are both given $10 000. If we assume that the more money a person has, the happier they will be, this will result in both the billionaire and the battler becoming happier. Now let us consider, realistically, by *how much* is the happiness of each of them likely to increase on being given the extra $10 000? The billionaire is likely to scarcely notice this (comparatively slight) increase in his wealth. We are assuming it will increase his happiness a little, but commonsense tells us it will probably only be increased by a fairly small amount. The battler, on the other hand is quite likely to be made *much* happier. Perhaps the extra $10 000 will enable him to feed his family properly for several months, or pay overdue rent and so prevent him and his family from being put out on the streets. Although both the billionaire and the battler receive $10 000, commonsense tells us this is likely to increase the happiness of the battler much more than that of the billionaire. This phenomenon is well known to economists and is an example of what is technically termed the *law of diminishing marginal utility*.[7]

In the light of this, let us consider the difference between distributions I and II. In Distribution I, B has only $100, in II he has

$100 000. So, in Distribution I, B is living in what we would regard as extreme poverty, while in II he is living in a fair degree of comfort. Commonsense tells us that B is likely to be a great deal happier in Distribution II than in I. On the other hand, A has $1 000 000 in Distribution I, and only $900 000 in II. Again, we are assuming that A will be less happy in II, but commonsense tells us that a person with only $900 000 is not likely to be immensely less happy than someone with $1 000 000. So, while B will be perhaps slightly less happy in II, A will be very much happier. So, the *total happiness* (of A and B combined) in Distribution II will (commonsense tells us) probably be greater than in Distribution I, *even though the total wealth is less.*

It is clear that these considerations reveal a flaw in the argument from utilitarianism to the conclusion that economic rationalism is morally best. Even if we agree that economic rationalism leads (close) to Pareto-optimality and hence (close) to the maximisation of the wealth in a community, it does not follow that human happiness will be maximised in the community. This is so even if it is accepted that more wealth means more happiness. Paradoxically, there can be more happiness in a community with less wealth, *even if* we accept that the more wealth a person has, the happier they will be.

There is another point that is worth noting here: the *greater* the difference between rich and poor, the more likely it will be that a more even distribution of wealth will produce greater happiness, even if it also produces less *total* wealth. If Smith initially has $100 000 and Jones initially has $130 000, then total happiness *may* be increased by redistributing wealth so that they both have $110 000. However, if Smith initially has $1 000 000 and Jones initially has only $100, then *almost certainly* total happiness would be increased if instead they both had $500 000. The more *unevenly* wealth is distributed, the less likely it will be that maximising wealth will also result in maximising happiness. So, the greater the gap that develops between rich and poor in a society, the less likely it becomes that the distribution of wealth can be given a utilitarian justification.

In summary, although it initially appeared that utilitarianism might provide a moral justification of the free market, it now appears more likely to provide a moral justification of governments taking steps to create a greater degree of equality of wealth than would come about under a free market. These considerations are, not surprisingly, very well known to economists. Some defenders of the free market have replied by calling into question some aspects of utilitarianism itself. Specifically, they have questioned whether it is possible to justify the claim that one distribution of wealth will bring more happiness to a community than another distribution. The difficulty they perceive lies in comparing one person's degree of happiness with that of another. (In the terminology of economists, this is the difficulty of 'interpersonal comparisons of utility'.) In order to accurately assess the degree of happiness of a group and compare it with that of another group, it appears we need to be able to literally compare the degrees of happiness of *different* people. But can we do this scientifically? Even if we do not demand that the degrees of happiness of different people be compared with *mathematical* precision, it is still unclear what entitles us to say that one person or one group has more happiness than another. Am I happier than my next door neighbour? How would I go about measuring or comparing our different degrees of happiness? Of course, it is possible to compare our incomes, the size of our houses, and so on. But how do we compare our *amounts of happiness*? Critics of utilitarianism say we cannot. We consider this type of criticism below in the section on evaluating utilitarianism.

ECONOMIC RATIONALISM AND THE 'BALANCED' LIFE

For most human beings, a good life is a *balanced* life. We can list the things that we think would go into making up a good life. Undoubtedly, one of the most important things would be certain material possessions: it is important to have a secure dwelling, food, shelter, heating, transport and so on. But obviously material possessions will not be the only thing that appear on the list. A full or satisfying life will have within it a certain amount of *productive* or *rewarding* work. But it will also have appropriate periods of leisure. It will contain time spent with friends and family; human relationships will occupy an important place. A balanced life will also contain a mix of intellectual and physical or sporting activities, and time spent on hobbies. It may also contain time devoted to culture and the Arts. Some other factors that will tend to make life better are security, freedom from stress, and a clean and healthy natural environment. Finally, for some people at least, it will also have 'meaning' — there will be time within it for religion or philosophy.

For most people, it is easiest to be happy if life contains some mix of these activities or aspects. A person who spends all their time working is likely to start longing for a rest or some leisure activity; but conversely a person who has nothing but spare time on their hands is likely to develop the desire to get involved in some kind of productive work, and so on. Of course, the right mix will vary from person to person: some people might be quite happy working seventeen hours every day, while others may find six hours a day to be plenty. Some people might only feel happy if they are constantly surrounded by other people; others may need far less frequent social contact. The right mix may vary from one person to another, but, for most us, *some* kind of mix or balance is necessary if we are to lead what we would regard as good or happy lives. Almost no-one would be happy living on an unrelieved diet of just one kind of activity.

Now, we have seen that there is very good reason to believe economic rationalism will lead to the maximisation of wealth for the society. Therefore, it may lead to maximisation of *material* well being — but will it lead to a *balanced* life? Will it tend to also give us those things on the list other than material possessions? It is not too difficult to see that there is *no guarantee* that it will provide us with those other things. Yet the situation is probably worse than that. *Pure economic rationalism would probably make it very hard for people to lead a balanced life.* We can see this if we remind ourselves again of the mechanism by which economic rationalists try to maximise efficiency. They do this by trying to ensure that the markets in society operate in ideal conditions. Let us recall what these ideal conditions would be like. One feature of the ideal market is that there are no public goods. This means that there would be no unemployment benefits, nor a minimum wage. Neither would there be trade unions, as these are a form of monopoly. There would not be any restrictions on when a person could or could not open their shop for business. In an ideal market, competition would be very intense competition: everybody would be doing the best they can to persuade customers to buy their products rather than those of their rivals. Obviously enough, under such conditions there would be a strong incentive to work as long and hard as you could: if one of your rivals were able to work harder and longer than you, then they might start to take away business from you — and you *must* do your very best to compete against your rivals because there would be no social security safety net to fall back on.

Of course, no government would find it politically possible to introduce an ideal market, and in chapter three we noted a range of other reasons why ideal markets are not possible. However, pure economic rationalism aims to get society as close as it can to an ideal market. Clearly, under conditions approaching ideality it would become harder to lead a balanced life. There seems to be good reason to believe that a greater and greater proportion of a person's time would be taken up with work. This would obviously make it harder to find the time or the energy to engage in leisure activities or sport. There would also be less time for the pursuit and cultivation of human relationships, or to take an active interest in the Arts or cultural matters. Under intense competition, with no safety net, levels of security will obviously be lower and levels of stress higher. There are also reasons why work would be a less intrinsically rewarding activity in an ideal market: obviously work is less likely to be a pleasure if you have to work very long hours, particularly under conditions of stress. Also, as Adam Smith noted, one important way of increasing output is the division of labour — but this can have the effect of making work boring and repetitive. Finally, and importantly, intense competition is likely to have negative consequences for the environment. Under intense competition, there is incentive for everyone to produce as efficiently as possible. One way of maximising efficiency is by growing larger than your competitors, since by doing that you can introduce more economies of scale. So all or most companies will be trying to grow as large as they can. Growth means more production, more consumption of natural resources and more pollution. Therefore intense competition will tend to lead away from a clean and unpolluted natural environment.

In summary, as society gets closer and closer to an ideal market it would become harder and harder to obtain those things *other than material possessions* that appeared on our list of what would make up a good, balanced life. It would be harder and harder to achieve a balanced life and, at least for most people, a balanced life is necessary for maximising happiness. So, the attempt to provide a justification of economic rationalism by appealing to utilitarianism seems to be flawed. Economic rationalism perhaps leads to a maximisation of material wealth in a community, but there seems to be good reason to believe that moving society closer to an ideal market would not lead to a maximisation of human happiness.

There is a natural response to this argument that is available to the economic rationalist. The argument just given claims that under economic rationalism it is harder for people to lead balanced lives. The argument asserts that a life might be better 'on balance' if less time were spent working and more time were spent on other things, even though this would mean less material wealth. But — so this response goes — in a free market, people are free to make whatever choices are in their own best interest. So, if a person really were better off earning less money but with more time for other things, then the person would choose that option. An economic rationalist might say that the fact that people do not choose that option, but continue to work hard shows that they would not be better off with a less wealthy but more balanced life. People will, in a free market, choose the option that maximises their own happiness.

However, it is not altogether clear that this reply is satisfactory. It assumes that it will always be an option *available* to people to choose less wealth but more time for other things. But perhaps it is not always an available option. It may be that a person is confronted with just two options: outperform your competitors or lose your job altogether. For example, a shopkeeper might have no choice but to stay open fourteen hours a day, offering goods for sale at the minimum possible price, or go out of business. An employee might have no choice but to do their very best to outperform their colleagues, or else be first on the list when the company needs to 'downsize'. The option of being without a job at all — particularly if social security is reduced or non-existent — may be worse than the option of working as hard as one can but not leading a balanced life. The option of having less wealth, but still having a satisfactory level of wealth while simultaneously having a more balanced life, might simply not be an option that is available. So, in summary, there is at least one serious reason to doubt whether economic rationalism would make possible a *balanced* life.

ECONOMIC RATIONALISM AND LEVELS OF HAPPINESS

In the previous two sections we looked at various reasons for believing that economic rationalism might not result in the maximisation of human happiness. The arguments of both sections appeal to commonsense principles such as: 'people are more likely to be happy if they can lead balanced lives', or 'a poor person is more likely to be made happier by an extra $100 than a billionaire would be'. There is nothing wrong with such arguments, provided they are constructed carefully and do not contain logical errors. But there is, of course, an entirely different method whereby we can attempt to evaluate the claim that by maximising the total wealth in a community, the economic rationalist can thereby also maximise the human happiness in that community. That other method is *empirical* rather than a priori. This way of determining whether total wealth makes people happier is by looking at *surveys* of the general population on matters relating to happiness. The aim of this section is to examine the results of such surveys.

A recent survey by the Dutch scholar Ruut Veenhoven compared different countries for levels of happiness.[8] The method used involved two steps: *first*, people were rated for 'subjectively felt' happiness by a range of psychological surveys; *second*, the measure of how happy people *felt* themselves to be was then multiplied by the average life expectancy for that country. So, for example, if in a given country most people reported that they subjectively felt themselves to have 'six units' of happiness when asked to rank themselves on a scale of 1 to 10, and if the average life expectancy in that country was seventy years, then the 'happiness rating' for that country would be $6 \times 70 = 420$. The idea was in this way to obtain a measure of how much 'total happiness' the average person in a given country was likely to experience.

In broad terms, the survey found that the developed Western nations were the happiest. However, among those nations, the most happy of all were not the free market economies, and not always the very wealthiest countries, but the social democratic countries of Sweden, the Netherlands and Iceland, with Iceland being the happiest country on Earth. It must be emphasised, however, that the experts remain uncertain just why these countries should be the happiest in the world, with one commentator remarking that 'any number of ... factors ... may ... have an impact on happiness ... and their proportional impact could be a matter for endless and inconclusive debate'.[9]

As we noted, Veenhoven's survey ranked countries for happiness by multiplying subjectively felt happiness by life expectancy. It is perhaps not particularly surprising that the developed Western countries should come out on top on such a measure, since their wealth makes possible high levels of medical care and public health systems, which in turn tends to allow people to lead longer lives. When we ignore life expectancy and concentrate solely on happiness as a subjectively felt experience, the picture becomes much more complicated, and in some respects extremely surprising. When the figures for subjective happiness are converted to percentages, the countries surveyed ranged from Iceland, with the highest figure of 85 per cent, to Moldova with only 59.8 per cent.[10] But consider the happiness ratings for the following three countries:

Bangladesh	75.0 per cent
France	74.5 per cent
Italy	72.3 per cent

In other words, one of the poorest countries on Earth — Bangladesh — had a higher rating for happiness as a subjectively felt experience than the comparatively wealthy European countries of France and Italy. Similarly surprising results can be found in the

Americas, where Colombia and the United States had exactly the same rating of 82.5 per cent. (The same rating, incidentally, as Australia.) Colombia even scored more highly than Canada, which received 79.2 per cent. Some other examples of countries that scored well on subjective happiness while having only fairly modest standards of material wealth are: China (75 per cent), India (75 per cent) and Mexico (75.1 per cent). These results suggest that material wealth would seem to have very little necessary effect on happiness as a subjectively felt experience.

It has long been thought that a crucially important factor in producing happiness is *social stability*.[11] This is borne out if we turn our attention to the causes of *unhappiness* in countries. The ten *least happy* countries surveyed were Armenia (62.5 per cent), Belarus (63 per cent), Bulgaria (61 per cent), Estonia (65 per cent), Latvia (66 per cent), Moldova (59.75 per cent), Romania (65 per cent), Russia (61.5 per cent), Slovakia (62.5 per cent) and Ukraine (61 per cent). One obvious feature of this list is that all of these countries were either part of the former Soviet Union, or were formerly under Communist rule. Communism itself does not necessarily produce unhappiness, as shown by the moderately high rating of 75 per cent from China, suggesting that possibly it is radical change, or the *transition* from one system to another (fundamentally different) system that is the most significant producer of unhappiness.

In summary, the figures do not appear to support the idea that great material wealth is necessary for happiness as a subjectively felt experience. Considerable levels of happiness can exist in great poverty. The figures also seem to suggest that perhaps it is not the presence or absence of wealth, or the presence or absence of any one political system, but *preservation of the underlying or fundamental social/political system* that is, on the whole, the most important single factor in enabling people to be happy. (Of course, to say this is not to deny that sometimes the existing system may be so bad people would be better off it was changed.) Yet the figures do not enable us to say with any degree of confidence what the main causes of happiness are.

However, one thing that can be said is that the figures would not seem to provide a great deal of support for the claim that high levels of material wealth produce happiness as a subjectively felt experience. The figures do lend support to the claim that high levels of wealth produce 'total happiness', measured as subjectively felt happiness multiplied by life expectancy; but even here there is evidence that social democratic countries tend to fare better than the more strictly free market economies.

These results, of course, have relevance for the attempt to provide a utilitarian justification of economic rationalism. Recall that the argument was that economic rationalism would maximise wealth, which would in turn maximise happiness. But we have seen that the empirical evidence does not show that wealth maximises happiness as a subjectively felt experience. It does tend to increase 'total happiness', when life expectancy is taken into consideration, but here the social democratic system would appear to be a more effective maximiser of happiness than economic rationalism.

EVALUATION OF THE MORAL THEORY OF UTILITARIANISM: IS IT POSSIBLE TO COMPARE THE DEGREES OF HAPPINESS OF DIFFERENT PEOPLE?

Earlier in this chapter we saw that utilitarianism appears to lead us to the conclusion that the total human happiness in a society would be maximised if there were a more even distribution of wealth than that brought about by perfect competition, even if doing so would result in less total wealth. For example, commonsense told us that it is very plausible to think that the following distribution of wealth:

Smith has $1 000 000

Distribution A

Jones has $1000

would produce less happiness than:

Smith has $400 000

Distribution B

Jones has $400 000

even though the total wealth in Distribution A is greater. This is what commonsense tells us. It is also, plausibly, a consequence of a law of economics known as the 'law of diminishing marginal utility'. However, some economists have noted a serious difficulty with this commonsense view. What does it *mean* to say that Distribution B produces more happiness than Distribution A? It means:

[(Happiness of Jones in Distribution B) + (Happiness of Smith in Distribution B)]

is greater than

[(Happiness of Jones in Distribution A) + (Happiness of Smith in Distribution A)]

But how could we possibly *verify* this? How could we possibly verify, for example, that Smith has more happiness than Jones? How can we compare one person's level of happiness with that of another? In fact, can we scientifically establish *how* happy another person is? There are, to say the least, profound conceptual difficulties with saying, for example, that the degree of happiness of person A *plus* the degree of happiness of person B *equals* the degree of happiness of person C. But it is just this type of comparison we must make if we are to show that the total human happiness under one distribution of wealth is greater than it is under another.

The 'degree of happiness' that a person has cannot be measured, and compared with that of another person in the same way that, for example, one person's height can be measured and compared with that of another. However, utilitarianism makes the assumption that we *can* carry out this type of comparison. The essence of this criticism of utilitarianism is that it makes use of the notion of 'comparing the quantities of happiness of different persons', which is *not a scientifically respectable notion*.

Around 1940, a number of leading economists became increasingly sceptical about this aspect of utilitarianism. It was felt that if economics was to be a scientifically respectable discipline, it ought to be possible to do it without postulating such a thing as a 'quantity of happiness', of which one person could be said to possess more or less than another. One such economist was JR Hicks.[12] He argued that it was possible to do economics *without* making this dubious assumption.[13] We need not concern ourselves with the details of Hicks's theory here, but, very roughly, his idea was to replace the notion of happiness (or 'utility') with the notion of the *satisfaction of preferences*. Suppose Smith has $10 to spend. If he chooses to spend it on item A rather than item B then, says Hicks, we may say Smith *prefers* item A to item B. The way a person chooses to spend their money indicates their *preferences*, and their spending it in that way enables them to satisfy their preferences. Hicks pointed out that the operation of the free market, under ideal conditions, would bring about a Pareto-optimal distribution of satisfaction of preferences. (We can say that a distribution of satisfaction of preferences is Pareto-optimal if any alternative distribution that enabled Smith, for example, to satisfy *more* of his preferences would mean that someone else would have to satisfy *fewer* of their preferences.) Hicks argued that it was possible to do economics making reference only to satisfaction of preferences, and not making any reference at all to anything like the 'total quantity of happiness' in a society, or even to the notion of one person being happier than another person.[14]

Hicks believed that by reforming economics in this way, he was making it more scientifically respectable. The notions of 'quantity of happiness' and of one person having more happiness than another are, as we have seen, beset with difficulties. If we demand of economics the same degree of rigour and objectivity we find in chemistry and physics, these things cannot be measured. But Hicks thought it *was* possible to tell objectively if Smith *preferred* A to B: he preferred A to B if he spent his \$10 on A rather than B. So, Hicks said, economists should deal merely with satisfaction of preferences and omit altogether any talk of maximising the total quantity of happiness, or of making one person or group happier than another.

One immediate consequence of Hicks's view is that economists, as economists, should no longer see their task as one of finding ways to maximise happiness. If they did see the role of economics in those terms, they would be placing at the core of their discipline a notion that was not scientifically respectable. But a perfectly respectable aim for economics, in this view, would be merely to find ways of ensuring a Pareto-optimal distribution of the satisfaction of preferences. In summary, Hicks objected to utilitarianism because it required economists to deal with the notions such as 'quantities of happiness', or of one person being happier than another person. But these were not scientifically legitimate concepts, so he developed another way of doing economics that did not require economists to deal with these questionable concepts.

Is Hicks's objection against utilitarianism a good one? It does seem to be true that we cannot know *with certainty*, or prove scientifically, that one person or group of persons has more total happiness than another. So, we cannot prove scientifically, or show with certainty, that a more equal distribution of wealth would produce more total happiness than a less equal distribution. Although it cannot be shown with certainty, it still seems to be a perfectly reasonable belief that a society in which everyone is comfortably well off will produce more total happiness than one in which one half is very well off and the other half lives in grinding poverty. If it is *reasonable to believe* that some course of action will bring about some result, isn't this enough on which to base our decisions?

Economists exhibit a range of views on this question. Kurt Rothschild, himself a noted economist, discerns two main schools of thought on the question of whether it is possible to compare the degrees of happiness (or 'utility') of different people.[15]

1   The 'hardline' position that since comparisons of the degrees of happiness of different people cannot be given any scientific, objective proof, they should not be made at all. For the hardliners, the only legitimate way of evaluating the condition of a group of people is by asking: is the distribution of satisfaction of preferences Pareto-optimal?

2   Others who maintain that although comparisons of the degrees of happiness of different people cannot be carried out with complete scientific objectivity, disciplines such as psychology and sociology can provide us with estimates of degrees of happiness which are reasonable enough.

Note that it is only the hardliners who are rejecting utilitarianism — the others are simply saying economists would need help from disciplines such as psychology to work out which distribution of wealth is best. However, if the hardliners are right, economists should give up any attempt to maximise human happiness. Also, it is hard to see what reason there could be, within the hardline position, why economists should aim for a more even distribution of wealth. Indeed, if the hardliners are right, economists should not attempt to aim for a society that is just, fair or morally right, since the concepts of 'justice', 'fairness' and 'moral rightness' are not strictly scientific concepts either.

Let us, for the sake of discussion, grant that concepts such as 'happiness', 'justice' and 'fairness' are not strictly scientific concepts. Does this mean that governments should leave out all consideration of such concepts? Here it is important to distinguish between economics as an explanatory science, and government policy informed by economic considerations. Economics as an *explanatory science* is merely concerned with explaining and predicting the behaviour of ideal and actual markets. Economics, in this sense, offers explanations of why particular events occurred; for example, it can offer explanations of why employment levels went up or why GDP went down. One thing that economics as an explanatory science does not do is make recommendations about what action governments ought to take. Economics as an explanatory science simply tells us what did, or could (under certain conditions), cause an occurrence. It does not, in itself, tell us how things ought to be. *Government policy*, on the other hand, does (implicitly) make a claim about how things ought to be. Suppose a government decides, for example, to increase its spending by 5 per cent. This is, clearly enough, based on the assumption that it is a good thing to raise government spending by this amount, and that doing so will result in a better state of affairs for the country. Put simply, economics as an explanatory science tells how things *are*, or how things will be in the future. Government policy makes recommendations about how things *ought* to be, or on how it would be good for things to be.

Should economics as an explanatory science deal with concepts such as 'maximisation of total happiness' or 'maximisation of fairness' in a society? This is a question for the experts, and it may very well be that the answer to this question is 'No'. But even if such concepts should not be used in economics as an explanatory science, it does not follow that they should be excluded from government policy. It remains possible that government policy should be informed by, for example, the values of the community. Of course it does not follow from this that the aim of government policy should be the utilitarian one of maximising human happiness, but the exclusion of this allegedly unscientific concept from economics as an explanatory science does not entail its exclusion from deliberations, made by governments, concerning the best thing to do. The hardliners might be right about economics as an explanatory science, but it does not follow that all non-scientific concepts should be excluded by government policy.

We should also note here that if we were to exclude all 'unscientific' concepts, or all unverifiable concepts, from our considerations in deciding the best thing to do, there would often be nothing stopping us from doing things that were highly *immoral*. For example, there is no way of objectively proving that a cat would really feel pain if I were to set it on fire, but no-one would claim that meant it was morally permissible to set the cat on fire. Or again, it is not possible to give a precise definition of the concept 'natural justice' in the way it *is* possible to give a precise definition of a scientific term such as 'valency'. It would be absurd to think that this meant it was permissible to embrace decisions which violated natural justice. The fact that some concept is vague or unverifiable does not mean it ought to be left out of consideration when we are deciding the right thing to do.

In summary, there are many concepts which are unscientific, or which cannot be objectively measured. Perhaps all such concepts should be removed from economics as an *explanatory science*, but it simply does not follow from this that all such concepts should be ignored when discussing the morally right thing to do. Neither does it follow that governments should omit all such concepts when deciding the best thing for a country.

IS THE NOTION OF PREFERENCE ANY BETTER THAN THE NOTION OF HAPPINESS?

Hicks said that while 'happiness', or 'utility', is not a respectable notion, the notion of 'preference' *is* respectable. He said that a person, Mr A, prefers good *b* to good *c* if he chooses to spend his money on *b* rather than on *c*. But does this show that the notion of preference is scientifically respectable? Has Hicks given us a satisfactory account of the notion of preference in scientifically acceptable terms? Robert Solo has argued that he has not. It is worth repeating Solo's brief but telling criticisms here.

> Mr A might have purchased *b* because he is an automaton pre-programmed to buy *b* and nothing but *b*. (Try to disprove that with only scientifically rigorous concepts.) Or Mr A could have bought *b* because he was told to, by his stockbroker, by his boss, by his wife, by his children, by his Aunt Matilda, and especially by that television commercial. He might have bought *b* in simple imitation of his neighbours. He might buy *b* knowing nothing about *c*, *d*, *e* or *f*; indeed without knowing anything about *b* either. His purchase might be as random as when he buys a numbered lottery ticket or bets on the throw of the dice.[16]

Solo's point is that trying to define the notion of preference in terms of a *tendency to purchase b* rather than *c* is really quite unsatisfactory. A person might be disposed to purchase *b* rather than *c* without having what we ordinarily take to be a *preference* for *b*. Rather, we would say a person has a preference for *b* if they *like b* more, or they regard it as more *desirable*. The notion of preference, just as much as the notion of happiness, involves private mental states such as *liking*. Hence, the notion of preference really seems to be in the same boat as the notion of happiness. Both refer to private, subjective states of a person; both resist definition in objective, publicly verifiable terms.

Of course, this does not show that utilitarianism does use only scientifically respectable terms. But it does seem to show that the alternative to utilitarianism offered by Hicks — the notion of a Pareto-optimal *satisfaction of preferences* — involves the same intellectual difficulties.

UTILITARIANISM AND JUSTICE OR FAIRNESS

We now turn our attention to a very different type of difficulty for utilitarianism. The type of difficulty we are about to consider — first formulated by JJC Smart — has much exercised moral philosophers. Imagine that you are a police officer in some small country town and a murder has been committed. There are only two suspects for the crime: a prominent local citizen and a wandering hobo. Now suppose that you personally happen to know that in fact the prominent local citizen is guilty (but you are the only person who knows this), yet that it would also be quite easy for you to frame the hobo. Moreover, let us suppose, you know for a fact that you could frame the hobo in a way which no-one else would ever discover. Should you frame the hobo and in this way get everyone else to believe the hobo is guilty?

Commonsense says that since you know that the prominent local citizen is in fact guilty, that's who you should announce is guilty. The difficulty for utilitarianism is that it seems to imply that the police officer should frame the hobo! The reason for this is that human happiness will almost certainly be maximised by saying that the hobo is guilty. If the police officer says the hobo is guilty then of course the hobo himself will not be very happy, but since no-one knows or (we will assume) cares very much about the hobo, no-one else will be made unhappy by the hobo being found guilty. However, if the prominent local citizen is found guilty, many people will be shocked and upset. So, the course of action which results in the maximisation of human happiness is saying that the hobo is guilty. Nevertheless, we feel quite strongly that it is not the morally right thing for the police officer to do. Since the hobo did not commit the murder, he does not *deserve* to be found guilty, and since the prominent local citizen did, he does. Justice would not be done by finding the hobo guilty, even though it would result in the maximisation of human happiness.[17] More generally, it appears that utilitarianism is not a wholly satisfactory theory of the nature of moral goodness because it leaves out the 'justice' or 'deservingness' dimension of morality.

It should not be thought that the general type of situation that we have just described with the hobo and the prominent local citizen is rare or unusual: it quite often happens in government action that overall happiness may be maximised by doing something that will bring considerable suffering to some minority who has done nothing to deserve that suffering. Suppose, for example, that the government is considering whether to build a new power station. If it does, then everybody in the state will be a little happier because their electricity will come to them more cheaply. However, let us suppose that there is a small community living next to the power station. They will have their lives made an absolute misery because not only will there be noise and fumes produced by the power station, but the fumes may be toxic. Nevertheless, it turns out that the total happiness to millions throughout the state getting slightly cheaper electricity is greater than the extreme misery caused to a very small number. So, according to utilitarianism, the construction of the power station is a morally good thing. But it is certainly far from obvious that it *is* morally right. What have the people living near to the power station done to deserve having their lives made a misery? If they have not done anything, then I think we would say it was wrong to cause them all that misery by building the power station.

Of course, a natural suggestion to make at this point is that the government should provide compensation to the people affected. While this is surely correct, and while such an approach may well result in more human happiness than either of the other two options considered, the essential difficulty for utilitarianism still remains. The difficulty is that utilitarianism still implies that the option of building the power station (without compensation) is *morally better* than the option of not building it, since it results in more overall human happiness than the option of not building it. But this is at least a very dubious claim. Again, where utilitarianism seems to go wrong as a theory of what is morally right, is that it leaves out the dimension of *justice* or *desert* (deservingness). If the people living near the power station have not done anything to deserve being made miserable, it seems to be morally wrong to make them miserable, even if doing so brings some slight benefit to a much larger number of others.

Of course, cases of this nature are not restricted to action taken by governments. Well publicised cases of this type also involve banks. A bank may close down a number of small rural branches. Doing this may help to ensure the bank's profits are maximised, and help the value of shares in the bank to go up, which will in turn help to ensure shareholders keep their shares in that bank. It may also help to ensure that the branches that continue to exist offer a cheaper service to their customers than would have been the case if the small rural branches had stayed open. In this way closing down the small rural branches may bring minor benefits to a very large number of people throughout the country. However, it may also bring severe hardship to people in the same towns as the small rural branches. Sometimes, closing the bank can begin a process which ends in the whole town 'closing', in turn causing other people to lose their jobs. A small minority undergoes severe hardship so that a much larger number gets some (usually fairly slight) benefit. It *may* be that the total happiness that comes to the many is greater than the total hardship that comes to the few. Yet we still have qualms about the moral correctness of this action because the few who suffer have not done anything to *deserve* their suffering. It seems that it is not morally right to cause undeserved suffering, even if by doing so we bring about some (slight) increase in happiness to very many others.

A related point is made by Karl Popper in his *The Open Society and Its Enemies*.[18] Popper says that there is a 'moral asymmetry' between causing happiness and avoiding causing harm or misery. What he means is that, while it is good both to bring happiness to our fellow human beings and to avoid causing them misery, there is a *stronger moral obligation on us to avoid causing misery.* This claim does seem to have considerable plausibility. Suppose I have $10 000 to give away and can give it to either A or B. A is reasonably well off, leading a comfortable enough but unexciting life. If I give the money to A, I will not relieve any misery, since A is not in misery, but I will turn A's unexciting life into a happy one. B, on the other hand, is leading a miserable life. If I give the money to B, I will turn B's miserable life into one which is free from misery. To whom should I give the money, A or B? I think we would say that the *stronger* moral obligation lies on us to give the money to B. Popper's claim that the *stronger moral obligation* lies on us to prevent misery seems to be quite plausible. But if Popper is right then utilitarianism is wrong. If, as Popper claims, our primary moral obligation is to avoid causing misery, then an action that causes misery may be morally wrong even if it also causes a greater amount of happiness. So, on Popper's view, it may not be right to build the power station or close the bank, even if doing so maximises happiness.

In summary, utilitarianism seems to be confronted with a problem. It seems to leave out the dimension of *justice* or *desert*, which most people feel *is* an important dimension of ethics and morality.

RULE-UTILITARIANISM

It should be noted that not all moral philosophers see points of the kind raised in the previous section as being *decisive* against utilitarianism. One way in which utilitarian philosophers have attempted to meet this kind of difficulty is by introducing another form of utilitarianism, known as rule-utilitarianism.[19] So far, we have been discussing the form of utilitarianism known as act-utilitarianism. According to act-utilitarianism, an *act* is morally right if it provides more human happiness than its alternatives. We have seen that this view has problems, and so the economic rationalist who appeals to act-utilitarianism may be trying to justify their own position by appealing to a discredited moral theory. But there is an alternative to act-utilitarianism known as *rule-utilitarianism*. This doctrine focuses (as its name suggests) on rules rather than acts. Might the economic rationalist do better if they try to rest their case on rule-utilitarianism?

According to rule-utilitarianism, a *rule* is morally correct if and only if human happiness would be maximised *were people to obey that rule*. According to rule-utilitarianism, an *act* is morally correct if and only if it is done in accordance with a morally correct rule. The nature of the difference between act-utilitarianism and rule-utilitarianism can be made clearer if we consider what each of them has to say about an activity such as *promise keeping*.

Should you always keep your promises? An act-utilitarian will almost certainly say 'No', whereas a rule-utilitarian may very well say 'Yes'. Suppose you promise to meet a business colleague at 3 pm, but it turns out that to do so you must abandon a friend who badly needs some support and encouragement. What should you do? Should you keep your promise and go to the 3 pm meeting, or should you stay with the friend who needs comfort? The act-utilitarian will say that the right *action* is the one that maximises human happiness. Since this is very likely to be staying with your friend, the act-utilitarian is likely to say in this case that the right thing to do involves breaking your promise to your colleague. But things may be quite different for a rule-utilitarian. For them the correct act is one done in accordance with a morally correct rule, and a rule is morally correct if everyone's conforming to it would maximise human happiness. The rule-utilitarian may say, 'Yes, it is true that in this particular case, the act that maximises human happiness involves breaking a promise; but suppose everyone went around breaking promises. No-one could rely on others to do what they had promised to do. The smooth and reliable running of society would be impossible. *In the long run* human happiness is maximised if people *do* stick to the rule: "Always keep your promises."' Therefore, according to such a rule-utilitarian, 'Always keep your promises' is a correct moral rule. Hence, this rule-utilitarian will say that, in the case under consideration, you should keep your promise to your colleague, because doing so conforms with a correct moral rule.

Rule-utilitarianism can give what many people would regard as a more plausible response to the example of the police officer who knows the hobo is innocent. If the police regularly went around condemning innocent people and letting criminals off, after a while the world might become a terrible place. So, plausibly, it would be much more productive for human happiness if the police conformed to the rule: 'Do not condemn people you know to be innocent'. In summary, it appears that rule-utilitarianism may be rather more plausible than act-utilitarianism.

Unfortunately, however, this does not appear to be of much help to the economic rationalist. Act-utilitarianism applies, first and foremost, to specific *acts*: an act is morally right if it maximises human happiness. Rule-utilitarianism applies, first and foremost, to *rules*: a rule is morally right if general conformity to it would maximise human happiness. Economic rationalism is something implemented by governments, but in this type of case the distinction between *individual actions* and *sequences of actions that conform to a rule* is rather arbitrary. If a government implements economic rationalist policies during a term of its office, is that a single action or a sequence of actions done in conformity to the rule: 'Maximise economic efficiency'? It could be seen as either. However, whether it is seen one way or the other, maximising economic efficiency is likely to bring suffering on some minority which has not done anything to deserve this suffering. For example, actions such as closing down banks or government services in remote districts, or reducing assistance to the disabled might maximise the total happiness in society, yet bring unhappiness to a minority who don't deserve it. If there is no clear distinction between a single action and a sequence of actions done in conforming to a rule, then economic rationalism runs into problems whether it is act-utilitarianism or rule-utilitarianism that is accepted as the correct theory of morality.

It is fair to say that most philosophers see examples such as those discussed above as indicating that there is probably something wrong with utilitarianism. Most philosophers would, I think, say that the burden of proof lies on utilitarians to show why we should continue to accept their view. In the light of this it seems safe to say:

> If a particular course of action maximises human happiness, but does so by causing significant suffering to some sub-group that *has not done anything to deserve it*, then the burden of proof lies on those who say the course of action is morally correct.

Let us now see what bearing this conclusion has on the argument for economic rationalism. As we have seen, one of the main mechanisms for implementing economic rationalism is the free market. In an ideal free market there is intense competition. One consequence of this intense competition is the *total* welfare of society is maximised (it is Pareto-optimal). This may, but also may not, result in the maximisation of human happiness. Another consequence of competition is that there will be winners and losers. Some will become very wealthy in competition, whilst others will go out of business. Thus economic rationalism does tend to increase the gap between rich and poor. Do the losers in competition *deserve* the bad things that come about as a result of competition; and do the winners deserve the good things? This difficult question is the focus of the next chapter. Here we note that if the answer to this question is 'No', then the moral argument for economic rationalism from utilitarianism has another flaw. *Even if* Pareto-optimality were to maximise *total* human happiness still we might not have a moral justification of economic rationalism. If it were to maximise total human happiness by inflicting suffering on those who had done nothing to deserve it, then it is at least debatable whether it is morally correct. The burden of proof would be on those who said it was morally correct.

SUMMARY

Let us now summarise the results of this chapter. The aim of this chapter has been to assess an argument for economic rationalism from the moral theory of utilitarianism. As we noted at the beginning of this chapter, it is possible to represent this argument as follows:

PREMISE 1   That course of action which brings about the greatest happiness for the greatest number is the action which is morally correct (the Principle of Utilitarianism).

PREMISE 2   Economic rationalism brings about the greatest happiness for the greatest number.

Therefore, economic rationalism is morally correct.

This argument is considered *valid* as the conclusion follows logically from the premises. The aim of this chapter has been to consider whether the premises are *true*. We noted that there are several reasons for doubting the first premise. *If* the markets in a society are ideal, or are close to ideal, then we can be sure that there is a sense in which the welfare of the society will be at (or at least close to) its maximum. But even advocates of economic rationalism agree that the wealth created will not be evenly distributed throughout society. There is good reason to believe that there can be greater total *happiness* in a society with somewhat less wealth, if that wealth is more or less evenly distributed. This will be so even if it is granted that the more wealth a person has, the happier they will be. Therefore, even if economic rationalism maximises total wealth it does not follow that it would maximise happiness.

It was also noted that for most people a happy life is a *balanced* life, but the intense competition that is likely to exist under economic rationalism would make it harder to lead a balanced life. Intense competition makes it more difficult to include a balance of work, play, human relationships and other activities engaged in for their own sake, and to live in a clean environment.

We then looked at statistical evidence that might be relevant to the question of whether economic rationalism would lead to a maximisation of human happiness. This statistical evidence did not support economic rationalism: we noted considerable happiness can exist in great poverty, and there is some evidence that the social-democratic system produces more happiness than economic rationalism. However, we also noted that these statistics ought to be interpreted with caution. In the light of these considerations it seems reasonable to conclude that the argument for economic rationalism from utilitarianism is confronted with serious difficulties.

We also briefly evaluated the moral theory of utilitarianism itself, first discussing the objection, made by a number of economists, that utilitarianism required us to postulate a quantity of 'happiness' of which it can be said that one person, or group, has more than another. But some economists had objected that postulating such a quantity was not scientifically respectable. The main point made in response to this objection was that, even if the notion of 'happiness', and related notions, ought to be removed from economics as an explanatory science, it does not follow that it should be removed from government deliberations concerning the best thing to do. Next, we considered the objection that utilitarianism left out the 'justice' or 'deservingness' dimension of morality. It was noted that while philosophers are divided on the question of whether utilitarianism is correct, it seems fair to say that the burden of proof lies on people who claim that it is a satisfactory theory of the nature of moral goodness. Rule-utilitarianism does not seem to help the economic rationalist any more than act-utilitarianism.

In our discussion of utilitarianism, we noted that a course of action does not seem to be morally correct if it produces maximum human happiness by causing some people to experience *undeserved* hardship or suffering. In intense competition there are, of course, winners and losers: some grow very wealthy, while others slave away for what is comparatively very little money, while still others lose to the competition, go bankrupt or lose their jobs. Clearly then, even if economic rationalism maximises total wealth, in the process it causes suffering. Is this suffering deserved? Do those who lose in competition *deserve* the pain they experience? And do those who are successful in the free market deserve their success? These are the questions we look at in the next chapter.

6

THE ARGUMENTS FROM DESERT

A popular form of moral argument for economic rationalism and the free market, especially among business people and some journalists, appeals to the concept of *desert* (or 'deservingness').[1] The operation of the free market will, according to the economic rationalist, maximise the amount of wealth in a community, but there is no guarantee that the wealth will be distributed equally.[2] It is likely, in fact, to result in great inequalities in the distribution of wealth with both billionaires and people living below the poverty line to be found in the same society. According to the argument from desert, there is nothing wrong with such vast inequalities of wealth because the operation of the free market distributes wealth according to *desert*: if a billionaire has acquired their wealth through the free market then they deserve it. Similarly, if a person becomes poor in the free market, they too deserve their lot; they deserve their poverty. The argument from desert says the free market gives people as much wealth as they *deserve*.

ECONOMIC RATIONALISM AND THE GAP BETWEEN RICH AND POOR

Everyone, whether they are an economic rationalist or not, agrees that economic rationalism may tend to increase the gap between rich and poor.[3] The way in which the introduction of highly 'free market orient-ed' economic policies can increase the gap between rich and poor is exemplified by the history of Britain over the last twenty-five years. In 1978, shortly before the election of Margaret Thatcher, Britain had one of the smallest gaps between rich and poor of any country on Earth. On one measure (the 'Gini coefficient') it had about the same gap as the most egalitarian countries — Sweden, Finland and Belgium — do now. Thatcher was elected in 1979 and at the same time the gap between rich and poor started to increase. It increased steadily throughout the Thatcher/Major years until about 1993, since which time it has more or less remained stable. Britain now has one of the most unequal distributions of wealth in the western world, on most measures coming in about second or third.[4]

Just how much economic rationalism can increase the gap between rich and poor can be seen by considering the recent economic history of Australia. Traditionally, Australia has prided itself on being an egalitarian country. It has seen itself as being different from both Britain, with its residual class system, and America with its multi-billionaires and its homeless and destitute. Up until the mid-1970s Australia was indeed more egalitarian than either of these countries; in fact, it was one of the most egalitarian countries in the world. However, in the mid-1970s Australia started to adopt what we now call 'economic rationalism'. This process began with the election of the Fraser Liberal government in 1975, and continued under the Hawke and Keating Labor governments, affecting the distribution of wealth in this country.

By the early 1990s Australia could no longer claim to be one of the world's most egalitarian countries. Indeed, by 1999 Australia and Britain were, on one measure, the two most inegalitarian countries in the industrialised world — a fact which requires some clarification. A recent United Nations survey calculated the degree of inequality of wealth in a country by determining the average income of the richest 20 per cent and the poorest 20 per cent of a country's population and finding the ratio between the two.[5] It should be noted that there are several ways of measuring the gap between rich and poor, and they can give different results. One other way is to compare the incomes of the richest 10 per cent with the poorest 10 per cent. Using this measure, in 1994 Australia had the fourth biggest gap between rich and poor in the developed world (behind the United States, Italy and the United Kingdom).[6] However, by using the Gini coefficient to calculate the gap between rich and poor, Australia comes out as second only to the United States.[7]

So, while different ways of measuring the gap yield different results, it seems Australia is ranked somewhere between second and fourth amongst the most unequal developed countries. This is in considerable tension with the image Australia often has of itself as the most egalitarian nation on Earth. Using these figures, it was found that the wealthy in Australia earn approximately ten times the wage earned by the poor. On this measure, the gap between rich and poor in Australia is now greater than that in the United States, and is *more than twice* the gap that exists in Japan, the Netherlands, Sweden, the Czech Republic and Spain. Australia has become (after Britain) the industrialised world's second most unequal country. (We should also observe that Australia currently has what is perhaps the 'driest' economic rationalist government in its history. As Britain now has a Labour government it is possible that in next few years Australia will overtake Britain as the most inegalitarian country in the industrialised world.) So, in about twenty-five years economic rationalism has taken Australia from being one of the most egalitarian countries in the world to very close to being the industrialised world's least egalitarian country. However, according to the arguments from desert, not only is there nothing wrong with this, it is in fact *morally how things ought to be*. Let us now examine these arguments from desert.

THE ARGUMENTS FROM DESERT

There are, in fact, two distinct versions of the argument from desert. We will call the first the merit version of the argument from desert, and the second the service version of the argument.[8] The *merit version* of the argument says that those who grow wealthy in the free market deserve their wealth because they have acquired it as a result of the application of meritorious personal qualities such as industry, creativity, intelligence, persistence and frugality. Conversely, those who are poor in a free market deserve their poverty because they have been lazy, profligate and foolish. The merit version of the argument says, therefore, that the free market confers wealth on individuals to the extent that they exhibit meritorious personal qualities.

The *service version* of the argument is a little harder to explain. We can approach this version of the argument by considering again Adam Smith's concept of the 'invisible hand'. How does a person grow rich in the free market? Clearly, by selling a lot of their products. Yet if a person is to sell their products at all, they must persuade customers to buy *their* products rather than those of their rivals, and this can be done only if they produce something the public wants that is cheaper than the products of their rivals, or better, or both. Therefore, if a businessperson is to grow rich in the free market, they must make available for sale to the public products that are what the public wants, and that are cheap, or good, or both. They will thereby have provided a service to the public. The service version of the argument from desert says that the free market confers wealth upon an individual to the extent that they provide that service to the public: those that grow wealthy deserve it because they have made available to the public products they want; those that are poor deserve their poverty because they have not provided this service.

There is a slight refinement that can be made to the service version of the argument from desert. In order for a person to grow rich, it is not enough that they sell some products to the public; they must sell many. But since people will buy a product only if it is cheap and/or good, a businessperson will grow rich if and only if they have supplied to public a *large number* of products that are cheap and/or good. Moreover, the larger the number of such products they have made available, the richer they will become. However, the larger the number of cheap and/or good products the businessperson has made available to society, the greater their total benefit to society: if they had not made those products available, then many people would instead have had to purchase poorer quality or more expensive goods, or no similar goods at all. Summarising this, we can say that the richer a businessperson becomes, the greater the number of cheap and/or good products the public will have purchased from them, and the greater the benefit the businessperson's efforts will have brought to the community. So, the argument goes, those who become wealthy under the free market deserve their wealth, because of the magnitude of the benefit they have brought to the community.

The aim of this chapter is to critically evaluate both the merit and service versions of the argument from desert. We will begin our discussion with the merit version of the argument.

THE MERIT VERSION OF THE ARGUMENT FROM DESERT

Advocates of the merit version of the argument from desert say that the free market confers wealth on an individual to the extent that the individual possesses meritorious qualities such as intelligence, industry, creativity. Yet we do not have to think about matters very hard to see that this is not always so. One factor that is often important in determining how successful an individual becomes is the wealth of their parents. Obviously, wealthier parents are able to send their children to better schools and support them for longer than parents that are not so wealthy. People also *inherit* wealth from their parents. It is beyond serious dispute that, typically, a person who has wealthy parents will usually be at least slightly more successful than a person with an otherwise equivalent set of abilities but who lacks wealthy parents. We would not say that the person had *deserved* that extra success by having wealthy parents.

Another factor that should not be overlooked in determining success is sheer luck. There is, of course, a very wide range of opinion on the question of to just what extent luck is responsible for an individual's success, but few people would wish to say it had absolutely no role to play at all. If one person was more successful than another because of luck, we would not say the extra success was thereby *deserved*.

The idea that success obtained through luck is not deserved should be borne in mind when we consider one specific type of the argument from desert. We fairly frequently encounter the claim that someone deserved their success because *they were prepared to take risks*. A course of action that is risky is, by definition, an action the outcome of which is, at least to some extent, beyond our knowledge or control. So, if a risky course of action is successful, its success must be, at least to some extent, due to luck and is therefore to that extent undeserved. Of course, this is not to say that success that is due to taking risks is wholly undeserved: to take risks requires courage and that is presumably a meritorious quality. Therefore, it follows from what we mean by the expression 'taking a risk' that the success must be *partly undeserved*.

There are certain skills and personal attributes which can bring success in the free market, but which we would be reluctant to say made that success deserved. For example, duplicity, or the ability to lie convincingly, may bring success but many would doubt that meant the success was deserved. Indeed, most of us would probably say a person exhibiting those qualities was more deserving of punishment than reward. A businessperson may grow wealthy through exercising their ability to dominate, manipulate or instil fear in others, but it is at least controversial as to whether it is morally right that they should receive reward for doing so. Conversely, there are skills which tend not to bring success in the free market but which seem, on the face of it, to be as meritorious as those which do. The skills of a poet or artist would, on the face of it, appear to be as intrinsically meritorious as those of many other occupations, but nowadays it is almost impossible to make a living as a poet or artist in the free market. If it is objected that the skills of a poet or artist are not really meritorious because people nowadays are not prepared to pay much for what they produce, then the objector is implicitly appealing to (some variant of) the *service version* of the argument from desert, rather than the merit version. Remember that what makes the merit version of the argument different from the service version is that the former says that some skills are intrinsically meritorious, or meritorious in virtue of their very nature, rather than in virtue of how the market responds to those skills. On the face of it, the skills of a poet or artist do seem to be as intrinsically meritorious as those of many other occupations, but the free market typically does not confer wealth on people who possess those skills.

The idea that the free market confers rewards on those who possess certain 'intrinsically meritorious' qualities becomes clearly untenable when we note that the qualities rewarded by the free market change over time. One very important factor that can produce a change in the skills rewarded by the free market is technology. Once physical strength may have been an asset, yet now it is virtually worthless. A 'photographic' memory may once have given a person a huge advantage in the free market, but with the development of electronic means of storing information this has become less of an advantage. The ability to do sums quickly in the head would once have been a great advantage, but the easy availability of the calculator means this is now almost no advantage at all. The qualities that bring success in the free market change as technology develops — there is no single set of qualities that brings success in the free market. Therefore, the idea that the free market brings success to those who possess some set of 'intrinsically meritorious' qualities seems to be very dubious indeed.

Of course, there are some very general qualities, such as intelligence and energy, which will always tend to produce success in the free market no matter how technology changes or develops. It is undoubtedly true that there is some degree of correlation between individuals who have these qualities and those who enjoy success in the free market; although we should remember it will only be a loose correlation, since other factors will also influence success. We will also find at least a loose correlation between success and the qualities of intelligence and energy in many systems other than the free market. In systems as different as the Catholic Church and the Soviet Communist Party, individuals possessing intelligence and energy have also had a better chance of enjoying success than individuals not possessing those qualities. If there is a loose correlation between success and meritorious qualities such as energy and intelligence in many systems other than the free market, the existence of such a correlation in the free market does not give us any reason to morally prefer the free market to those other systems.

So far in our discussion we have not questioned the assumption that qualities such as intelligence and energy are intrinsically meritorious. But is this assumption true? There is, of course, no doubt that any system that has a chance of actually working must confer rewards upon people who possess these qualities. However, the question we are presently considering is not: Will the free market work? or Will other systems work? The question is whether it can be given *a moral justification*. The suggestion under consideration is that the free market is morally justified because it gives rewards to those who possess intrinsically meritorious qualities such as intelligence and energy, and who therefore *deserve* their rewards. However, does the possession of these qualities really mean those who have them deserve their rewards?

We can approach this question by considering another personal quality which, very probably, does, at least to some extent, increase an individual's chance of success: that is, *good looks*. There are many occupations in which possession of good looks is an advantage. Sales is an obvious example: a salesperson who is good looking will probably have at least a little more success in getting people to buy things than an otherwise equally skilled salesperson. Educating, lecturing and public speaking are other areas where an attractive appearance can be an advantage, and, of course, the industry where an attractive appearance, especially for women, is almost mandatory is television. In any occupation involving a significant degree of 'people contact' it will probably be at least something of an advantage. Yet would we say that a person who attained their success through good looks *deserved* their success? I think we would be a little reluctant to give an unequivocal 'Yes' to this question. For some reason, success achieved through good looks seems to be less deserved than success obtained through intelligence and energy.

Why is this so? At first we might be inclined to say that possessing good looks does not enable a person to do their job any better, but this is at least debatable. One perfectly good measure of how well a salesperson is performing their job is how many sales they achieve. If having good looks enables a person to achieve more sales, then it *does* enable them to do their job better. One measure of how well a television presenter is doing their job is how much success they have in getting people to watch their show and thereby increase ratings. So, it seems, there are quite reasonable indicators for measuring a person's success in a job where having good looks is considered an advantage. However, I think we still have doubts about saying that a person who becomes successful *because* of their looks thereby deserves their success.

Another reason we may have for doubting that a person who is successful because of their looks deserves their success is because one is generally either born with good looks, or is not. If a person is born with good looks, they did not have to *do anything* to get their good looks; they did not acquire them through their *efforts*. So, if a person is successful because of a quality they were born with and did not acquire through their efforts, we would be reluctant to say the success was deserved. However, this overlooks the fact that it is possible, to some extent, to improve one's appearance by one's efforts. Similarly, as intelligence is thought to have a significant genetic or hereditary component, the claim that success gained through good looks is not deserved because 'you are born with them' would apply with equal force to the claim that success due to intelligence is not deserved either.

Many of the qualities that increase a person's chances of success are not qualities that have been gained through that person's efforts. Energy undoubtedly contributes to success, but energy levels would seem to depend at least in part on how strong and vigorous a person's body is, and that has at least a genetic component. Certain types of personality would seem to aid success more than others; for example, in many working environments an extroverted and outgoing personality will be more advantageous than a more reserved, introverted one. Yet whether a person is an extrovert or an introvert seems to be determined largely by genetics, and certainly by early childhood. If energy, creativity and an extroverted personality are not qualities a person has acquired through their efforts, but have just acquired 'through the luck of the genetic draw', it is not clear why success gained as a result of these qualities is any more *deserved* than, say, success gained as a result of the range of advantages that come from having wealthy parents.

Of course, there is no doubt that, if society is to function, more rewards must be conferred on people who exhibit intelligence, energy, creativity and so on, than those who do not. But the question is whether this is morally right, rather than something which, although unjust, practical necessity forces us to do. We have seen that there are a range of reasons for saying it does not seem to have any *moral* justification. The reasons for rewarding people with these qualities are *practical* rather than moral.

THE SERVICE VERSION OF THE ARGUMENT FROM DESERT

In view of the difficulties associated with the merit version of the argument from desert, it is natural to turn to the service version of the argument. The service version of the argument, we recall, says that people who grow rich in the free market have made available to the public many products that are cheap and/or good; they have thereby rendered a valuable service to the public and so they deserve their wealth. It is useful to distinguish two sub-versions of the service version, which we will call the benefit version and the satisfaction of preferences version. According to the *benefit version*, those who grow wealthy in the free market deserve it because they have made available to the public products which benefit them; they have provided a benefit to the public by providing them with cheap and/or good products. According to the *satisfaction of preferences version*, they deserve their wealth because, by making such products available for sale, they have enabled consumers to *satisfy their preferences*.

That these two versions of the argument are different can be brought out when we consider that it is possible for a person to voluntarily buy a product which does not benefit them, and can even harm them. Cigarettes are arguably an example. The cigarette manufacturer makes available to the public a product that many people buy, and the cigarette manufacturer may grow rich as a result; however, the cigarette manufacturer has not made available to the public a product which *benefits* them. So, it seems to be possible to grow rich in the free market without bringing a benefit to the public. Consequently, we cannot say that it is always true that a person who grows rich in the free market deserves their wealth because they have brought some benefit to the public. The benefit version of the argument therefore contains a slight 'wrinkle'.

At first it might be thought that the *satisfaction of preferences* argument does better. Although the cigarette manufacturer does not benefit the public, they do seem to enable the public to satisfy their preferences by making cigarettes available to them. They are giving the public 'what they want', and, it appears, it could be argued that the cigarette manufacturer deserves their wealth because they have enabled people to satisfy their preferences. However, it turns out that, on closer examination, this version of the argument fares little better than the benefit version. An important reason why people choose to buy products such as cigarettes, even when they know they are harmful, is because they are addicted to them. Do we feel that a person who grows wealthy by making available to people a product to which they are addicted, and is harmful, thereby *deserves* their wealth? In at least some cases we are prepared to answer this question with an unequivocal 'No'. For example, most of us would agree that a dealer in crack cocaine does not deserve their wealth. There are, of course, a number of reasons why the sale of cigarettes is not exactly parallel, but still, we may have serious reservations about saying that a person deserves their wealth if they have obtained it by enabling those addicted to a harmful product to satisfy their preferences. So, the satisfaction of preferences version of the argument also runs into difficulties with the case of addictive, harmful products.

It is natural for an advocate of the free market to respond to this objection by denying that they reveal any *serious* difficulty with their position. It is, after all, quite easy to modify the free market so that the difficulty does not arise. All that needs to be done is to prohibit the sale of products that are harmful and addictive. This certainly does not mean getting rid of the free market altogether, it just means modifying it in a fairly minor respect. The advocate of the free market can perhaps still maintain that, provided it is modified in this way, it still confers rewards upon people who provide a valuable service to the community by making available products that are cheap and/or good.

Unfortunately for advocates of the free market, this is only the first in a long series of modifications that would need to be made if the service version of the argument is to have a chance of being tenable. We have already noted that the merit version of the argument from desert runs into difficulty with occupations such as the artist and poet. The qualities required to be a good artist or poet seem as intrinsically meritorious as those of many other occupations, but it is almost impossible to make a living as an artist or poet in the free market as it exists nowadays. These occupations also create a difficulty for the service version of the argument. Let us suppose a man buys a painting. We will suppose he does not buy it as an investment, but instead just likes the look of it and wishes to hang it on his wall. How much will he pay for it? As a rough approximation, we can say the amount he will pay for it will be determined by the amount of pleasure he will get from looking at it as it hangs on the wall: the more pleasure he thinks he will get, the more he will pay the artist. So, again as a rough approximation, we can say that the amount of money the artist will get will be determined by the amount of pleasure the painting will give to the person who buys the painting. So far, it seems as though matters are pretty much in accord with the service version of the argument from desert: the artist provides the purchaser with a certain amount of aesthetic pleasure and receives a proportionate amount of money. However, on closer inspection it turns out that the artist quite probably gives more than she receives. If the purchaser puts the picture on his wall, he will receive aesthetic pleasure from looking at it, but so will the other members of his family and visitors to the house who look at the painting. The man's enjoyment of the painting does not prevent others from also enjoying it; in this respect the painting is a non-rival good. He may pass the painting on to his children, who can continue to enjoy it. There is, in principle, no limit to the number of people who can derive enjoyment from looking at the painting.

Matters are rather different with a product like a hamburger or a bar of chocolate. A person who buys a hamburger and eats it thereby deprives others from eating it. The person who pays for the hamburger is (provided they are the one who eats it) the sole recipient of the benefits of it. They buy the hamburger because they think the benefit they will get from it is greater than the amount of money they pay out to the hamburger maker. But, at least for the average person, the benefit they get from the hamburger would not be a lot greater than the amount of money they pay for it. Consequently, the money the hamburger maker gets is 'roughly commensurate' with the benefit they confer on the hamburger consumer. However, since the hamburger consumer gets *all* the benefit from the hamburger, the reward the hamburger maker receives in payment is roughly commensurate to the *total benefit* that comes from the supply of the hamburger.

We can now see one important reason why artists get what is plausibly 'unfair treatment' in the free market. When one person enjoys a work of art, whether it is a painting, poem, novel, sculpture or whatever, they do not destroy the ability of another person to get just as much enjoyment out of it. A work of art can go on producing enjoyment indefinitely for any number of people other than the purchaser of the work of art. Indeed, it may go on providing pleasure to people long after the artist is dead, but the reward the artist receives will only be (roughly) commensurate with the amount of aesthetic enjoyment the *purchaser* will get. Therefore, it is possible, and very often will actually be the case, that the benefit the artist confers on society as a whole will be much greater than the reward received from the sale of their art. So, the case of *art* constitutes a clear counter-example to the service version of the argument from desert since, according to that argument, the free market confers rewards upon individuals to the extent that they render a valuable service to society. However, the services that artists render to the community will typically be greater, and in some cases much greater, than the rewards they get in the free market.

Even a very cursory examination of the history of art confirms that the benefits artists confer are generally much greater than the rewards they get from the sale of their art. Probably the most famous example of this is Vincent van Gogh, who lived his life in extremely modest circumstances but whose works have since brought pleasure to many millions of people, yet he is certainly not an isolated case. Readers who examine the history of art will find that it is not at all unusual for famous artists to have lived their lives in poverty.[9]

Although artists perhaps represent the clearest case of people whose reward is much less than the benefit they provide, there are a number of other occupations of which this is also true. The situation arises wherever a product is a non-rival good — that is, one person's enjoyment does not prevent others from enjoying it — that has an *indefinitely long lifespan*. Obviously, books and poems have this characteristic. If one person reads a book or poem they do not prevent another person from reading it, and books and poems can exist for a very long time: far beyond the lifetime of the author. Other important examples are discoveries and inventions. We are all familiar with the saying, 'Give a man a fish and he eats for a day, teach him how to fish and he eats for the rest of his life.' Actually, this underestimates the benefit that can come from *discovering*, for example, how to catch fish. If a woman in a village discovers how to catch fish, she confers a benefit not just on the others in the village for the rest of their lives, but also on their descendants. People who are not yet alive benefit from her discovery. Since many of the beneficiaries of her discovery have not even been born when the discovery is made, they cannot pay the inventor for the benefit she has brought to them. The reward the inventor will get will be less than the free market can confer. This point applies, of course, not just to ways of catching fish, but to any discovery the benefits of which continue way beyond the lifetime of the discoverer.

More generally, for the creators of anything that endures for a very long period of time — ideas, concepts, theories, as well as works of art and scientific inventions — the benefit they confer on society as a whole will tend to be greater than the reward they get under a free market. Such activities constitute another counter-example to the service version of the argument from desert.

Another difficulty for the service version arises when we consider charity work. Much charity work is entirely voluntary. The free market does not confer rewards on those who, for example, supply food or shelter to the destitute for the simple reason that the recipients of these services are not able to pay. Yet it is surely the case that charity workers are providing a service to the community. Conversely, a financial expert who advises the wealthy on tax minimisation may even be doing the community as a whole a disservice, yet they may be paid well for what they do. These points show that it is a mistake to think that the free market confers rewards on those who provide a service that is of benefit to the community; it would be closer to the truth to say it confers rewards on people to the extent that they provide services to those who are best able to pay.

So far, we have not yet considered what is perhaps the most obvious class of people who provide a valuable service to the community, but who would receive no reward at all in the free market. These are the providers of the services we considered in chapter one: lighthouse keepers, footpath, road and street lighting constructors, the police, the army and so on. For a variety of reasons it is not possible for a person to make a profit by offering these services in the free market, but we would agree that these services are of benefit to the community. So again, the free market does not confer rewards upon individuals to the extent that they provide to the community a service that is of benefit.

In this section we have looked at a range of occupations which provide to the community something of benefit, but which the free market either does not reward at all, or the reward it provides is systematically less than the benefit the activity brings to the community. This shows that the service version of the argument from desert has many counter-examples. There is yet another moral we can draw from the discussion of this section. Every now and again we hear the claim made that various activities — art, scientific research and so on — should be treated as a business, no different from any other business. However, this claim

overlooks the fact that these activities *are* different from other businesses: the benefit they bring to the community is systematically and sub-
stantially greater than the reward the free market confers upon their
practitioners. Arguments from desert attempt to provide a moral justification for the free market by claiming that it gives rewards to people
that are commensurate with the benefits they bring to society by making available high quality, low cost goods and services. Clearly, in this
argument it is assumed that it is morally right that the reward people get
should be commensurate with the benefit they confer upon society.
(Otherwise, the argument would not be a moral *justification* of the free
market.) Yet we have just seen that the benefits which certain people in
a free market, such as artists and scientists, bring to society are greater
than the rewards they receive. So, if 'justice is to be done', if the rewards
they get are to be commensurate with the benefits they confer on society, it is morally appropriate that society give them *more* reward than
that which the free market by itself gives them.

A VARIANT ON THE ARGUMENT FROM DESERT: IT IS WRONG TO PROVIDE ASSISTANCE TO STRUGGLING PRODUCERS

One occasionally hears commentators say that it is wrong for the government to give assistance to struggling producers because that is to
'reward inefficiency while punishing efficiency'. What is meant by this
claim? The thinking behind it is as follows. Why should some producer
be struggling? The reason — according to this line of thought — must
be because they have been inefficient. Had they been efficient, that is,
had they succeeded in producing many high quality goods cheaply, then
they would not be struggling. Now, where would the government get
the money to support these inefficient producers? Clearly, it would only
come from taxes, and those taxes would mostly come from people and
companies that are making a lot of money. But why would these producers be making a lot of money? Clearly, because they *are* efficient. So,
supporting struggling producers involves taking money from efficient
producers and giving it to inefficient producers; it is rewarding inefficiency while punishing efficiency.

This argument is really a version of the argument from desert. Why
should it be thought to be wrong to take money from efficient producers? Clearly, because it is thought that in efficiently supplying cheap
and good products, those producers have deserved their money.[10] It
may also be thought that efficiency is a meritorious personal quality,
akin to industriousness and frugality. Similarly, why should it be
thought to be wrong to give money to the inefficient? Clearly, because

the inefficient have *not* supplied cheap and good products, and so do not deserve the money. It may also be thought that inefficiency is a bad personal quality, like laziness or profligacy. For these reasons it is thought to be wrong to give money to the inefficient and take it from the efficient.

Plainly, this reasoning is a version of the argument from desert. Consequently, it possesses the strengths and weaknesses of that argument: it has a certain amount of truth to it, but it also has many counter-examples.

STATUS AND THE FREE MARKET

We have already noted that in a free market there will be a tendency for the gap between rich and poor to increase. Now, it may very well be the case that, with the operation of the free market, the poor do not necessarily grow poorer in absolute terms — although we should also observe that there is some evidence that the 'typical' person will actually tend to become slightly worse off.[11] But whether, in absolute terms, average people become better or worse off in the free market, the *divide* between the rich and the rest increases. Many people may respond to this by saying, 'So what? If the poor and the majority of the people in the middle do not become any worse off, does it really matter if the rich get even richer?' It may even be claimed that if the rich get richer while everyone else remains more or less the same, it is a good thing since the *total* amount of wealth in the community is increased. However, one important aspect that is left out by this is the 'status' or 'standing' people will have in a community. Consider the following two situations.

> SITUATION ONE A particular person, who we will call 'A', earns about $25 000 per annum. This is enough to ensure that A can eat satisfactorily, has a roof over his head, a car, is warm in winter, and so on. Moreover, in situation one, everyone else in A's society earns pretty much the same as A.

> SITUATION TWO Again, in this situation, A earns $25 000 per annum. As in situation one, this is enough to ensure that A's basic needs are met: he has enough to eat, is warm in winter and has a car to drive. However, in this society everybody else earns about $250 000 per annum and so has much larger, more expensive homes; they drive what to A are luxury cars, they are more expensively and fashionably dressed, and so on.

In which situation is A likely to be happier? We are confident that A is *likely* to be happier in Situation One. Of course, we can easily imagine circumstances in which A was happier in Situation Two: for example, if he had a boring or soul destroying job or a miserable home life in Situation One. But if A was to be happier in Situation Two, there would need to be some additional factor making his lot worse in One, or better in Two. It is only commonsense that, in Situation Two, the sheer fact that A was 'at the bottom of society's heap' would tend to be a *minus* for A. Most would regard being 'at the bottom of the heap' as a negative or undesirable thing. So, although A is as materially well off in both situations, he is plausibly less well off in Situation Two, simply by virtue of occupying the lowest position in society.

These remarks illustrate an important point about status. Status 'behaves' in a very different way from money or material goods. A person who has only one loaf of bread, or only one dollar, obviously has less than a person who has ten loaves of bread, or ten dollars. However, the person who only has one loaf of bread still has a small quantity of something good: having the loaf of bread is a 'positive' rather than a 'negative'. A person with low status does not have less of some good thing than a person with high status. Having low status is actually a negative thing. People with low status do not have *less* of something good; rather, they have something *negative*. Low status is unpleasant. This creates a variety of difficulties for arguments from desert. The basic difficulty is quite simple. According to the argument from desert, the reward a person gets in the free market is determined by the benefits they bring to society by making available for sale products that are cheap and/or good. Yet this concentrates only on a monetary reward. Another form of reward that society is capable of conferring on a person is high status or prestige. Conversely, low status or lack of prestige is a 'negative' which society is capable of inflicting on an individual. (Recall that low status seems to be not merely a lack of something that is good, but something that is actually bad.)

We can regard the total reward that society confers on an individual to be a function of factors that include both the monetary reward and the prestige associated with their occupation or achievement. We have seen earlier in this chapter that the argument from desert does not show *monetary* rewards to be distributed according to desert. But even if it did there would still be a potential problem with the argument from desert: does the free market ensure that *total* reward (that is, monetary reward + factors including prestige) will be conferred on individuals in accordance with desert? It is easy to think of situations in which it seems the free market would not confer 'total reward' in accordance with desert. Let us suppose that for some reason the occupation of 'widget making' enjoys very low status. This will be, for the widget maker, a negative or bad thing, lowering the total reward they receive from society. Yet it is hard to see how this lowering of the total reward could be deserved. If the widget maker is providing a valuable service to the community in providing widgets, and not in addition doing it any harm, we at least need to be given some argument as to why the 'negative' of low status is a thing that is deserved.

It might be argued that the free market does contain within it a mechanism for compensating the widget maker for their low status. If widget making is a low status occupation, then fewer people will be attracted to it. But if fewer people are engaged in making widgets then, so the argument goes, the supply of widgets will go down and so their price will go up. Therefore, each widget maker will be able to make more profit on the sale of their widgets and so will receive a higher income. This higher income will, according to the argument, satisfactorily compensate them for the low status of their occupation. However, this argument does not stand up under closer examination. In particular, the argument is not tenable if there are few people in work anyhow, if the degree of social security support for people without a job is low, or if there is considerable social stigma attached to being without a job. Let us consider a person who is considering whether or not to become a widget maker. Whether they will choose to do so will depend upon the other options available to them: they will, presumably choose to become a widget maker if it is the best of the options available to them. If it is very hard to get a job, it may be that the only options open to a person are either being a widget maker or having no job at all. They will, therefore, choose to be a widget maker if it is *better* than not having a job. And if, for a number of reasons, being without a job is very unpleasant, people will rationally choose to be a widget maker, even if it has very low status. Therefore, the low status of being a widget maker need not result in any shortage of people employed in making widgets, and so need not result in an increase in the profits that go to widget makers. That is, the operation of the free market need not compensate people for the low status of their occupations.

It should also be observed that this difficulty is not at all improbable or unlikely. The situation just described will occur when the potential employees are faced with the choice of either being in a low status occupation or being without work. People with limited qualifications or experience frequently are in exactly that position. The jobs that are low paid usually have low status attached to them *because* they are low paid. The free market will not ensure that people in such jobs are compensated for the low status of their occupation.

In a society in which a person gains status *simply from having a lot of money*, or suffers low status from having little or no money, it is as if the rich are paid twice, and those who are poor have what little benefit their money gives reduced even further. Not only does the money the rich have enable them to buy large houses and expensive cars, the sheer fact that it is a lot of money also 'buys' them status, too. The money the poor receive may enable them to buy or rent a small house, but the sheer fact that the quantity of money they get is small means they have low status. Since low status is a bad thing, the total reward they get from society (including monetary reward + status) is reduced.

HOW IMPORTANT IS A PERSON'S 'POSITION' IN SOCIETY?

A very natural response to the considerations given above is: 'Very well, perhaps the free market does not confer status according to desert, but so what? Perhaps low status is an unpleasant thing, but it is not seriously harmful. The inability of the free market to confer it according to desert is a minor imperfection, and, after all, obviously no system is going to be perfect. So, this is hardly a serious criticism of the free market.'

I suspect that the above response is likely to be fairly common, but there is some reason to believe that it is false. First, there is the evidence of commonsense. In wealthy countries, people spend most of their time working for things that are not necessary in order to meet their material needs. For example, a car costing only a few thousand dollars will get you from A to B at exactly the same speed (the speed limit) as one costing ten or even a hundred times as much. So why do people buy the more expensive car? Few people would seriously dispute that factors such as 'prestige', 'status' and 'presenting a good appearance to the world' play a very important role. Many of the other things people often buy are more than is necessary for their material well-being; consider, for example, the size and appearance of their house and additions to it, the appearance and brand name of clothes, and so on. Again, I don't think many people would seriously dispute that the pursuit of status often plays a pretty significant part in people going after these things. However, if people spend so much of their money and energy pursuing status, it must be fairly important to them. So, these fairly commonsense observations indicate that status is quite important.

There is a body of medical evidence which indicates that status is very important in determining health and life expectancy. It is crucially important to understand that, according to some recent studies (which we will shortly discuss), the reason why high status means better health (and low status means poorer health) is *not merely* because people with high status can afford better medical care — although that is undoubtedly also a factor. Rather, the evidence indicates that status itself affects health. That is, according to these studies, the sheer fact that a person is at the top of the social pecking order will tend to improve their health, while the sheer fact of being at the bottom will have a negative effect on it *independently* of the quality of the medical care they receive.

One recent book on this topic is Richard Wilkinson's *Unhealthy Societies*.[12] According to Wilkinson, the causes of dying in poor countries are very different from those in wealthy countries. In poor countries, infectious diseases are the main cause of mortality, while in wealthy countries they are mainly degenerative diseases and diseases which are a consequence of an affluent lifestyle, such as heart attack, stroke and obesity. Wilkinson focussed on developed, wealthy countries, however, not all such countries are equally wealthy. Let us consider two groups of people — one group in a very wealthy developed country and another group in a developed but not so wealthy country — that enjoy a similar standard of living in material terms (both groups may contain individuals who earn on average about US$20 000 per annum and enjoy a similar degree of access to medical care). You might expect both groups to enjoy more or less similar health, but this is not what Wilkinson found. His study consistently found that the groups in the wealthier countries experienced poorer health than their materially equivalent groups in the not so wealthy countries. The factor related to their poorer health was not lower income, nor lack of access to medical facilities, but simply their having lower social status in their country.[13]

Wilkinson also made a significant discovery concerning the relation between the *absolute* wealth of a country and the health of its citizens. He found that, once a country became 'wealthy enough', no additional wealth improved the health of its citizens.[14] The citizens of a very wealthy developed country enjoy no better health than the citizens in otherwise equivalent, but less wealthy, developed countries. He concludes that a person's position in their country's *social order* has more impact on their health than their income and believes this supports the idea that it is social status itself which affects a person's health. He further concludes that in the developed world it is not the richest countries that have the best health, but the most egalitarian: the health of a country's citizens is better if there is an even distribution of wealth in the country, but worse off if there is a large gap between rich and poor.

It must be stressed that Wilkinson's findings do not show that wealth is irrelevant in determining the state of health of the people in a country. If a country is poor, then increasing the wealth of its citizens is a very effective way of increasing their health. But once the wealth of a country rises to a certain level, then increasing the equality of distribution of its wealth is *a more effective way* of increasing the health of its citizens than further increasing the absolute amount of wealth.

The claims just considered might be greeted with scepticism. 'How', it might be asked, 'could the sheer fact that a person is at the bottom of the social ladder affect their health? Low income or lack of access to medical care could of course affect a person's health; but if a person has access to these things, how could their merely occupying a position of low social status have an influence on their *health*?' The answer to this question, according to Wilkinson, is partly psychological (or in his terminology, 'cognitive') and partly biochemical. He describes many ways in which factors such as social stress, poor social networks, low self-esteem, high rates of depression, anxiety, insecurity and the loss of a sense of control can predispose people towards disease.[15] If people at the bottom of society's social order are more prone to those psychological conditions, then, according to Wilkinson, it should be not be surprising that their lower status should be associated with poorer health.

It is worthwhile here to briefly give a few examples of the mechanisms by which these psychological and social conditions can affect health. One example given by Wilkinson concerns the thymus gland, essential to the healthy functioning of the immune system.[16] Anatomical studies have shown that this gland is often shrunken in the poor and Wilkinson says this is caused by chronic stress. In this way, claims Wilkinson, the poor may become more prone to disease. In another case, early studies had revealed that age-adjusted death rates from heart disease are four times higher for low-status civil servants than for high-status civil servants.[17] A study by Eric Brunner has found that the cause for the higher death rates amongst low-status civil servants is due to elevated levels of low-density lipoproteins and fibrinogen, which increase the likelihood of clogged blood vessels and heart disease.[18] Brunner further concluded that the elevated levels of these substances in low-status civil servants is due to chronic stress.[19] We can summarise the causal relationship postulated by Wilkinson and Brunner as shown in figure 6.1:

Figure 6.1

Let us now see how these claims by Wilkinson and others might bear on the argument from desert. We have already noted that the free market does not confer status according to desert. One natural response to this is to concede that the free market is, perhaps, imperfect in this respect, but to claim that this is only a *minor* flaw, on the grounds that status is of only minor importance. Low status — it may be argued —

may be unpleasant but it does not do people any actual harm. However, if the claims of Wilkinson and Brunner are correct, it might not be true that status is a trivial or unimportant thing. Their investigations suggest that low status increases people's propensity to disease and lowers their life expectancy. Moreover, it appears that it does this by affecting their *psychological state*. If being at the bottom of society's ladder can so affect a person's state of mind that their life expectancy is actually reduced, it can hardly be said to be unimportant. If their claims are correct, the failure of the free market to distribute status according to desert is therefore a serious flaw. This, of course, leaves unanswered the question: *are* the claims of Wilkinson and Brunner correct? This is a question which can only be answered by further empirical investigation by the experts.

AN ETHICAL ASSUMPTION OF THE ARGUMENTS FROM DESERT

In the final section of this chapter we will consider a fundamental *ethical* assumption upon which the arguments from desert are based. The advocates of these arguments say that the free market confers rewards upon individuals in a way that is commensurate with what those individuals have rendered to the rest of society, or with their meritorious qualities, and hence in accordance with what they deserve. In this chapter we have seen that while this claim may be true as a first approximation, it also has a wide range of counter-examples and difficult cases. Even if it *were* the case that the free market always gave people no more and no less than they had deserved, would that constitute a moral justification of the free market? If it is to constitute a moral justification, then it must be morally right that people are given wealth in accordance with what they have deserved. This might, on the face of it, seem like a claim that is obviously true, but when we look at it more closely it starts to look rather more dubious. It is useful to distinguish between the following two questions.

1 Is it morally correct that a person who, through their activities, has earned or deserved some benefit, should receive that benefit?

2 Is it morally correct that a person who has not done anything to deserve some benefit should *not* receive that benefit?

The answer to the first question is presumably, 'Yes', but let us consider the second question more closely. We can approach this question by considering an imaginary example. Suppose you encounter a complete stranger drowning in a swimming pool. Should you save this person? We will assume you are a strong swimmer and, although you would have to experience some unpleasantness if you were to jump in and save them, you would not be in any real danger from drowning yourself. But, let us also suppose that the person is a *complete stranger* to you: they have never saved you from drowning, neither have they ever rendered any other kind of service to you, nor done you any favours. We can also suppose that you know for a fact that the person slipped into pool because they did something foolhardy, like dancing on the diving board. We would say it was the person's own fault that they had slipped into the pool. I'm pretty sure that, even in such circumstances, we would still say you *ought* to save the person. We would morally condemn someone who said, 'Well, this drowning person has never done anything for me, so why should I save them?' We would also morally condemn someone who refused to save the drowning person on the grounds that they (the drowning person) had been foolish or silly. So let us grant that you morally ought to save the person; but has the person done anything to *deserve* being saved by you? If they have never had any contact with you at all, it is hard to see how they could be said to have deserved to be saved by you. So, the person has not done anything to *deserve* your saving him, but still, it is morally right that you should save him. It still seems to be morally right to save the person even though it is through their own foolishness that they are in this situation.

Let us now consider again the claim raised in the second question — that if a person has not done anything to receive some benefit then it is morally right that they should not receive that benefit. Is this claim always true? The case of the drowning person just considered shows that sometimes, at least, it does not seem to be true. It *is* right to save the drowning person even though they have not done anything to deserve being saved.

To what extent do these considerations cast into doubt the argument for the free market from desert? It may be suggested that the case of a person who is, for example, starving because they cannot get a job in the free market, and a person who is drowning in a swimming pool, are not really the same. It may, for example, be claimed that a person who is starving only has themselves to blame for their predicament: if only they had tried harder, or shown more initiative, then perhaps they would not be starving. While this may or may not be true, it is not clear how it saves the argument from desert. Remember that it seemed to be right to save the drowning person even if they had fallen into the pool as a result of their own foolishness. So even if, in the free market, a person is starving because they have been foolish or lazy, it is at least unclear whether it is right to let them starve. Another reason that may be given for saying that the two cases are not the same is that, while the person in the pool may very well drown, it is unlikely that a person without a job would literally starve: they may eventually find some way of supporting themselves. But again it is not clear how this does much good for the argument from desert. It would surely be right to save the person even if there was only a *possibility* they might drown.

What this suggests is that even if the free market distributed rewards according to desert there would still at least be a question as to whether the free market was thereby morally justified. In particular, there would still be a question as to whether the market was morally justified if it conferred no benefits at all on those who had not contributed anything to society. Of course, it is a matter of fact that some people feel it *is* wrong to withhold all kinds of benefit from people who have not made a contribution to society. The principle that a person should not receive a benefit unless they have done something to deserve it is at least controversial. So, it seems at least *questionable* whether the free market would be morally justified even if it distributed benefits according to what had been deserved.

SUMMARY

Throughout this chapter we have critically examined versions of the argument from desert. We noted that there are two versions of this argument: the merit version and the service version. The merit version of the argument asserts that the free market confers rewards upon individuals to the extent that they exhibit meritorious qualities, such as industriousness and intelligence. However, we saw numerous difficulties with this argument: sometimes the free market confers rewards upon people who exhibit qualities that do not seem to be meritorious, and fails to confer rewards upon people who do. The idea that there is some set of fixed, intrinsically meritorious qualities rewarded by the free market also runs up against the difficulty that the precise set of qualities which leads to success in the free market changes with time, and with the development of technology. Perhaps it is true that there are some qualities, such as energy and intelligence, that will always tend to be rewarded in the free market, but there are also many other institutions, other than the free market, in which those qualities will tend to lead to success.

Next we considered the service version of the argument from desert. We noted that there is an important class of occupations that does not receive in the free market the reward that is commensurate with the benefit they render to society. These include the occupations that produce non-rival goods that also have an indefinitely long lifespan. These goods therefore have a potentially unlimited capacity to confer benefits on society. Some important examples of occupations that produce goods of this nature are: artists, writers, scientists and inventors. A consideration of these occupations also showed the incorrectness of a currently popular tendency to treat these occupations — and indeed all occupations — as if they were just another business, no different from any other business.

We then noted a general difficulty for both the merit and service versions of the argument from desert: the inability of the free market to confer *status* according to desert. It was noted that some investigators have found that status, or people's position in the social hierarchy, is so important it even affects their life expectancy. If their findings are correct then the inability of the free market to confer status according to desert may be a serious shortcoming.

Finally, we noted that one basic assumption of the argument from desert is at least questionable. The argument assumes that if a person has done nothing to deserve a particular benefit, then there is nothing morally wrong with them not receiving it. If this were correct, it would mean there was nothing morally wrong with letting a drowning stranger die or a poor, jobless person starve.

In conclusion, while the claims of the arguments from desert might be true 'as a first approximation', or at least roughly true for some occupations, they also have a range of counter-examples. However, there is another idea which came up in this chapter which is worth re-iterating. In discussing the effects of status on health we noted that, according to Wilkinson, once a country attains a certain degree of wealth, further increases in wealth do not serve to improve the health of its citizens, but increases in the equality of distribution of wealth *do*. This at least suggests, but does not prove, the following hypothesis: it is appropriate for a community to increase its wealth up to a certain level, but once it reaches that level, further increases in wealth start to become less important than other aims. This is a theme to which we will return later in this book.

7

SOCIAL DARWINISM

In the previous chapter we considered the idea that perhaps the free market confers rewards upon people in accordance with what they deserve. However, we also found that, although this may be correct as a rough first approximation, it has many counter-examples. We noted that there are instances in which the free market confers rewards upon those who do not appear to deserve it, and do not confer rewards on those who do. Now, a natural response to this might be: 'Of course the free market is not always going to be fair. The real world is never perfectly fair. In the real world, the rewards will go to the strong, or the dominant, or the cunning. Others who might be equally 'deserving' but who lack these qualities will miss out. This is just the way of nature and since we live in the real world, not some morally perfect utopia, we just have to put up with this.' If we encounter someone who argues in this way, we have met someone who is advocating something close to a form of *social Darwinism*. It is this doctrine that forms the focus of this chapter.

Social Darwinism is nowadays less popular as a way of defending the free market than it once was, but it is still worth discussing for two reasons. The first reason is that it was once an *extremely* popular form of argument, with rich businessmen and famous economists publicly proclaiming that what happened in the business world was nothing more than nature's law of the survival of the fittest applied to the economic realm — and history has shown that ideas that were once extremely popular can have a way of making a comeback. The second reason for discussing social Darwinism is that one of the ideas that forms a key ingredient of it is still influential. Social Darwinists say it is *natural* that the strong should prosper and the weak fall by the wayside. What may be, and often is, implicit in this is the idea that if it is *natural*, then it is *good*; and the idea that 'if it's natural, it's good' is one that seems to have an ongoing appeal. Up until fairly recently, it was frequently used as an argument against all forms of sexuality other than the heterosexual. Nowadays its most popular use is probably in defence of various environmental causes, and against developments such as the genetic modification of foods. The idea that 'if it's natural, it's good' is one that does not seem to go away. So it is still worth discussing the way in which the idea has been claimed to justify social Darwinism.

SOCIAL DARWINISM AND ECONOMIC RATIONALISM

We have seen that economic rationalists say the primary goal of policy should be the maximisation of economic efficiency, and the most effective means for achieving this goal is a free market operating under ideal conditions. According to this view, the function of government is to try to ensure that society moves as close as possible to an ideal free market. In such a state, each company is competing against its rivals who are producing the same or similar products. Those companies that are able to make the products efficiently will survive and prosper. Those that don't will not be able to survive: they will go bankrupt, or be taken over, or just become smaller and smaller. There will, that is, be a struggle for existence in the market, with the fittest, or most efficient, surviving and the less efficient eventually dying out. Eventually, so the argument goes, the market will be populated only by those companies that are maximally 'fit' — by the maximally efficient producers.

Of course, all this bears a clear analogy to Darwinian natural selection, or the process whereby organisms in the natural environment struggle for existence against their rivals: the unfit are eliminated and only the fit survive. In fact, it is tempting to see the process whereby the inefficient producers are eliminated and the efficient producers survive as simply Darwin's law of the survival of the fittest applied to the economic realm. This parallel has been used as the basis for a moral justification of the operation of the free market. The argument proceeds as follows. Darwinian natural selection is a *natural* process and because of the close analogy between Darwinian natural selection and the process of the survival of the fittest, or most efficient in the marketplace, it can be said that the latter is a natural process, too. It is further claimed, that which is *natural* is also morally good, or morally appropriate. Therefore, it is concluded, the process of the survival of the most efficient in the marketplace is a morally good, or morally appropriate, process. This argument is a defence of social Darwinism.

Social Darwinism can be summed up in three short sentences. The law of the survival of the fittest is natural. The natural is good. So, in human society, the law of the survival of the fittest should prevail.

It is very important to understand that a person who advocates social Darwinism is doing a lot more than simply claiming, 'the theory of evolution is true'. The theory of evolution is a hypothesis — widely accepted by biologists — about how the living organisms we see in the world around us evolved from species that existed in earlier times. It is a hypothesis about how, in the natural world, things have happened. It is not, in itself, a claim about how things morally ought to have developed, and neither is it, in itself, a claim about how they morally ought to develop in the future. *In itself*, Darwin's theory of evolution has nothing to say about matters of morality at all. Moreover, Darwin himself was not an advocate of the moral view known as social Darwinism.[1] Consequently, it would be an error to think that *social* Darwinism is 'proved to be true' by the discoveries of Darwin. It is also a mistake to think that social Darwinism is merely 'the application of Darwin's discoveries' to the social sphere. Someone who merely applied Darwin's discoveries to the social sphere would see human society as being a realm in which, as a matter of fact, the fit survive and the unfit are wiped out. Yet social Darwinism is not just the belief that as a matter of fact, the fit survive and the unfit die. Social Darwinism is the belief that that is how human society *morally ought to be*: the social Darwinist says it is morally right that the fit should survive and the unfit die out, not just that that is what actually happens.

HISTORICAL BACKGROUND TO SOCIAL DARWINISM

Social Darwinism is, historically, an important intellectual movement. Perhaps the most famous social Darwinist was Herbert Spencer. A contemporary of Darwin, Spencer actually hit upon a version of the theory of evolution seven years before Darwin first published his *Origin of Species*. Spencer also coined the phrase 'the survival of the fittest'.[2] But, unlike Darwin, Spencer was primarily concerned with *human* evolution. He did not develop the theory of evolution as an account of the development of plants and animals. He was, moreover, primarily concerned with the development of mental characteristics rather than physical ones. Spencer was, like Darwin, influenced by the nineteenth century thinker Thomas Malthus, who had observed, in his *Essay on the Principle of Population*, that populations, whether of animals or humans, tend to increase *faster* than the resources upon which they rely.[3] He reasoned that this meant that eventually a population must become too large for the resources — land or food supply — upon which it depends. So, overpopulation is inevitable.

Spencer saw that when population rises to the level where it surpasses the resources available — when there is not enough to go around — there will inevitably arise competition for the scarce resources. He believed that those possessing skill, intelligence, self-control and the power to adapt through technological innovation would survive in the struggle for scarce resources, while those who lack those qualities would not. Spencer therefore regarded competition for scarce resources as the means by which the human race would be improved. He thought that the process would eventually lead to a state in which all possessed those admirable virtues. For Spencer, competition is the process whereby mankind would eventually be led to a state of perfection.

Spencer's ideas were eagerly embraced by some of the leading businessmen of the time. For example, Andrew Carnegie wrote of his encounter with Spencer's ideas:

> I remember that light came as in a flood and all was clear ... I had found the truth of evolution. 'All is well since all grows better' became my motto, my true source of comfort. Man was not created with an instinct for his own degradation, but from the lower he had risen to the higher forms. Nor is there any conceivable end to this march to perfection. His face is turned to the light; he stands in the Sun and looks upward.[4]

And John D Rockefeller said:

> The growth of a large business is merely a survival of the fittest ... The American Beauty rose can be produced in the splendour and fragrance which bring cheer to its beholder only by sacrificing the early buds which grow up around it. This is not an evil tendency in business. It is merely the working out of a law of nature and a law of God.[5]

The general message of Spencer's philosophy was that evolution would lead mankind 'onward and upward' to a state of happy perfection. It would, unfortunately, lead to suffering on the part of the unfit, but this was an inevitable, although regrettable, consequence of the process. Overall, Spencerian philosophy was optimistic. He did, however, strongly condemn organised or institutionalised attempts to help the less fit members of society. Consider, for example, the following extraordinary passage.

> To aid the bad in multiplying, is, in effect, the same as maliciously providing for our descendants a multitude of enemies. Doubtless, individual altruism was all very well, but organised charity was intolerable:

unquestionable injury is done by agencies which undertake in a whole-
sale way to foster good-for-nothings, putting a stop to that natural
process of elimination by which society continually purifies itself.[6]

Another advocate of social Darwinism was William Graham
Sumner. Although Sumner shared Spencer's view that society does,
and should, conform to the principles of Darwinian natural selection,
in temperament he was very different from Spencer. While the latter
optimistically looked forward to human perfection, Sumner grimly
and puritanically emphasised the element of constant struggle in competition. Like Spencer, Sumner's social Darwinism led him to condemn practices which attempt to help the less fit members of society.
He wrote:

> Let it be understood that we cannot go outside this alternative: liber-
> ty, inequality, survival of the fittest; not-liberty, equality, survival of the
> unfittest. The former carries society forward and favours all its best
> members; the latter carries society downwards and favours all its worst
> members.[7]

Despite the rather harsh and joyless character of his message, and
despite a cold personal manner, Sumner was a highly successful lectur-
er at Yale, where his classes were extremely well attended. However,
unlike Spencer, he never gained the favour of the business elite. It
appears that the ruthless integrity of his views made him equally likely
to denounce both his enemies and his would-be allies.

Social Darwinism, as an intellectual movement, was most influential
in the last quarter of the nineteenth century, and in the period of the
twentieth century leading up to the First World War. Since then, it has
been a minority view, but it has a perennial appeal, especially with some
groups of the political far right. Moreover, social Darwinism, in a broad
sense, need not be restricted to extreme right wing groups. I am sure
the reader will have encountered people who argue that it is 'only natural' that the fit should survive and prosper.

THE ARGUMENTS FOR SOCIAL DARWINISM

There are, broadly speaking, four main arguments for social Darwinism.

1 The argument from the moral goodness (or the moral permissibili-
  ty) of that which is natural.
2 The argument from the inevitability of the process of evolution.
3 The argument that evolution will lead to a state of human perfection.
4 The argument that it will minimise suffering in the long term if we
  now let natural selection weed out the weak.

THE ARGUMENT FROM THE MORAL GOODNESS OF THAT WHICH IS NATURAL

The idea that the natural is good is often appealing, but on closer inspection it can start to look much less plausible. Usually, when people say that something is 'natural', what they mean is that it is found in nature; but many of the things we find in nature are the *opposite* of what we would normally regard as morally good. Lions will rip out the throats of young gazelles, cuckoos will throw other chicks out of the nest they have invaded, some wasps will lay eggs in live caterpillars which hatch and proceed to devour the still-living caterpillar, and so on. The claim that such things are morally good is certainly strongly in conflict with what we normally understand by 'moral goodness'. Killing, and the causing of pain and suffering are what we typically regard as paradigm cases of that which is *not* morally good. So, the person who claims that which is natural is morally good at least owes us some kind of an account as to *why* we ought to accept that the brutal and violent aspects of nature which don't appear to be morally good, actually *are* good.

Perhaps the most common argument is that these apparently brutal aspects of nature are just nature's way of keeping things 'in balance' — it is nature's way of ensuring that no one species becomes too numerous while no other species is driven to complete extinction. However, we should not overlook the fact that species *do* become extinct simply as a result of natural forces, and that other species, such as eucalypts in Australia, do come to dominate a particular region. Evolution doesn't keep all species 'in balance', at least if this is taken to mean that it prevents species from being wiped out completely while preventing others from becoming dominant.

Another common argument is that the lion, for example, which rips out the throat of the gazelle is just obeying its instinct. More generally, the acts of cruelty we find in nature are not performed by agents who have knowledge of moral right and wrong, but are merely performed by 'dumb animals' simply following their instincts, and which therefore cannot be morally condemned for what they do. It is, consequently, a mistake to see what goes on in nature as morally wrong. This argument is, as far as it goes, perfectly correct: animals cannot be morally condemned for what they do if they have no knowledge of right and wrong, and so there is very considerable plausibility in the claim that what goes on in nature is *not* morally wrong. But the same reasoning also shows that what goes on in nature is not morally right, either. If animals blindly following their instincts in ignorance of right and wrong shows that nature is not morally wrong, then equally, it shows it is not morally right. It shows it is morally neutral. Therefore, it does not show that what is natural is also morally good. There are also, of course, problems with carrying this idea over to the business world, since humans *can* tell the difference between right and wrong.

A variant on the claim that the natural is good is: *unnatural is bad*. Note that the claims, 'natural is good' and 'unnatural is bad', are *not* logically equivalent. To say that the natural is good does not rule out the unnatural being good, too. We find social Darwinists, such as Sumner, arguing as follows: 'organised charity, socialism, and so on are contrary to the law of nature, and so are morally bad'. This argument does not quite establish that social Darwinism *is* morally good but, if valid, it does perhaps establish that the alternatives to it are morally bad. So, if valid, it perhaps gives a reason to *prefer* social Darwinism, from a moral point of view, to the alternatives. However, the claim that the unnatural is bad is difficult to defend. Bandages are undoubtedly unnatural, but I do not believe anyone would thereby condemn the practice of putting a bandage on a cut finger as morally iniquitous. Probably most of the things we do in modern life — travel by car, watch television, work at a computer and eat processed food are unnatural, but few people would be persuaded that meant they were *morally* wrong (although they might be condemned on the grounds that they were bad for your health).

It is also fair to observe that people who use the argument, 'It's unnatural, therefore it is wrong', do so *selectively*. Some people condemn homosexuality on the grounds that it is 'unnatural', but such people (apart from ignoring studies which show that many species of animal do indeed take part in 'homosexual' acts) rarely advocate, say, nudism on the grounds that we do not find animals wearing clothes. Some argue against drugs on the grounds that they are 'unnatural' substances, but this condemnation is often not extended by such persons to other unnatural substances such as medicines, artificial sweeteners or food preservatives. If we were *consistent* in rejecting everything that is unnatural, we might end up having to go back to the cave. The view that, 'If it's unnatural, it's morally wrong', is therefore *very* difficult to defend.

People who defend social Darwinism may be guilty of the fallacy of attempting to derive 'ought' from 'is'.[8] A person is guilty of this fallacy if they argue that since some state of affairs is as a matter of fact the case, it morally ought to be the case. A social Darwinist would be guilty of this fallacy if they argued that since it occurs in nature that only the fit survive and prosper, it is morally right that only the fit *should* survive and prosper. However, this does not logically follow at all. To say that in nature only the fit survive and prosper is to simply to say how things seem to be, but asserting *how things are* is to do something different from asserting *how things morally ought to be* for the very simple reason that it is possible for the way things are to be morally wrong. It does not follow automatically that since things *are* a particular way, they morally ought to be that way. Moral philosophers call the belief that you can infer how things ought to be from the way the are 'the fallacy of attempting to derive "ought" from "is"'. It is also sometimes claimed that social Darwinism commits the *naturalistic fallacy* of attempting to define moral goodness in 'naturalistic' terms.[9]

Social Darwinists claim that the operation of the free market approximates closely (or more closely than any other system) the process of natural selection, or survival of the fittest, in the natural world. But is this claim true? The first thing to note is that the free market is a very long way from the 'state of nature'. The free market requires people to recognise the rights of ownership and private property and to accept the custom of paying for goods; that is, of not taking from someone else a particular good that one wants unless prepared to give a quantity of money, or something else of equal value, in exchange. It will also require the existence of a government to ensure that people conform to this practice, and punish those who do not. It should also be observed that 'fitness' in the state of nature is a very different thing from 'fitness' in the free market. An individual who is fit in the state of nature will, perhaps, be someone who is physically strong, or who is able to run fast. However, possession of those qualities is not likely to bring an individual much success in the free market nowadays. Conversely, an individual who is supremely fit according to the standards of fitness applicable in the free market — say, Bill Gates or John Paul Getty — is unlikely to count as very fit in the state of nature. At least on the face of it, the free market does not closely resemble the state of nature.

Even if we overlook these points, there is still a difficulty with the idea that the free market most closely approximates the state of nature. The difficulty is that the particular version of the free market that most closely resembles the state of nature is not one that any economic rationalist would wish to advocate. For example, the version of the free market most closely resembling the state of nature would allow, for example, *false advertising*. We find a close analogue of false advertising in nature when some species mimic the appearance of other species to their own advantage. Deception is a very widespread aspect of animal communication, but not many advocates of economic rationalism would say there should be deception in the free market. More generally, the version of the free market that most resembles the state of nature would have no government intervention at all; but economic rationalists, as opposed to 'extreme free marketeers', do not advocate no government at all. Economic rationalists see the role of government as preserving competition and moving society closer to an ideal market. This will involve, for example, preventing the formation of monopolies and collusive pricing, preventing theft, maintaining honesty in advertising and providing at least those public goods necessary for the efficient running of the free market but which cannot be provided by it. Therefore, economic rationalists do not advocate the version of the free market that most closely resembles the state of nature. Hence, economic rationalism cannot be justified on the grounds that it most closely resembles the state of nature.

THE ARGUMENT FROM THE INEVITABILITY OF THE PROCESS OF EVOLUTION

One argument for the free market that is prominent in the writings of both Spencer and Sumner appeals to the inevitability of the process of the survival of the fittest.[10] The idea is that natural selection is an unavoidable or inexorable process. Governments might try to arrest this process, but the best they can hope to achieve is a temporary slowing down of it. Eventually, the natural forces that favour the fit will win out. As just presented, the above considerations do not constitute a moral justification of the free market. However, there are two lines of thought which, if valid, would show at least that it is not the case that governments should try to do anything to alter the processes that would take place under the free market.

The first line of thought proceeds as follows. There is a well-accepted principle of moral philosophy which is summarised by the saying, '"ought" implies "can"'. What this means is that a person ought to do something only if they can do it, or are able to do it. The reader is invited to consider the following questions: Should you travel back in time and prevent Hitler from ever having been born? Is there a moral obligation on you to do this? Obviously, you *can't* do it as it is not possible for you to do it, but is there a moral obligation on you to do it? Pretty clearly, *if it is not possible* to do something, such as travel back in time and stop Hitler being born, then it is not appropriate to say that you nevertheless have a moral obligation to do so. You have a moral obligation to do something only if you *can* do it. Conversely, if it is not possible for you to do something, then there is no moral obligation on you to do it.

Now, all of this has relevance for the morality of the free market. As we have noted, advocates of social Darwinism see the 'survival of the economically fit' as an irresistible 'law of nature'. According to these thinkers, governments might try to prevent this by, for example, legis-lation designed to help the economically weak, or taxes designed to dis-tribute wealth from the economically strong to the weak. But all of this is considered by them as futile as a child on a beach building sand walls trying to prevent the tide from coming in: eventually, failure is inevitable. Similarly, so this argument goes, eventually the economical-ly strong will assert themselves over the weak. Therefore, say the social Darwinists, it is not possible for governments to prevent the economi-cally strong from prospering any more than it is possible for them to successfully legislate against the law of gravitation. Anyone, including a government, ought to do something only if they *can* do it. Since it is not possible for a government to stop the economically strong winning out over the weak, *it is not the case that they ought to try.*

If the above claims are correct, governments should not try to prevent the social and economic outcomes that are going to occur anyway due to the operation of the free market. This does not con-stitute a moral justification of the free market, but, if valid, it does show there is nothing morally wrong with letting the free market have free reign. There is, however, another closely related argument which, again if valid, has a slightly stronger conclusion. It aims to show that it is morally wrong to try to interfere with the survival of the fittest in the free market. Like the first argument, it starts from the premise that it is not possible to interfere with the survival of the fittest in the free market and therefore it is futile to try. But, with the second argument, it is further asserted that it is morally wrong for a government to spend money on activities which are futile — to do so would be a waste, and to waste scarce resources is morally wrong. Therefore, it is argued, it is morally wrong for governments to try to alter the (supposedly inevitable) process of survival of the fittest in the free market.

Let us critically examine these arguments. First, we should note that there is probably some truth to the claim that the 'survival of the fittest' is like some inexorable force of nature, such as the incoming tide, which cannot be stopped. This is not just true in the biological sphere, it is probably, at least to some extent, also true in the econom-ic sphere. It is probably inevitable that, no matter what economic sys-tem is implemented, the industrious, the intelligent (or the cunning) and the resourceful will tend to do better than people who lack these qualities. Some degree of inequality, in which the 'fit' are better off than the 'unfit', is almost certainly inevitable; but it does not follow from this that the degree of the inequality that exists between the fit and the unfit is beyond our control. Indeed, it is easy to see that it is to some extent under government control. 'Progressive' systems of taxation, laws against the formation of monopolies, the minimum wage, death duties and social security are all means by which the extent of inequality in a country can be reduced, even if it cannot be eliminated altogether. Perhaps the law of the survival of the fittest means some degree of inequality is inevitable, but it does not follow that the degree of inequality that would be produced in a totally deregulated free market is also inevitable. (In a similar way, perhaps perfect *justice* is unattainable, but that does not mean that a government should stop trying to formulate laws which are as just as they can make them.) Perhaps it would be futile for governments to try to completely eliminate inequality, but it does not follow that it is futile for them to try to reduce it. So, any argument for governmental inaction from the inevitability of the survival of the fittest fails.

THE ARGUMENT THAT EVOLUTION WILL LEAD TO A STATE OF HUMAN PERFECTION

This is the argument that is especially prominent in the writings of Spencer, and which also seems to have persuaded such important business figures as Rockefeller and Carnegie. It is, however, probably the argument that has fared worst with the passage of time. Part of the reason why the argument is now in such disrepute is the association it has with movements such as eugenics and Nazism;[11] however, the argument is also based on an assumption that biologists now recognise to be false. It is simply not the case that evolution carries life towards a state of perfection. Evolution tells us that the fittest will survive, but the fittest need not be closer to perfection than the unfit. Typically, we think of one thing as being closer to perfection than another if it has more value than the other; a thing which *is* perfect is a thing that has supreme value. The products of the survival of the fittest need not be perfect in this sense. If the human race were wiped out by some virulent and incurable virus, not many of us would be inclined to say the virus was closer to perfection, or of more value, than human beings. It has sometimes been claimed that if there were a nuclear war then humans and other mammals would be wiped out, while cockroaches and scorpions would survive, but few would claim that this meant cockroaches and scorpions were of more value. So, the organisms that succeed in the struggle for existence need not be closer to perfection, or of more value, than those that do not.

One story of survival of the fittest that is often given concerns the *peppered moth*, a species of moth which inhabits the forests of England. There are two varieties of this moth: one with lighter coloured wings, the other with darker. Throughout most of history the lighter coloured moth was more numerous. The moth with darker wings could be more easily seen by birds because their darker wings stood out more clearly against the leaves of trees, making them an easier target for predatory birds. In that environment, the moths with lighter coloured wings were fitter, or better able to survive in the struggle for existence. During the Industrial Revolution the factories in England emitted a great deal of soot, which settled on leaves, making them darker. As a consequence, the darker peppered moths became better camouflaged than the lighter coloured moths, and their numbers increased. Eventually, the darker moths came to outnumber the lighter moths: with a change in the environment in which they lived the darker moths had become fitter. But then, in the 1980s, with the rise of the environmental movement, factories reduced the quantities of soot they pumped out into the atmosphere. This meant the leaves became clean of soot and so the lighter coloured moths once again became more numerous. What this story shows is that natural selection is not leading organisms towards some final state of perfection. Rather, as the environment changes, so what counts as fitness also changes. What evolution does is ensure that organisms change so they can survive in the environment at the time; different features ensure survival in different environments, but there is no reason to suppose this process is leading to a final state of perfection.

Just as there is no reason to suppose that evolution in the natural world will lead to perfection, so is there no reason to believe that the survival of the fittest in the free market will lead to human perfection. As we have already noted, what counts as fitness in one economic environment need not also count as fitness in another. We should also remember that some characteristics that may aid survival in both the free market and the natural environment, such as the ability to successfully deceive or mislead one's rivals, are not usually thought of as constitutive of human perfection. Conversely, some human beings who we might see as exemplifying at least aspects of human perfection, such as saints, might perform rather poorly in a free market. There seems little reason to suppose that the operation of the free market would select those characteristics that are constitutive of human perfection.

The idea that if we let the free market operate untrammelled, then the law of the survival of the fittest will ensure that eventually the human race will be populated by people who are intelligent, industrious, frugal and so on, is based on a misunderstanding of how evolution actually works. This can be illustrated if we consider in detail how some characteristic might be naturally selected. We will focus our discussion on a particular characteristic that is beneficial to the survival of a species, such as thick warm coats in polar bears. In any population of polar bears, there will be some degree of variation in coat thickness, with some having thicker coats than others. We will assume that having a thicker coat gives a polar bear a greater chance of survival in the Arctic winter conditions and therefore of living long enough to be able to reproduce than those polar bears with thinner coats. If having thick coats is something that polar bears pass on to their offspring, the next generation of polar bears will have, on average, slightly thicker coats than the previous generation. But note, it would be a mistake to think the next generation of polar bears would have thicker coats than their parents; they would in fact, on average have coats of the same thickness as their parents. However, if the members of the previous generation which lived long enough to become parents tended to have thicker coats, the next generation will, on average, have thicker coats.

There are two main points that we need to note from the above discussion. For natural selection to increase the prevalence of some characteristic in a population, the following conditions are necessary:

1 The characteristic involved must be heritable, which allows the genes for that characteristic to be passed from parent to offspring.
2 Members of the species who do not possess the characteristic will not live long enough to mate and reproduce (or they will have a lower probability of doing so).

It is now easy to see that the operation of the free market — at least as conceived by the economic rationalist — will not ensure that the population will eventually become intelligent, industrious or frugal. These characteristics may be, at least in part, heritable, but the real difficulty for the free marketeer is caused by the second condition. In our society, people who are not particularly intelligent, industrious or frugal *do* live long enough to mate and reproduce, and our society would have to be changed in a very radical way indeed for such persons not to survive. Even if all government assistance, such as unemployment benefits, free education and medical care, were removed it would still be possible for people lacking the nominated qualities to live long enough to reproduce by receiving support from their parents. The fact is that in any society which has even a remote chance of being brought into existence, natural selection will not eliminate those lacking in intelligence, industriousness or frugality. So, natural selection will not bring about the type of society that the social Darwinist envisages. Therefore, the argument for the free market from the claim that it will eventually lead to a state of human perfection is untenable.

THE ARGUMENT THAT IT WILL MINIMISE SUFFERING IN THE LONG TERM IF WE NOW LET NATURAL SELECTION WEED OUT THE WEAK

We are all familiar with the following moral dilemma: suppose you are in a lifeboat with eight people, and that if all eight stay in the boat then the boat will almost certainly be overturned in the approaching storm; and even if it should survive the storm there is not enough food for all eight to survive before being rescued. On the other hand, if there are only five people in the boat, it probably would not capsize in the approaching storm, and there would be enough food to survive until rescued. What should be done? Should all eight people be allowed to stay in the boat, meaning that all eight might end up drowning or starving, or should three be thrown out of the boat before the storm arrives, so that the five remaining will probably survive?

Spencer argues that planet Earth is like the lifeboat. Recall that he said that 'organised charity' was indefensible because it would leave future generations with too many mouths to feed. What he is suggesting is that unless we let the unfit die out, the result further down the track, when the Earth's population becomes too great for its resources to support, will be mass starvation. However, as an argument for the free market in modern societies, this is plainly unsound. As we noted in the previous section, in modern societies the 'unfit' do not die out: they fail to prosper, but they do not starve. Moreover, Spencer's argument is based on the assumption that the only, or at least the most effective, means of population control is allowing the unfit to die of starvation. Whether or not this assumption was tenable when Spencer wrote, it is hardly tenable now that we have modern techniques of birth control. We should also not overlook the fact that even if it were politically possible to allow the 'unfit' to die of starvation, which it undoubtedly is not, such a course of action would produce a violent response on the part of those left to die, and may even bring about a political revolution. The idea that we should or could limit population growth by letting the unfit die cannot be taken seriously.

SUMMARY

Let us now summarise the results of this chapter. The aim of the second part of this book is to critically evaluate attempts to find a moral justification of economic rationalism and the free market. Historically, one of the most important attempts to provide a moral justification of the free market has come from social Darwinism. In this chapter we examined four social Darwinist arguments. We saw that the argument that appealed to *the moral goodness of that which is natural* is in many respects flawed. There seem to be many examples of things that are natural but not morally good and, conversely, many things that are morally unexceptionable yet not natural. The argument from *the inevitability of the survival of the fittest* was seen to be flawed because it does not justify the social Darwinists' claim that attempts to better the lot of 'less fit' groups within the community are bound to be futile. The argument from the claim that *natural selection in the free market will, in the long run, lead to a state of human perfection* was seen to be based on a now discredited conception of the nature of evolution. Finally, the argument from the claim that *it is better to let natural selection weed out the unfit now than let billions die of starvation in the future* seems to make bizarrely unrealistic assumptions about what the poor would 'lie down and take', and about what types of society might actually exist. It also assumes starvation is the only way of limiting population growth.

So, in conclusion, we may say that all the attempts to provide a moral justification of the free market using social Darwinist ideas fail. However, we can also say a little more than that. As TH Huxley remarked, doing the morally right thing often consists of doing the precise opposite of what nature demands.[12] Kindness, charity, forgiveness and a concern for justice are often precisely the opposite of that which most increases the chances of survival in nature, or success in the free market. For this reason, a society which most closely resembles the 'struggle for existence' that we find in nature is more likely to be immoral than moral. The fact to which the social Darwinist draws our attention: the resemblance between the survival of the economically fit in the free market and the biologically fit in nature, is therefore more likely to furnish us with a moral refutation rather than a moral justification of the free market.

8

THE ARGUMENT FOR THE FREE MARKET FROM THE NOTION OF VOLUNTARY EXCHANGE

Let us begin by reviewing the discussion so far. The core idea of economic rationalism is that governments should aim to maximise economic efficiency, and one important device for maximising economic efficiency is the free market. The first fundamental theorem of welfare economics tells us that under *ideal conditions* the free market will produce a state of Pareto-optimality, in which resources are allocated in a society so that efficiency is maximised. Of course, everyone — whether they accept economic rationalism or not — agrees that these ideal conditions are unattainable, but advocates of economic rationalism say that governments should nevertheless aim to approach them as closely as possible, since by those means the economy of a country can be brought closer to Pareto-optimality and thus maximum efficiency. However, even if a country were brought close to a state of maximum efficiency, at least one important problem would remain. Although maximum efficiency would maximise the *total* amount of wealth in a country, there is no guarantee that it would be evenly distributed. In fact, the operation of the free market tends to produce great inequalities of wealth: it makes some people billionaires while others live below the poverty line. So, while the operation of the free market might maximise the total amount of wealth in a community, there is a serious question as to whether the state of affairs to which it would give rise would be morally justified.

In this chapter we will consider an argument that has proved very influential amongst contemporary political and philosophical thinkers. The argument was developed by the Harvard philosopher Robert Nozick in his book *Anarchy, State and Utopia*, and appeals to the notion of a strictly *voluntary exchange*.[1] If Nozick's argument is sound, it means that there is nothing morally wrong or unjust about the vast inequalities of wealth that can arise in the free market, provided those inequalities arise as a result of strictly voluntary exchanges between individuals. Indeed, Nozick makes the further claim that attempts to remove inequalities of wealth, by, for example, redistributing money from the rich to the poor, are actually *unjust* if those inequalities initially arose from strictly voluntary exchanges. As Nozick's argument is rather complex, it is worth giving an overview of it before we consider it in detail.

OUTLINE OF NOZICK'S ARGUMENT

Let us consider a community of individuals. In this community, some may have more property than others. This 'property' may be money, material goods, land or any other kind of 'holdings', to use the term favoured by Nozick himself. Is this situation *just*? For Nozick, the distribution of wealth in the society as a whole is just if, and only if, it is just that each individual has the amount of property they do, in fact, have. What this means can be made a little clearer if we consider a very simple community consisting of three individuals. We will call these individuals Smith, Jones and Brown. Let us suppose Smith has $X, Jones has $Y and Brown has $Z. Is this situation just? For Nozick, the situation as a whole is just if, and only if, in each case it is just that Smith has $X, Jones has $Y and Brown has $Z. What this means is that, for Nozick, the question of whether the distribution of wealth in society as a whole is just is reduced to the question of whether the amount of wealth held by any individual in that society is just. Under what circumstances is it just that a particular individual have the quantity of wealth they do in fact have? Under what circumstances would it be just that, for example, Smith had $X? Nozick says it is just that Smith should have $X if, and only if, the *manner in which he acquired those $X was just*.

We now reach the crucial step in Nozick's argument. He says that if Smith acquired his $X through *strictly voluntary exchange*, then he acquired his $X in a just manner. More generally, according to Nozick, if in the free market people acquire their wealth through strictly voluntary exchange, then they have obtained it in a just manner and so it is *morally just* that they should have the particular amount of wealth they do have. He then makes the final step of arguing that, since it is just that in a free market each individual should have the amount of wealth they in fact end up with, it therefore follows that the distribution of wealth in a society as a whole, that arises as a result of the operation of the free market, is also just. Nozick also draws the further conclusion that since this distribution of wealth is just, any alteration to this distribution of wealth, by, for example, taxing the rich and giving it to the poor, must therefore be unjust.

THE DETAILS OF NOZICK'S ARGUMENT

The above is, in broad outline, a summary of Nozick's argument. We will now fill in some of the details in this broad outline. For Nozick, that a particular individual has $X is *just* if, and only if, the manner in which they acquired that $X was just. In the above rough outline we said that a person justly acquires their $X if they obtain it through strictly voluntary exchange. Actually, Nozick has a bit more to say about just acquisition. We need to distinguish between the case in which something is *not* already owned by someone else (such as a tract of wilderness) and the case in which it is. Following Nozick, we will call the acquisition of something not already owned 'initial acquisition'. Nozick develops an account of the conditions under which the initial acquisition of some entity is just. We need not concern ourselves with the details of this account here, but roughly, he says that an initial acquisition of an entity, such as a tract of land, by a person is just if the person increases its value by his own labours (perhaps by turning the land into a productive farm), provided that in so doing he does not infringe on any pre-existing rights of other people to make use of the land.

Nozick also develops an account of transfer of ownership. He says one person can justly acquire ownership of an item from another by sale or trade, or by receiving it as a gift. For a person to acquire an object by sale or trade *justly*, the exchange must be *strictly voluntary*; that is, the choices made by the parties involved in the transfer must be made without any form of coercion. Nozick says that an offer of exchange is coercive if it is accompanied by the use of force or the (explicit or implicit) threat of force. So, in Nozick's view, a person acquires something justly through sale or trade if the exchange was made without either the explicit or implicit threat of force.

For Nozick, a distribution of wealth in a society as a whole is just if it arose from some initial distribution that was just — by a just means of initial acquisition or transfer. Therefore, for Nozick, the operation of the free market will result in a just distribution of wealth if two conditions are met.

1 The *initial* distribution of wealth was just.
2 Any alteration of the distribution of wealth occurred by just means;

in particular, if changes in the distribution of wealth occur as a result of the operation of the free market, then they do so by strictly voluntary exchange (that is, exchange free from explicit or implicit threat of force).

Nozick further supports his claim that changes in wealth that come about as a result of strictly voluntary exchange are just by asking us to consider the following example. Suppose that the basketball player Wilt Chamberlain signs a contract guaranteeing him 25 cents of every ticket sold in which he plays. After a season of baseball, 1 000 000 tickets have been sold and so he acquires $250 000. The exchanges involved here are strictly voluntary as people freely choose to pay their money for their baseball tickets. Assuming that the distribution of wealth prior to Chamberlain signing his contract was just, the distribution of wealth after the baseball season is over (and Chamberlain is $250 000 wealthier) will, according to Nozick, also be just since it took place as a result of strictly voluntary exchanges. So Nozick claims that, even though Chamberlain may now be much wealthier than most people, the distribution of wealth would still be just. Would a government be justified in *redistributing* wealth, taking some of Chamberlain's money and either giving it to those who were less well off or spending it for their benefit? Nozick's answer to this question is 'No' — since Chamberlain acquired his money justly he therefore has a *right* to the money. Consequently, to take some of his money from him and give it to the poor would be a violation of Chamberlain's rights. (A similar idea was once expressed by the noted economist Milton Friedman, who once described taxation designed to help the needy as 'robbing Peter to pay Paul.)

CRITICAL EVALUATION OF NOZICK'S CLAIM

Although Nozick increases the plausibility of his case with his 'Wilt Chamberlain' example, it is not too difficult to think of other examples where his position is much less plausible. The key question is this: is Nozick right to claim that if something was acquired in a strictly voluntary exchange it was thereby acquired justly? Let us imagine that an old gold prospector has spent many years gathering gold dust on his claim out in the middle of the desert. Over the years he has acquired many hundreds of thousands of dollars worth of gold and eventually decides to give up his life as a prospector and live in comfort in the city. So he loads up the bags of gold on his horse and heads off to the nearest homestead, several days ride away. On the way his horse unfortunately panics and he is thrown from it, together with the bags of gold; he watches as the horse rides off with all his food and water supplies. A few days later he arrives at the homestead, still carrying the bags of gold, but dying of thirst and exhaustion. He asks the homestead owner for water, food and a bed to rest in. However, the homestead owner realises that the prospector is carrying bags full of gold, and also perceives that the prospector is dying of thirst. So the homestead owner says, 'I will give you all the water you want, but you must give me the gold in the bags.' At first the prospector refuses, pleading with the homestead owner and appealing to his conscience, but the homestead owner will not budge. Eventually the prospector realises he must either hand over the bags of gold or die of thirst, so he reluctantly hands over the bags of gold and in return, the homestead owner gives him all the water he wants.

In this imaginary example we feel strongly that the homestead owner did not acquire the gold *justly*. The homestead owner took advantage of the prospector's situation in a way we do not feel was right. But notice that the homestead owner acquired the gold through strictly voluntary exchange. The homestead owner did not exert force on the prospector to give him the gold; neither did he threaten the prospector with force, yet we still feel that he acquired the gold unjustly. This example, therefore, would appear to be a counter-example to Nozick's claim that if a person acquires some good through strictly voluntary exchange, then it has been justly acquired.

Why was the homestead owner's acquisition of the gold unjust? This is not an easy question to answer. It is not that the homestead owner gained more from the transaction than the prospector: the prospector gained his life. Neither did the homestead owner use coercion. We might be tempted to say the exchange was unjust because the prospector had a lot more to lose from the transaction not taking place at all; but this cannot be right — the exchange would have been just had the homestead owner asked a fairer price for the water *even though* the prospector would still have had a lot more to lose from the exchange not taking place at all. We get a little closer to the truth, I think, if we say that the homestead owner used the prospector's position to extract an unfair price for the water. This, of course, raises the question: what would have been a *fair* price for the water? And this is, of course, an instance of the more general question: what is the *fair* price for anything? This is a very complex question, which could form the subject matter of a book in itself.

Although it is very difficult to define a just exchange, it is pretty clear that the exchange between the prospector and the homestead owner is unjust. Moreover, one factor which makes this unjust exchange possible is the fact the prospector was *compelled* to accept it because he would have undergone extreme suffering if he did not accept it. He had to accept an exchange which he would not have accepted, had the amount of suffering he would have experienced been more nearly equal to that of the homestead owner. It is because the homestead owner *took advantage* of this inequality that the prospector was forced to accept an unjust exchange. In the light of this we may assert the following principle (P1).

> If A acquires from B, by *a strictly voluntary exchange*, some good G, then A's acquisition of G may not be just if B would experience vastly more suffering than A if the exchange did not take place at all.

Note that the above principle merely asserts that A's acquisition of G *may* be unjust, not that it *will* be. For it to be unjust, A must at least take advantage of B's situation. The principle also leaves vague just *how much* more suffering B must experience than A. It seems plausible to say the exchange may be unjust if B has *vastly* more to lose, but obviously there will be 'shades of grey'. Some exchanges, such as that between the prospector and the homestead owner, are clearly unjust, since the homestead owner takes advantage of the fact that the prospector will lose his life if the exchange does not go ahead. Some other possible exchanges might not be so clearly unjust, but may nevertheless in some degree cast doubt on the justice of a person's acquisition of some good.

Although the above example involving the prospector and the homestead owner is, of course, an extreme case, in a highly 'unfettered' free market we could expect situations to arise which at least approximate this one. In a highly unfettered free market there would be no minimum wage, nor benefits for those without a job. Situations could arise where a person who cannot find a job would have to beg or starve. An employer taking advantage of this situation could conceivably get new employees to agree to work long hours while paying them no more than a subsistence wage. If no coercion was used in getting employees to agree to this, the exchange between the worker and employer would count as strictly voluntary. But, if we grant P1, then Nozick's argument that acquisitions which occur as the result of strictly voluntary exchanges in the free market are thereby just, is not valid.

It may be objected that in the situations described (the prospector and the homestead owner; the worker who must accept the low wages or starve) the exchanges are not strictly voluntary. In both cases, threats are implicit: in the former case, the homestead owner (implicitly) threatens to let the prospector die of thirst; in the latter the employer implicitly threatens to let the prospective employee starve or be reduced to begging. In both cases there is the implicit threat of harm that would come from not giving aid. This consideration may or may not show that the exchanges are not strictly voluntary. Even if they are not strictly voluntary, this is of little aid to the advocate of Nozick's defence of the free market. Clearly the type of exchange described could occur in a free market, and is highly likely to occur at least sometimes in a totally unfettered free market. We feel strongly that such exchanges are not entirely just, so Nozick's argument, as a defence of the free market, fails.

Although we must judge as unsuccessful Nozick's argument for the claim that wealth obtained through voluntary exchange is thereby justly acquired, another part of his position is pretty much unaffected by this conclusion. Nozick also says that since wealth acquired in the free market is acquired justly, people have a right to wealth acquired in this way, and so if governments were to use (the threat of) force to extract taxes from people, they would be violating people's rights. *This* conclusion of Nozick's still retains some force. Although there is no guarantee that wealth acquired by voluntary exchange will be acquired justly, it is surely *possible* that it will be. So, in any actual economy, it is likely that some voluntary exchanges will be just, although others may not be. What, then, is a government to do? If it taxes everyone, it will tax some people who have acquired their wealth justly, and if Nozick is right this will involve violating at least *their* rights. One option would be to tax only those who acquired their wealth *unjustly*, but working out who those people are would be extraordinarily difficult. It seems therefore that, if Nozick is right, governments must either tax no-one, or violate at least *some* people's property rights.

Is Nozick right in claiming that *if* a person has acquired their wealth justly, governments are not justified in using (the threat of) force to extract taxes from them? This question is considered in the next section.

NOZICK AND PROPERTY RIGHTS

We will now consider another hypothetical example, which reveals a different flaw in Nozick's position. Let us suppose Smith and Brown go camping in an area of wilderness, accompanied by Smith's young daughter. While in a remote area, Smith's daughter is bitten by a spider and Smith realises that his daughter must be given an antidote very quickly or she will die. They are too far away from civilisation for Smith to get her there in time; however, Brown possesses the antidote. Smith asks Brown to give him the antidote so that he can save his daughter, but Brown refuses, stating that he bought the antidote out of his own money and it is therefore his property. Unfortunately, Smith does not have any money with him to purchase the antidote from Brown. Smith pleads with Brown, pointing out that his daughter will die if she does not get the antidote, but Brown will not change his mind. Finally, Smith decides to take the antidote from Brown by force: he takes it from Brown's pack, Brown grapples with him but Smith pushes him away and gives the antidote to his daughter.

Were Smith's actions morally justified? In considering this question, we can assume that Brown justly acquired the antidote by paying a pharmacist for the antidote in an interaction that was a strictly voluntary exchange, and in which neither party would have suffered if the exchange did not take place. So, Brown's ownership of the antidote was, we may assume, perfectly just. But even so, we feel sure that under the circumstances Smith *was* morally justified in taking the antidote from Brown by force.

It is important to understand what Nozick would say about this case. Nozick would agree that Brown did *not* act morally in refusing to give the antidote to Smith. As we shall discover in the section in this chapter on giving assistance to the poor, Nozick agrees that those who are well off have a moral duty to assist the poor and needy, so he would undoubtedly assert that Brown morally ought have assisted Smith. But I believe Nozick is nevertheless committed to saying that, since Brown had justly acquired the antidote, he had a right to the antidote, and hence in taking the antidote from him by force, Smith was violating Brown's property rights. For this reason Nozick would condemn Smith's gaining possession of the antidote *by force*. Thus, Nozick's position here is highly counterintuitive. We feel that if his daughter was going to die, Smith was justified in using force to acquire the antidote and, given that it was the only way available to him of acquiring it, it would have been wrong for him not to use force.

For Nozick, property rights, or the right to ownership of that which is justly acquired, is an *absolute* right: if someone has acquired some good justly, it is always wrong, according to Nozick, to take it from them by force. But this does not seem to be correct. There do seem to be possible circumstances in which it is morally right to take, by force, some good which has been justly acquired. If so, Nozick is wrong to say that property rights are 'absolute'.

A Nozickian might possibly respond to the above argument by conceding that if someone's life is in danger, then it may be permissible to violate a person's property rights, but insist that is the *only* circumstance in which it is permissible to do so. However, this is highly dubious, as can be seen if we modify the example given above. Let us suppose that, instead of the spider bite being fatal, it would merely make Smith's daughter extremely ill, and perhaps place her at risk of permanent health damage. Even so, I think we still feel confident that Smith would be justified in using force to acquire the antidote from Brown. Neither is it necessary that it be Smith's *daughter* who was endangered: if it had merely been a child placed under his care for the holiday we still feel, I think, that he would have been justified in using force to get the antidote from Brown. In view of these, we may assert the following principle (P2).

> Although having justly acquired some good G may give A a *prima facie* right to that good, it is not an absolute right. If A's continued possession of the good G would bring about sufficient harm to others, then it may be morally justified to use force to take G from A.

As with P1, P2 is very vague; but if it is granted that P2 is correct, then once again Nozick's defence of a totally unfettered free market fails. For Nozick's argument to be sound, it must never be morally right for governments to violate an individual's property rights by (threat of) force, no matter what the consequences of not doing so are. However, if P2 is correct, it is sometimes justified.

Of course, the situation described concerning Smith's daughter is an extreme one, but in a totally unfettered free market it is easy to imagine circumstances which are morally very close to it: for example, if a proportion of the population was extremely wealthy while another section was literally starving in the streets. Nozick's argument does not succeed in establishing that it would be morally wrong, in such a situation, for a government to use (threat of) force to distribute money from the rich to the poor.

So far in this section we have argued that Nozick's claim that property rights are *absolute* is very implausible and in conflict with our moral intuitions. It should be noted that Nozick himself does not argue for the absolute character of the property rights that he defends. Instead, he simply appears to regard it as self-evident that if a person has justly acquired some good then they have an absolute right to it. What plausibly is self-evident is that if a person has justly acquired a good, they have a strong claim to it; but what is not self-evident, and indeed seems to be false, is the idea that the claim is so strong that it overrides all other moral considerations. Nozick's claim that property rights are absolute therefore ought to be rejected.

RAWLS'S ALTERNATIVE CONCEPTION OF A JUST SOCIETY

One important argument against Nozick's claim that property rights are 'absolute' and never to be over-ridden, comes from John Rawls.[2] Rawls points out that if the system of voluntary exchange is allowed to run for many generations then, inevitably, some people would grow rich while others would become poor. Rawls invites us to consider the bearing this has on the *children* of the people in such a

system. Children born to rich parents will have much greater oppor-
tunities than those born to poor parents. Those born to rich parents
will have a much wider range of choices and a much greater chance
of leading the type of life they want to than will the children of poor
parents. But, Rawls points out, there is nothing very *just* about this
situation. Whether a person is born into a rich or a poor family would
seem to have more to do with the luck of the draw than anything to
do with justice or fairness. A child who is born into a rich family has
not done anything to *deserve* being born into that family. Rawls sees
the fact that some people are born into rich families, where they will
be able to lead comfortable lives, while others are born into situations where they will have nothing to look forward to but grinding
poverty as an *injustice* produced by the operation of the system of
voluntary exchange. For this reason, Rawls rejects Nozick's claim
that the system of voluntary exchange gives rise to situations that are
always just.

Rawls also provides a general criterion for deciding whether a given
way of running or organising society is just. He asks us to imagine we
are located behind a 'veil of ignorance' where we have no information
about our own race, sex, abilities, religion, or social or economic class.
In order to understand what Rawls is suggesting, it might help us to
imagine ourselves existing as 'minds' or 'souls' in some 'heaven', or
realm, before our birth and even before our conception. When inhabit-
ing this realm, we had no idea at all about the sort of conditions into
which we would be born. We did not know whether we would be born
male or female, black or white, rich or poor, or whatever. Neither did
we have any knowledge of what type of *society* we would be born into,
be it Communist, social democratic, a free market economy or tribal
Amazonian, for example. Of course, Rawls is not actually suggesting we
once were in this state of complete ignorance concerning whereabouts
we would 'end up'; he is rather suggesting that imagining we are behind
this 'veil of ignorance' will help us to decide whether or not a particular form of society is *fair* or *just*.

Rawls asks us to suppose that, from behind this 'veil of ignorance',
we can choose the type of society in which we will live. But, crucially,
this choice must be made while we are ignorant of what our own conditions will be in that society: we do not know whether we will be a rich
person or a poor person in that society, or black or white, male or
female, and so on. So, for example, while we could choose to live in a
society with a free market economy, we could not choose to be a rich
person in that society. Or, we could choose to live in a racist society, but
we would not know whether we would be born in to that society as a
white person or a black person, and so on.

Rawls's key suggestion is this: let us imagine a person, located behind this veil of ignorance, who merely wishes to make decisions that are in their own interests; a society is *just*, says Rawls, *only if such a (self-interested) person would choose to live in that society*. So, for example, Rawls says a self-interested person would not choose to live in a racist or sexist society if they did not know what race or sex they would end up being, and so, on this test, racist and sexist societies are not just. Neither would such a person, he argues, choose to live in a society divided into rich or poor, or in which some are born into lifelong poverty while others go through life enjoying every comfort, and so he says these societies are not just either. Rawls also says his 'veil of ignorance' test leads to some more surprising conclusions about the nature of a just society. Would a self-interested person choose to live in a society in which the bulk of life's rewards went to the intelligent and talented, while the rest had to accept much less? Remember that, from behind the 'veil of ignorance', the self-interested person does not know whether they themselves would be talented and intelligent, or untalented and unintelligent. So, Rawls argues, the self-interested person would not choose to live in a such a society; and so, on his criterion, such a society would not count as just.[3]

Rawls develops his conception of a just society in great detail in his book *A Theory of Justice*. Commentators see his conception of a just society as highly egalitarian.[4] It is beyond the scope of this chapter to carry out a detailed adjudication between the rival conceptions of a just society developed by Nozick and Rawls, but we can at least note that there does exist a well-formed alternative to Nozick's view. Moreover, while Nozick's account leads to some highly counter-intuitive consequences (such as the 'just' acquisition of the prospector's gold by the homestead owner), Rawls's view does not seem to have such implausible consequences.

NOZICK ON ASSISTANCE TO THE POOR

As we have already noted, Nozick believes governments are never justified in using force, or the threat of force, to take taxes from the wealthy to spend on the poor. He thinks that the fact that some people would grow poor in the free market is unfortunate, but it is not unjust. However, he does believe that the wealthy have a *moral obligation* to help those who are less well off. He says the wealthy ought to help the poor, but that this aid should be *voluntary*, rather than the result of government coercion. There are, however, a number of difficulties with this proposal. One problem noted by Allen Buchanan is that, to be maximally effective, aid to the poor must be well co-ordinated.[5] However, it is unclear whether purely voluntary aid could be as well co-ordinated as that provided by government with all its information and resources. Moreover, it is also extremely unclear whether purely voluntary aid would be sufficient to ensure that the poor lived in a tolerable degree of comfort. This problem would be especially acute in times of high unemployment. Since most people try to minimise the amount of tax they pay, it is unlikely that they would *voluntarily* give out an amount comparable to that which they are now compelled to pay as tax. We should also note here that a recent survey has shown that most of the people in Australia earning over $500,000 give nothing to charity.[6] The idea that voluntary methods of assisting the poor would be as effective as taxation based methods does not seem realistic.

It is worthwhile briefly considering how Nozick would respond to these objections. He would agree that it would be a very unfortunate thing if the poor were left without satisfactory forms of assistance, but, for Nozick, this would be the lesser of two evils. It would be an even greater evil, in his view, if governments took money from the rich by force (or the threat of force) and gave it to the poor, since this would involve violating their rights. In his view, taxing the rich and giving money to the poor is committing an injustice (violating people's rights) to fix up a situation which, although unfortunate, is not actually unjust. However, Nozick's claim that it is a greater evil to tax the rich than it is to let the poor starve, seems very dubious. Consequently, Nozick would need a very powerful argument to persuade us of the claim that a person's having acquired their wealth through strictly voluntary exchange gave them an absolute right to that wealth. However, he has not given us any such argument. His 'Wilt Chamberlain' example makes the claim seem plausible, but other examples, such as the example of Smith's daughter bitten by a spider, make the claim seem rather less plausible. He has not given us any compelling, general reason to believe people always have an absolute right to what they have acquired through strictly voluntary exchange. So, we cannot say Nozick has established that it is always a greater evil to tax the rich rather than let the poor starve.

SUMMARY

Let us now summarise Nozick's argument. He has presented a case for an 'absolute' free market; that is, one in which governments do not tax the rich to help the poor. We have seen that Nozick's argument is based on two assumptions.

1 If a person acquires some good through strictly voluntary exchange, then they have acquired it justly.

2   If a person has acquired some good justly, then their right to that
    good is *absolute*; in particular, it is never morally justified to use
    force, or the threat of force, to deprive them of that good.

However, both these assumptions are extremely dubious. The first
assumption need not be true if one party to the exchange would suffer
much more than the other from the exchange not taking place at all. So,
for example, in a totally unfettered free market, if a worker must accept
the terms offered by their prospective employer or starve, the employer may not have justly acquired the benefits of the worker's labour. The
second assumption need not be true if, for example, *not* taking by force
from a person a good they had justly acquired would cause sufficient
human suffering: if, for example, people would starve to death if the
good is not taken. Since Nozick's argument is based on two extremely
dubious assumptions, we may conclude that his defence of a totally
unfettered free market fails.

The failure of Nozick's first assumption also enables us to stipulate
a condition that must be met if the operation of the free market is to be
morally justifiable. If an employer is to acquire their wealth *justly*, it
must be the case that any exchange between the employer and employees be just. This is *more likely* to be so if employees would not experience great suffering, were the exchange not to take place at all. (For
example, it is more likely to be met if it is not the case that they would
otherwise starve.) But for *this* condition to be met, it must always be
possible for them to fall back on a source of livelihood that would
enable them to live in at least tolerably comfortable conditions. The
only way this can be assured, of course, is through government provided assistance. So, from this perspective, unemployment benefits are not
strictly a form of charity which the rich gives to the poor. Assuring that
the unemployed live in tolerably comfortable conditions thereby
increases the likelihood that contracts between prospective employees
and employers are just and, therefore, for the wealth thereby acquired
by the employers to be *justly* acquired. It helps to both ensure that
prospective employees are not the victims of an injustice, and that
employers acquire their wealth justly.

9

ECONOMIC DEMOCRACY AND THE MAXIMISATION OF LIBERTY

In this chapter we consider four more moral arguments for the free market. The arguments of this chapter have two things in common. First, they place greater emphasis on the *political* dimensions of the decision to adopt the free market than do the arguments considered so far. In particular, the arguments focus on the notions of democracy and liberty. Secondly, they are arguments that are prominent in the writings of the economist Milton Friedman, who is perhaps the most generally well known economist who champions the free market. An examination of Friedman's arguments will be the primary focus of this chapter.

The first argument we will consider states that the free market provides a mechanism whereby democracy can be implemented in the economic realm; in other words, the free market is just the implementation of democracy in the economic realm. The other three arguments claim that the free market ensures that liberty is maximised.

THE FREE MARKET AND ECONOMIC DEMOCRACY

Let us begin by considering the idea that the free market is a means by which democracy is implemented in the economic realm. The basic idea is this. In buying a particular item the purchaser is telling those making and selling the item that it is wanted, and the more people buy that item, the more the view is expressed that it is wanted. This in turn encourages the production of more items of that kind. However, if no-one buys an item of a particular kind, then the message will get through that no-one wants it, and so people will stop making it. The operation of the free market can be regarded as a sort of continuous referendum in which people are being asked, 'Do you want this particular product?' If enough people vote 'Yes', it will keep getting made; if they don't, it won't. So in the free market 'the will of the people' determines what gets made: it is democracy in the economic sphere.[1]

There is, to be sure, an element of truth in this claim, but when we look at it more closely it becomes a little more dubious whether we would wish to apply the positive or approving term 'democracy' to it. In order to see this, let us imagine a possible society like ours, in that governments are decided by elections, but with a difference. Let us suppose that in this other society, every (adult) person got to vote, but the amount their vote *counted* depended on how wealthy they were. For example, let us suppose, if you had $100 000 then your vote counted as one vote; if you had a million dollars, your vote counted as ten votes; if you had a billion dollars it counted as ten thousand votes, and so on. Would such a system be 'democratic'? Well, in one sense it would obviously be democratic, since governments were determined by the result of elections, rather than by inheriting a crown, or by military takeover; but in another sense it would *not* be democratic. Consider a community of 10 000 people who each have, on average, $100 000, with the exception of one person who is a billionaire. The billionaire votes for party A, the 9999 others all vote for party B. Using this system of voting, the vote of the billionaire would outweigh all the others and party A would win. Whether such a system would be 'democratic' or not, it clearly would lack a feature which we especially value in those systems that we generally call 'democratic': that one vote means one value. Whether we call it 'democratic' or not, this would not be the type of system of which we approve.

Of course, in our society we do not always manage to achieve 'one vote, one value'. A vote in an electorate with a small population is 'worth more' than a vote in an electorate with a large population — but this is considered an *imperfection* of our system, and electoral boundaries are drawn with the intention of getting closer to 'one vote, one value'. That each vote should carry one value is an aim of our system which we try to achieve, although it is not always achieved with absolute accuracy.

It is now quite clear why the free market cannot be regarded as a means of implementing economic democracy, in the sense of 'democracy' which we especially value. The free market can perhaps be regarded as a continuous referendum in which people vote on which products should keep being made and which should not, but it is not a referendum in which each person has just one vote. It is rather more like a referendum in which the number of votes each person has is proportional to the amount that they spend. A person who spends more has more 'votes' than a person who spends less, and if there were a person who had no money at all, they would have no 'votes'. So, although there is perhaps a sense in which the free market can be seen as a continuous referendum, it lacks the 'one person, one vote' aspect which we especially value in a democracy.

It might be objected here that although some people obviously have much more spending power than others, the very wealthy spend most of their wealth on items which could be called luxuries. However, on the every day necessities of life, such as milk, bread, potatoes and washing powder, the poor and the rich spend roughly equal amounts. So, at least as far as these necessities go, the market does approach a referendum in which each person's preferences count for no more and no less than any other person's.

While there is an element of truth to this claim, there are two points that need to be made: (1) the absolutely destitute do not have a vote even on the necessities; and (2) there is one necessity of life in which a person has a 'vote' only if they are moderately well off, and that is in the housing market. The type of house that gets built will be determined by the preferences only of those rich enough to buy one — and not every person is in that position.[2] If the housing market is like a referendum, then it is like one in which a person gets a vote only after their income rises above a certain level.

We noted above that electoral boundaries are often redrawn to ensure that the value of each person's vote remains more or less the same. We believe it is a good thing that each person should have a (more or less) equal input into how the country is to be run, and so we take steps to ensure 'one vote, one value'. This suggests the following thought: if the free market is to be morally justified *because* it provides a means of implementing democracy in the economic sphere, should we perhaps take steps to ensure that each person has (more or less) the same number of 'votes' in the economic sphere? What this would mean, of course, is that the government would take action, by means of taxation and aid to the poor, to move towards an equalisation of spending power. If we regard it as morally right that we should try to achieve (more or less) 'one vote, one value' when it comes to deciding governments, does consistency demand we should also try to move in this direction in the 'continuous referendum' which decides what should be produced in the free market?

This is clearly a complex question, and we will not attempt to fully address it here. However, it is worth noting that some of the reasons we have for valuing 'one vote, one value' in the political sphere also apply to the economic sphere. For example, one reason why we believe in 'one vote, one value' is that the type of government that is in power will affect all people who live under the government, or who are subject to its laws. So, each person should have an equal say in determining the nature of the government and hence there should be 'one vote, one value'. But clearly this also constitutes a reason for 'one person, one value' in the economic sphere, since each person living in a country will be affected by the economy of that country. Of course, not every citizen will be *equally affected* by a change in the economy, but neither will each citizen be equally affected by a change in government.

Of course, a natural objection to this argument is that governments are clearly restricted to individual nations; however, we are (increasingly) living in a 'global' economy. There is a sense in which a person is 'directly' affected by the government of a nation if they are a citizen of that nation and subject to its laws. Since they are subject to the laws of that country and no other, we regard it as appropriate that, by means of voting, they have some say about the character of the government that makes those laws. Yet in the economic realm the situation is quite different. I live in Australia, but I, and other Australians, do not just buy products made in Australia: we may buy cars made in Korea, clothes made in China, television sets made in Japan, and so on. So we affect, and are in turn affected by, the economies of many other countries in what we choose to buy. It would be utterly unrealistic to expect that the spending power, not only of all people in Australia, *but also of all the people in all its trading partners*, should be made equal. This is simply not possible. So the ideal of 'one person, one value' in the economic realm is obviously unattainable.

While the above argument does have cogency, its force should not be overestimated. Although it is true that the choices that Australian consumers make will have some bearing on what gets made overseas, they will, of course, have a much greater influence on what gets made here. And, of course, any change in the goods and services originating in Australia will have a much greater effect on the citizens of Australia than it will on the citizens of any other country. So, while the idea that the free market is a continuous referendum determining what gets made in Australia is not completely accurate, it still has some truth to it. So, if the principle of 'one person, one value' is still accepted, the argument that we should move towards the equalisation of spending power retains some, although limited, force.

Another reason for having 'one vote, one value' in the *political* sphere comes from a general sympathy towards egalitarianism. However, if there is a general sympathy towards egalitarianism, it would also support a tendency towards equalisation of spending power.

Let us now summarise the results of this section. We have considered the argument that the free market is morally justified because it is a means of implementing democracy in the economic realm. The free market, we noted, could perhaps be regarded as a continuous referendum, in which people 'voted', by buying certain goods rather than others, on what should continue to be made. However, it quickly became apparent that there is one respect in which the free market as it is, and especially the free market as it would exist under a strict economic rationalism, is *not* 'democratic'; in fact, it is a long way from 'one person, one value'. Since it is compatible with huge differences in individual spending power, it is also compatible with huge differences in 'economic voting power.' So the 'continuous referendum' that is the free market lacks one feature we especially value in democracy: its *egalitarianism*, whereby each person's vote counts for no more and no less than anyone else's. Therefore, the argument for the free market from 'economic democracy' is flawed.

THE FIRST LIBERTARIAN ARGUMENT: THE FREE MARKET ENCOURAGES OTHER TYPES OF FREEDOM

The central idea of this argument is that the free market leads to a maximisation of liberty in a society. There are, of course, many different types of freedom, one important type being economic freedom. However, it is not the only one — other types include: political freedom, religious freedom, freedom of speech, and so on. Now, in a free market economic freedom is maximised: people are free to enter into whatever work contracts they want, and to sell and buy whatever they want. Defenders of this argument claim that if the free market is introduced into a society, then not only will it bring about economic freedom, it will also tend, with time, to bring about an increase in the other forms of freedom as well. That is, if the free market is introduced into a society then the *immediate* consequence will be an increase in economic freedom, but in the longer term it will also tend to bring about an increase in other forms of freedom, such as political freedom and freedom of speech. If it is granted that the maximisation of freedom is a morally good thing, then the considerations just given constitute an argument for the moral desirability of the free market.[3]

Clearly, at the core of this argument is the empirical claim that if the free market is introduced into a society, then there will follow an increase in the other forms of freedom. But is this claim true? There is considerable evidence that it is: there is more political freedom and freedom of speech in free market Western economies than there is, or was, in countries using communist or 'command' economies, such as the former Soviet Union, Albania, Romania and North Korea. So there does seem to be *some* evidence that *lack* of economic freedom is

156 • THE ETHICAL CASE

associated with low levels of other freedoms, and that the free market is associated with higher levels of the other freedoms.

One reason for the correlation between the free market and other forms of freedom is that with the introduction of the free market comes greater wealth and this in turn means (at least for some) more leisure, more time to think about general political or philosophical questions, more education, and the possibility of contact with ideas other than those with which one has grown up. This 'opening up' encourages the development of a diversity of political, religious and ethical ideas, which may result in more freedom.

Another reason for the connection between economic and other freedoms is explored in some detail by Friedman.[4] In a free market, a business person must obtain the materials with which they conduct their business from whomever it is that supplies the cheapest and best materials of that type. If they insist on buying their materials only from, say, Caucasians or Christians, when others are able to supply the same things more cheaply, they may well go out of business. In the free market you must deal with whomever is able to supply you with the best goods, irrespective of race or religion. This will, according to Friedman, tend to foster a greater degree of tolerance to those of different races and religions.[5]

Friedman also gives a reason why freedom of speech will have a greater chance to flourish in free market economies than in command economies. For freedom of speech to *flourish*, it is not enough for people to merely have the right to say unpopular things. They also need to be able to *publish* or *distribute* those unpopular views; for example, to be able to publish books or articles, to have access to television 'air time', and to be able to have access to public halls for meetings. Friedman points out that doing these things requires money, and that in a communist or command system, that money would have to come from the government. But, he says, such governments would be unwilling to spend significant amounts of money supporting views that were critical of them, or which might lead to a lessening of their own power. So, Friedman says, free speech is unlikely to flourish in a communist or command economy. In a market economy, on the other hand, a publisher *will* publish books critical of the existing system if enough people are likely to buy them. The owner of a hall will hire it to a group of communists or anarchists or atheists if the takings at the door with make it worthwhile. As Friedman himself says, 'The suppliers of paper are as willing to sell it to the *Daily Worker* as to the *Wall Street Journal*.' In a market economy, it is not government approval, but whether there is sufficient interest in the public at large to make the manufacture and sale of something financially worthwhile. For this reason, says Friedman, free speech is more likely to flourish in free market economies.[6]

However, when we look at things more closely, the picture seems to become rather more complicated. One complication emerges when we consider several northern European and Scandinavian countries. These countries enjoy a high level of freedom in general and exhibit tolerance towards divergent religions, political beliefs, and cultural and social views. However, the economic systems of these countries are a long way from being *unconstrained* free market economies. They are, rather, heavily regulated free market economies with levels of taxation that enable the provision of extensive social welfare services, and are often called 'social democratic' economies. The degree of economic freedom in these countries is lower than that in the United States; nevertheless, at least in some points in its history, the United States exhibited lower levels of the other, non-economic freedoms than the Scandinavian countries. For example, the United States has exhibited high levels of intolerance towards communism and so was not, at least during the 'McCarthy era', a country in which there were particularly high levels of either freedom of speech or political freedom. Atheism and advocacy of the theory of evolution have experienced a degree of intolerance in some parts of the United States comparable with that experienced by communism. So, the idea that economic freedom is correlated with other forms of freedom does not always seem to hold.

Perhaps the most dramatic counter-examples to the idea that economic and non-economic freedoms 'go together' emerge when we consider a number of dictatorial military regimes which nevertheless accepted a fairly unfettered free market economy. Some South American countries, such as Chile under Pinochet, are examples of this. So, there is evidence that while a *moderately* free market tends to increase other forms of freedom, *extreme* free marketeerism, and certain types of free market, may tend to bring about a decrease in freedom.

There is a simple mechanism whereby the introduction of pure economic rationalism, or an unfettered free market, into a country that had previously had a constrained market, may lead to a decrease in non-economic forms of freedom. Under a completely free market, employers and prospective employees are free to negotiate contracts. It will, of course, be in the interests of the employer to have the employee working for as little money as possible, as this will help the employer to make their products as cheaply as possible. How low will wages go if employees and employers are free to engage in individual contracts? Under *pure* economic rationalism, there would be neither trade unions nor a basic wage (as it is a contractual inefficiency), so unless employment levels are virtually 100 per cent, if one person turns down a wage offer because it is too low, someone else will accept it. In this case wages would tend to decrease due to intense competition. If the alternative is starvation, then there is at least the danger that wages would tend to decrease to just above starvation level. However, matters are rather different for those at the other end of the spectrum. Under intense competition, it will be vital for a company to get the best possible person to be their CEO. At the highest level, if the best person for the job turns down a salary offer, there is no guarantee there will be someone else around nearly as good who will accept it — perhaps the next best person will be decidedly inferior to the very best person. There will therefore be intense bidding amongst companies for the very best people. This will have the effect of raising the salaries of those at the top and, in fact, this is what we are seeing with executive salaries now.

So removal of restrictions in the labour market would naturally tend to produce lower wages for those people whose jobs can be done just as well by many other people, while those who occupy positions close to the apex of the pyramid, and who do their job significantly better than their next best rival, will receive astronomical amounts of money. Of course, this state of affairs is likely to lead to dissatisfaction on the part of those at the bottom of the scheme. If this dissatisfaction becomes severe there is a danger that they may try to change the economic system of the country, or replace it with another one; or they may advocate change in other ways, by protesting and striking. Also, having many poor people may increase levels of crime. How might a government respond to all this? It might give the protestors what they want by ensuring, for example, a minimum wage, or it might tax the rich more heavily to pay for schemes to help the poor. However, such actions would move *away* from pure economic rationalism: they would involve increasing the degree of regulation of the market, or increasing the number of public goods. Another *possible* response would be to use force, or the threat of force, to stop the protests and strikes. This might involve outlawing unions, prohibiting public assemblies and the giving of speeches, or the publication of views critical of the present system. In other words, there is a danger that a completely unrestricted market — which maximises *economic* freedom — would bring about a reduction in political freedom, freedom of speech, and freedom of association and organisation. The maintenance of pure economic rationalism may, and is even reasonably likely to, lead to a decrease in the other, non-economic forms of freedom. The claim that increasing *economic* freedom will always bring about an increase in other forms of freedom too, is a claim for which there is little supporting evidence.

A related difficulty has been noted by Karl Popper in his publication *The Open Society and its Enemies* in which he writes of 'the paradox of freedom'. He says, 'Freedom ... defeats itself, if it is unlimited. Unlimited freedom means that a strong man is free to bully one who is weak and to rob him of his freedom ... [In an unrestrained free market] the economically strong [person] is still free to bully one who is economically weak, and to rob him of his freedom ... for those who possess a surplus of food can force those who are starving into a "freely" accepted servitude, without using violence.'[7] For Popper, unrestrained economic freedom is likely to lead to some people having to sell themselves into slavery in order to avoid starvation. In this way, unrestrained economic freedom leads to a lowering of overall freedom since some are reduced to servitude. This is, for Popper, an instance of the 'paradox of freedom' that unrestrained freedom leads to a lessening of freedom. As a liberal, Popper sees the maximisation of freedom as a desirable goal; he therefore proposes that an unrestrained free market be replaced by one in which the state protects the 'economically weak from the economically strong' and sees to it that 'nobody need enter into an inequitable arrangement out of fear of starvation or economic ruin'.[8] We see once again that the most a purported defence of unrestrained free market, or pure economic rationalism, does is support a *moderate* free market. Extreme free marketeerism and pure economic rationalism turn out to be unjustified.

Another difficulty in the libertarian position can brought out by considering more closely the notion of freedom. Why should it be desirable to maximise the amount of freedom that people have? One answer is that by maximising people's freedom we thereby maximise their ability to choose what is, *for them*, 'the good life'. Human beings exhibit tremendous diversity in their goals, preferences, values and ambitions, so it would be a hopeless task for a government to try to give to each person exactly what it is they want. What then are governments to do? One answer is that the role of the government is simply to try to set up the conditions that would enable each individual person to choose for themselves what would be 'the good life' for them. The role of government, in this view, is to try to set up conditions that enable society to exist in a peaceful, orderly state, without degenerating to crime or chaos, but which otherwise places as few constraints as possible on how people are to live their lives. If people have as few constraints as possible on them then they will be, in this view, free to choose the type of life they want to lead. This is a sketch of the political position sometimes called 'liberalism'.[9]

Oversimplifying a little, we can say that the core of liberalism is that governments should ensure people are *free* to choose the type of life they want to lead. But let us look a little more closely at the notion of freedom. The *Oxford Dictionary* defines freedom as 'personal or civic liberty; liberty of action' — therefore freedom is defined in terms of liberty.[10] 'Liberty' is defined by the same dictionary as 'a right or power to do as one pleases'. For our purposes, the important point to note is that there are two quite different notions involved in this definition of liberty: one is the notion of *right*, the other of *power*. To say that a person has the right to do something is very different from saying they have the power to do it. Presumably, I have 'the right' to lift a 500 pound weight above my head as there is no law which says that I must not do this. But I do *not* have the power to lift a 500 pound weight above my head; I am simply not strong enough. If we see 'freedom' as defined in terms of liberty, there will, therefore, be two aspects to the notion of freedom. One aspect links freedom with the *right* to perform some action, the other with the *power* to do it.

Ordinarily, we would only say that a person is free to perform some action if they have both the right and the power to do it. For example, if I lived in a society in which people were forbidden by law from lifting 500 pound weights above their heads, we would not say I was free to lift them above my head. But suppose there is no such law, and I still could not lift a 500 pound weight because I was not strong enough. Would we say I was *free* to lift the 500 pound weight above my head? Of course, under such conditions I would be free to *try* to lift the weight. But trying to lift a 500 pound weight above your head is a very different thing from actually doing it. Although we would say I was undoubtedly free to try to lift the weight, we would hesitate to say that I was actually free to lift the weight. The ordinary notion of freedom therefore seems to contain within it *both* the notion of having the right to do something *and* the notion of the power or ability to do it.

These considerations have relevance for liberalism. For liberals such as Friedman, the role of government is to make sure people are free to choose the life they wish to lead. However, if the account of the notion of freedom given above is correct, this means ensuring that people have both the right to do what they want, *and* the power or ability to do it. The way to make sure people have the right to do what they want is to minimise the number of laws prohibiting people from doing what they want. But how would a government go about ensuring people have the power or ability to do what they want? This, of course, is a very difficult question, but it is surely the case that if a government is to ensure people have the ability to do what they want, the government must do more than merely have as few laws as possible constraining people's activities. One way of ensuring people have the ability to do what they want is by ensuring they all have the *means* to do so, which is likely to involve ensuring everyone has enough money to do what they want. Such a conception of the role of government is, of course, far from that envisaged by Friedman, but if we recognise that the notion of freedom seems to contain within it both the notion of the right to do something and the power to do it, it is the conception to which Friedman's liberalism seems to lead us.

THE SECOND LIBERTARIAN ARGUMENT: ANY ALTERNATIVE TO THE FREE MARKET IS AN UNJUSTIFIED IMPOSITION OF VALUES ON A COMMUNITY

Is any alternative to a completely unfettered free market *morally justified*? In particular, are governments morally justified in, for example, attempting to bring about a distribution of wealth that is more even than that which the free market confers? According to the argument under consideration, they are not justified because any attempt to do so would involve the *imposition* of the government's own values on the population. For example, suppose a government was in power whose members were all devout churchgoers, and they made it compulsory for everybody to go to church. We can suppose that the *motives* of the government were entirely selfless and noble: they really believed that this was the morally correct thing for people to do and that everyone would be better off if they did this. However, most of us feel that a government would not be morally justified in making everyone go to church; they would be imposing their own values on the rest of society which they are not justified in doing, no matter how well intentioned they are. Similarly, so this imposition argument goes, a government which quite genuinely believed it was morally right that wealth should be distributed from the rich to the poor would still be imposing its own values on the population at large, and that is something they do not have a right to do.[11]

However, it is clear that there are a variety of reasons why this argument is flawed. One point worth noting is that — like the 'if it's natural, it's good' argument we encountered when discussing social Darwinism — people tend to use this argument selectively. If advocates of this argument were to apply it consistently, it would also be used against any government action designed to prevent people from taking addictive drugs such as heroin or crack cocaine. (We should observe, however, that some advocates of the argument accept this extreme conclusion.) A second point is that, while almost all of us — even regular churchgoers — would probably feel it would be wrong for a government to *force* us all to go to church, forcing the rich to pay taxes that will help the poor is another matter. There is a well established tradition not just of the well off paying taxes that will help the poor but of them being *required* to do so. Moreover, any party that announced that it would abolish all taxes that have so far been used to help the poor, or who said that from now on payment of such taxes would be voluntary, would not likely be elected. What this seems to show is that the belief that well off people should be required to pay taxes that will be used to help the poor is not something that is imposed on our society by a government, it is rather a belief that is widely held *within* in our society. It is not imposed, but *already there*.

However, if these considerations are correct, a puzzle arises: If the idea that the rich should be compelled to pay taxes to help the poor is already widely present in society, why should compulsion be necessary? If the value really is already there in society, won't (most) people simply obey it of their own free will? Why should compulsion be necessary to get the rich to pay their taxes? Here we should note that the two claims, 'I believe that the rich should be made to pay taxes' and, 'I, myself, would not pay taxes if doing so were not compulsory' are not necessarily in conflict. If a rich person was concerned about the assurance problem discussed in chapter one, they might believe that the rich ought to be made to pay taxes, but still refuse to pay the taxes themselves if the taxes were not compulsory. They might, for example, think that if taxes were voluntary then no-one else would pay them, and therefore under such circumstances there would be no point in paying taxes themselves. A person could also easily believe this *and* believe that the benefits that come from everybody paying taxes are so great that taxation should be compulsory.

Another possible reason why a person could believe *both* that the general population should be made to pay taxes, and that they themselves probably would not pay them if they were not compulsory, is because they fear they would succumb to weakness of the will (or 'akrasia') if taxes were not compulsory. Most of us suffer from akrasia from time to time. If a person says, 'I know I should cut down on the amount of alcohol I consume or the amount of chocolate I eat, but I am just too weak. I succumb to temptation', then that person suffers from akrasia or weakness of the will. Similarly, if a person were to say, 'I know I still ought to pay taxes even if they weren't compulsory, but I am afraid that if they were not compulsory the temptation to spend that money on myself might be too great', that person might be suffering from akrasia. The point is, it is perfectly possible for a person to consistently say *both*, 'I think payment of taxes should be made compulsory', *and also*, 'I don't think I would pay them if they were not compulsory'. The puzzle is, therefore, not a genuine problem.

It is worth noting that even if a community did not value egalitarianism, there is still a reason why, for example, taxing the rich and giving the money to the poor need not be a case of governments *imposing* their values on the rest of the community. Let us recall one aspect of liberalism: people have all sorts of values and preferences. It would be folly for governments to attempt to give to each person what he or she wants, so all that governments ought to do is to maintain the conditions in which each person is free to pursue what is, for them, 'the good life'. However, we have also noted that the notion of freedom seems to entail both the notion of a *right* and a *power*. Therefore, part of a government's job of maintaining the conditions under which each person is free to live the type of life they want would involve ensuring that each person has the power to do that; and it is plainly the case that part of ensuring each person has the power to live as they wish is ensuring they have the *means* to do so. However, if a society contains some people who are very rich and others who are very poor, it is highly likely that the means to live the type of life one wishes will not be equally distributed throughout that society. Since the ordinary notion of freedom seems to contain within it the notion of power or means, it follows that in such a society, the *freedom* to pursue the type of life you wish to lead will not be equally distributed either.

In chapter five we noted that if great inequalities of wealth exist in a society, it is extremely plausible to think that total *happiness* would be increased if the wealth were distributed more evenly. It is similarly plausible to think that if wealth were more evenly distributed, then the total freedom to pursue the type of life one wishes to lead would also be increased. Intuitively, it seems plausible to say that if $100 000 was taken from a billionaire and given to someone who had nothing, the freedom of the billionaire to lead the life of her choosing would hardly be diminished at all, but the freedom of the poor person to lead the type of life he wanted would be very substantially increased. So, *total* freedom in a society may be maximised by taxing the rich and giving it to the poor.

We can now see how a government's actions in bringing about a more even distribution of wealth need not involve the government imposing its values on the community, even when the community itself does not place any great value on equality. Governments, according to liberalism, should not impose their views of how people ought to live on the population. Their role, rather, is to simply maintain the conditions in society which ensure that each person is free to live their life as they wish. We have seen that taxing the rich and giving it to the poor is a way of doing just that: it increases the total freedom within society for each person to pursue the type of life they wish. It does not involve governments imposing their own values, rather, it involves governments helping to ensure each person has the freedom (the right and the power) to live according to his or her own values.

The idea that governments should not impose their own values on the population creates a problem for the economic rationalists themselves. Recall that economic rationalism is different from extreme free marketeerism. The main difference is that the economic rationalists will try to get society as close as it can to an ideal market, but the extreme free marketeer will not try to do this. Getting society close to an ideal market will require government action, such as requiring governments to step in to prevent the formation of monopolies. Plausibly, such government action would be a case of a government imposing its own values (in particular, its belief that the value of efficiency outweighs all other values) onto society as a whole. If the imposition argument works against attempts to produce a more even distribution of wealth, it also works against economic rationalists attempts to maximise efficiency.

One natural response for an economic rationalist to make at this point is to claim that action to stop the formation of monopolies does not involve the imposition of values. If a monopoly is formed in some area, then people have less choice in that area: they are forced to buy a particular brand of product. Stopping the formation of monopolies therefore helps to ensure that the number of choices that people are free to make are maximised. Therefore, far from being an imposition on people's freedom, it is a means by which the number of choices that people can make is maximised. It is a way of *increasing* people's freedom. However, in the light of the discussion of the previous argument, there is an apparent flaw in this argument. We saw that *pure* economic rationalism is reasonably likely to lead to a reduction in some non-economic forms of freedom, such as the freedom to form trade unions, and might easily lead to a reduction in other forms of freedom as well, such as the freedom to strike and the freedom of political association. The claim that pure economic rationalism maximises overall freedom seems rather dubious and we may therefore conclude that if the imposition argument is effective against attempts to produce a more equal distribution of wealth, it is also effective against economic rationalism.

THE THIRD LIBERTARIAN ARGUMENT: THE FREE MARKET PRODUCES ORDER AND STABILITY WITHOUT COERCION

According to this argument, although free markets require some coercion to produce stability, they require much less than command economies, such as communist economies. So how will life proceed under a free market? Under a free market, if people are to obtain the necessities of life, they must offer for sale to the community some product or service that the community wants, and it is up to each individual to decide what product or service they will offer. They will also buy from others whatever goods or services they want. In this way, an ordered society will arise naturally: people will get up, go to work, sell their labour and buy what they need. But this order will arise even though each individual freely chooses what sort of goods or labour they will sell to others, and what sort of products they will buy from others. This orderly life arises from thousands upon thousands of free choices made by individuals in the community. Of course, *some* coercion will be required: there will need to be police with the authority to use force, or the threat of it, to stop thieves from taking what they want from others. Also, since the police will need to be paid, and since it is implausible that private enterprise could make a police force a profitable enterprise, there will also be at least some taxes that people will *be obliged* to pay. Even so, the amount of coercion that will exist in such a society will be much less than in a command economy, where each producer is told by some central planning agency what it is they must produce. So, the free market produces order with much less coercion than a communist command, or totalitarian, economy. Friedman expresses the idea as follows.

> Fundamentally, there are only two ways of co-ordinating the economic activity of millions. One is central direction involving the use of coercion — the technique of the army and the modern totalitarian state. The other is voluntary co-operation of individuals — the technique of the market place.[12]

If we grant the very plausible assumption that freedom from coercion is a good thing, this argument surely shows that there is a respect in which a free market is preferable to a command economy such as a communist economy. However, it is much less decisive if it is taken to be an argument for a totally unrestricted free market rather than one which tries to lessen the gap between rich and poor. In the previous section we noted that if a totally unfettered free market is to be stable it may have to outlaw trade unions and restrict political freedom and freedom of speech. But to do this is clearly to (at least threaten to) coerce people in other ways. A free market which lessened the gap between rich and poor, and which also permitted political and other non-economic freedoms, may have less overall coercion than a strict economic rationalist society.

SUMMARY

In this chapter, four arguments for free market economics and economic rationalism focussing on the notions of democracy and liberty have been considered. All have some force, but they all fall well short of providing a justification of either economic rationalism or an unrestrained free market economy. The argument that the free market is nothing more than democracy applied to the economic realm failed because the form of 'democracy' exemplified by the free market comes nowhere near to ensuring 'one vote, one value'. The rich get many more 'votes' than the poor. Since 'one vote, one value' is something we especially value in democracy, the free market lacks a property we find particularly valuable in democracy. The argument that the free market maximises other (non-economic) forms of freedom as well is at best only partially true. While there is reason to believe that a moderate degree of economic freedom will tend to increase the other freedoms, there is also reason to believe that total economic freedom, such as we would find in a completely unrestricted free market, might bring with it the need to actually reduce other freedoms.

The third argument we considered was that if governments were to act with the intention of bringing about, for example, a more even distribution of wealth than that produced by the free market, they would be imposing their values on others. But this need not involve the *imposition* of any value, if the community already places value on equality. The final argument was that the free market produces order and stability without coercion. We noted that while this argument seemed effective against command economies, it is much less effective against, for example, social democratic systems.

In summary, the arguments considered in this chapter fail as defences of economic rationalism and the unfettered free market. Moreover, they fail for a similar reason: the free market does not ensure the degree of egalitarianism necessary for the preservation of the form of democracy we value, which includes non-economic forms of freedom.

10

CONSERVATISM, THE FREE MARKET AND ECONOMIC RATIONALISM

In this chapter we will consider the complex relations between free market, economic rationalism and the general philosophical perspective of conservatism. It is useful to begin by considering just what is meant by the term *conservative*. As a rough first approximation, we can say that a conservative wishes to leave things as they are. Typically, a conservative will be opposed change, but most realistic conservatives will not oppose *all* change. A conservative will generally approve of a change if they are convinced that the change is necessary for the survival of society, but otherwise they will oppose it.[1] A conservative can be contrasted with a *reactionary*. Roughly speaking, while a conservative wants to leave things as they are, a reactionary wants to go back to the way things were and reverse at least some of the more recent changes in society. Since 'reactionary' is a pejorative term, to call someone a reactionary implies that they want to reverse the (beneficial) changes that have occurred in society and go back to 'the bad old days'. A conservative can also be contrasted with what we might call a *progressive*. A progressive will approve of a change in society if they are persuaded that society will be better off if that change is made. But for a conservative, it is not enough for someone to have made a good case for a change in society. For the conservative, the change will be warranted only if the very nature of society itself would be threatened if the change were not made.

THE CASE FOR CONSERVATISM

Why would anybody choose to be a conservative rather than a progressive? There are, of course, many different reasons a person can have for being a conservative, here we will focus on just one strand of argument commonly found in conservative thought.

I happen to know very little about cars. Now suppose I have a car which, although it 'gets me from A to B', does not work very well. It sometimes stalls, is hard to start, is slow and consumes large amounts of petrol. Should I try to fix the car myself? Recall that I know almost nothing about how cars work. So, if I were to lift the bonnet and try to fix it myself I would almost certainly end up making things worse. My *intentions* are good: I am trying to get the car to run better, but if I don't know how cars work, then my (well intentioned) efforts will almost certainly end up making the car run even worse than it already does. So what I should do is take it to someone who knows how to fix it.

Conservatives maintain that human societies are so complex no-one really understands how they work. They hold that, with respect to human society, all of us, including experts such as politicians and senior public servants, are more or less in the same position as I am with my car: they don't know how societies work, so any attempt — even a well-intentioned attempt — to make it run better will probably have the opposite effect. It should be stressed here that the conservatives themselves are *not* claiming that they know how human society works. They are rather advancing the thesis that it is so complex that nobody, including themselves, understands it. This is sometimes referred to as the *complexity thesis* of conservatives.[2] A statement of this view was given by Edmund Burke in his *Reflections on the Revolution in France*. Burke wrote:

> The nature of man is intricate; the objects of society are of the greatest possible complexity: and therefore no simple disposition or direction of power can be suitable either to man's nature or to the quality of his affairs.[3]

Why do conservatives believe that human society is this complex? Here it will help to give just a broad outline of some common strands of thought in conservatism. One argument for the complexity of society is the length of time over which it has evolved. Our society consists of very many institutions, customs, habits, rules, conventions and 'ways of doing things' that have slowly evolved over countless years in responses to people's needs. They represent the efforts of millions who have lived before us, over the millennia, to develop a system that works. Such a system, conservatives claim, is too complicated for any single human being to comprehend. The most we can hope to do is to make some tiny, incremental improvement to some small aspect of it, but any attempt to replace society as a whole with some 'better' version would almost certainly result in disaster.

The basic idea of conservatism can perhaps be illustrated by a simple example. Consider a very small human group, such as a family or group of persons living together in a house. Let us suppose they are living together more or less harmoniously, then a new person moves into the house. This will often result in some kind of disruption to the way things were. Prior to the new person moving in, the people in the house had arranged various ways of living together harmoniously. They will have, perhaps only half consciously, arranged certain habits, customs or ways of doing things that enable them to live together without overly inconveniencing the others. But when the new person moves in there will often be at least some disruption to this. In fact, it may be that the people only become aware that they have certain customs or habits after the new person comes in and, in some way or another, creates an obstacle to the carrying out of those habits. From the conservative point of view, there are two important points to note about this story. First, many of the consequences of the new person moving in may have been unforeseeable by the people involved. But if the consequences were not foreseeable even by those living in the house, this seems to show that even a social system as simple as a family may have hidden dimensions of complexity, of which its own members are not aware, or of which they become aware only when they start to break down. The second point is, of course, that a human society as large as, say Australia, is immensely more complicated than a single family. It is therefore even less likely that any person should fully understand how a society as complicated as Australia, or any other country, works.

Although no single individual fully understands how a social system as large as a whole country works, each individual knows enough to 'do their bit' in helping to make it work. Each day every individual gets up, goes to work, interacts with others, makes decisions, purchases certain items, perhaps sells other items, and so on. They know what *they* must do to get through the day successfully. Each individual, whether they perform some lowly job in some corner of a small company, or whether they are the head of a large corporation or government department, or even the Prime Minister, has a knowledge of what *they* must do each day, what tasks they are to perform and what decisions they must make each day. But no-one has a complete knowledge of the whole system, neither did any one individual design the whole system. Yet, each day, the system *works*. Trains arrive (more or less) on time, letters are delivered, the supermarket shelves are stocked with food, and so on. All this despite the fact that no one single individual is responsible for ensuring that all this happens. How can this be? The conservative answer is that our society has slowly evolved over an immense period of time: ways of doing things that worked were retained, while those that did not were eliminated. Gradually, over the centuries, this process of trial and error has developed into the immensely complicated social system we have today. No individual is responsible for designing it — it is so complicated that no single individual *could* design it. Yet it works.

It is generally part of the conservative position that if some way of doing things is found to help society work, it is retained — people simply *keep doing it*; if not, it is rejected. Parents who have learnt to do it teach their children to do likewise. Copying or imitation is the means by which ways of doing things are passed from one generation to another, and so the way of doing things becomes a tradition or custom. Now it is also part of the conservative position that as traditions are passed on from generation to generation, the original point of 'doing things in that particular way' may be forgotten. People may just continue to follow the tradition unthinkingly; they may say, 'we just do things this way because we have always done them that way'. Conservatives say that just because people come to follow a tradition 'unthinkingly', and without wondering why they do things that way, it does not follow that doing things that way has ceased performing a valuable function. Consider, for example, the custom of leaving a field 'fallow' for one year in every three. This has the effect of maintaining satisfactory levels of fertility in the soil. Now it is certainly conceivable that in some farming communities people may have forgotten *why* they leave fields fallow. It may have simply become a tradition they follow unthinkingly; but, of course, leaving the fields fallow would still have the *effect* of maintaining their fertility, even if the farmers had forgotten it does. For conservatives, following traditions unthinkingly is not a bad thing, since the mind is thereby enabled to focus on other new problems.

For conservatives, human society consists of a vast system of customs, institutions, traditions, habits and ways of doing things that all fit together to produce a social system that works. All these aspects of society are *interconnected*, so that changing one part of the social system can have all sorts of unexpected changes elsewhere. Recently a woman was interviewed on television who discussed the impact of changes in divorce laws. Here is a rough paraphrase of what she said. I should stress that I am giving this account of what she said *not* because I agree with it, but because it is a good illustration of certain aspects of a conservative point of view.

In the 1970s in Australia changes in the divorce laws were implemented. The concept of 'no fault divorce' made it much easier for couples to divorce. As a consequence, there was a very significant increase in the number of divorces. This meant that there was also an increase in the number of single parent families. Now, for a variety of reasons it is more difficult to keep a child at school for a long period of time in a single parent family than it is in a two parent family. Part of the reason for this is, of course, financial, but there is also a variety of non-financial support and assistance that a two parent family can offer to a child staying at school which is harder for a single parent to offer. So, children in single parent families tend to leave school earlier than children in two parent families, which means it is harder for them to find a job. Therefore, unemployment rates among children from single parent families tend to be higher. But unemployed youth also have a higher than average chance of being involved in vandalism, drug abuse and petty theft, so the children of single parent families have a greater probability of being drawn into those activities. Once you make just a small change in things at one point, the whole system can start to unravel.

As mentioned above, this paraphrase is not given because I agree with it. It is rather intended as an illustration of the conservatives' view that our society is an interconnected whole, and that changing one small part of it (such as the divorce laws) can have all sorts of unexpected consequences elsewhere. Because they feel our actions are likely to have unintended and unforeseen consequences, conservatives are extremely wary of change.

Finally, conservatives tend to be sceptical about the powers of reason. It is sometimes said by non-conservatives that they are 'hostile to reason'. This should not be interpreted as meaning that they say reason ought to be abandoned altogether, or that we ought to give ourselves over to wild abandon or irrationality. Rather, conservatives say that, since society is so complex, any attempt to use reason to improve it, or to come up with a better society, should at least be treated with great scepticism, and will very probably fail. It is probably more accurate to say that conservatives are not opposed to reason as such. (How could they be, when they are prepared to use *arguments* to support their own position?) Instead, they are opposed to what they see as the over-confident use of reason to attempt something which (they believe) is too complicated for human beings to do.

VON HAYEK'S CONSERVATIVE DEFENCE OF THE FREE MARKET

Some thinkers have used conservative arguments in defence of the free market. Probably the most eminent advocate of such arguments is Friedrich von Hayek. In this section we will consider von Hayek's defence of the free market against alternative economic systems.[4] Von Hayek is principally concerned with arguing for the superiority of the free market over other systems in which the economy is organised by some central planning authority. We have already noted that, for conservatives, human society is so complex that no single human can understand how it works. Yet, it does work because each individual knows what *they* must do, each day, in order to contribute their own bit to the running of society. (Each individual knows to go to their place of work, what duties they must perform, whom they are to interact with, and so on.) The order of society arises from each individual's activities meshing together with those of others, despite there being no central co-ordinating body telling each person what to do and whom to interact with. In von Hayek's terminology, the order of society arises *spontaneously*. It is a product of human activity, but not the intended consequence of plans to bring about that order.

Let us consider how much information must be possessed by an individual operating in the free market. Suppose a small businessman makes and sells tables. He will need to know sources of wood, and he has to be able to choose the best source of wood for his needs. He will also need to know how much wood this supplier will be able to make available to him, and how much it will cost. Finally, he will also need to have at least a rough knowledge of how many tables he is likely to sell on a single day and respond to changes in demand. This information will be provided from his own experience of roughly how many tables he has sold each day in the past. Now, all this is a fairly limited, manageable amount of information, and so long as the table maker has this information, he will be able to conduct his business satisfactorily. He will, moreover, have reasonably easy access to this information because of his location in society.

Now let us consider how much information would be required by a central planning authority to successfully run a command economy. The central authority would tell the table maker how much wood to acquire from which timber yard, and how many tables he would need to make available to the public over a given period of time. But in order to guide the table maker wisely, not only would they need to know what type of timber was best for the table maker to acquire, they would also need to be sure the timber yard could supply him with enough timber. And in order to do this they would need to know what other manufacturers will be using this timber yard — so they would need to know what other timber users there are in the district, what their sources of timber will be, how much timber they will use, and whether the timber yard will be able to supply their needs. This in turn may depend on a range of other factors, such as the demand for the products made by the other timber users. Also, of course, the central planning authority would need to tell the table maker how many tables to make, which depends on how many people in the district of the table maker are likely to need tables, and what type of tables they will need. Moreover, the central planning authority will need to do this, not just for one particular table maker, but for all table makers throughout the country — and not just for the makers of tables, but for *all kinds of businesses whatsoever*. The authority will need to consider how all these businesses will interact with each other in providing for public needs, and will also need to have a detailed knowledge of what, in each district of the country, the public will need or want. Clearly, the amount of information that must be gathered and co-ordinated to do this is overwhelming.

The amount of information each *individual* needs for the free market to operate successfully is manageable, and the location of each individual makes the required information easily accessible to them. However, the amount of information needed by a *central planning authority* is immense, is not easily accessible, and the problem of co-ordinating all this information so that each part of the system interacts smoothly with the others is staggering. According to von Hayek there is, in principle, no limit to the size to which a free market can grow, since each participant in it will only need a limited manageable amount of information in order to conduct their business effectively. However, there *is* a limit to the use of a planned or command economy: it is limited by the capacity of human beings to co-ordinate quantities of information. Von Hayek argues that when economies become very large they simply become too large to be managed by a central co-ordinating body. Any such body trying to manage an economy the size of, for example, a whole country will have to make decisions on the basis of highly imperfect information, and will be unable to co-ordinate all the information to ensure the economy runs effectively. Such a central, co-ordinating body will be in the position I am in when I try to fix my car: their intentions may be good, but because of the highly imperfect state of their knowledge, they will probably end up making things worse.

Von Hayek's claim that the free market will be much more effective at distributing resources in an economy than a command economy which attempts to distribute them by means of a central planning authority seems to have been widely accepted. Yet even if his claim is accepted, it does not follow that a totally unfettered free market is justified, neither does it follow that there can be no role for governments in controlling or constraining the activities of the free market. There are, broadly speaking, two types of ways in which a government might try to 'improve' on what the free market does.

1 The government might try to do what the free market does better than the free market itself; for example, it might try to allocate resources more effectively than the free market.

2   The government might set up certain rules that must be observed by those operating within the free market and let the free market run along according to those rules.

Von Hayek says that if a government attempts the first method, it will fail due to the reasons already given; but as von Hayek himself points out, the arguments given do not show that governments ought not try to affect the operation of the free market using the second method. One way that a government can control the operation of the free market is by prohibiting the sale of certain products, such as heroin; or it can modify its operation by, for example, levying taxes on people. For von Hayek, such actions by government need not be objectionable. So long as these taxes are well publicised and are in place over a long period of time, their existence need not be incompatible with the smooth running of the market.[5] The government, as it were, sets up some rules on the operation of the free market and then the free market itself, operating within these rules, continues to carry on its extraordinarily complex processes of allocating resources.

The importance of this distinction between two ways of controlling the operation of the free market can perhaps be made clearer by considering an example, not from economics, but from sport. It would be quite realistic, for example, for the chairman of the football league to exert some control over the way games of football are played by changing some of the rules, such as changing the conditions under which a player would receive a 'yellow card'. The players could learn these new rules and proceed to play games of football in accordance with these new rules; but it would not be feasible for the chairman or coach or captain of the team to try to control a game of football by telling each individual player what to do at each moment, for example, by telling player 18, 'Now run eight metres forward, swerve to the left and pass the ball to player 16.' Each *individual* player is able to move around the ground appropriately because they only have their relations to the rest of the game to consider: each player has a limited amount of information to deal with and so they are able to play effectively. But if a chairman or a coach tried to tell each player what to do at each moment that play was actually in progress, the result would obviously be a complete mess. A chairman could set up rules for play and the players themselves could learn to play according to those rules, but if the chairman tried to tell each player how to move around the game, rather than leaving the decisions up to them, the result would be chaos. Similarly, according to von Hayek, a government can set up the rules by which the free market is run; for example, by saying that certain types of things are not to be bought and sold, or that products must be produced according to safety standards, or that certain amounts must be paid to the government as tax. However, what a government should not attempt to do is to tell each individual company the exchanges with other companies it is to make within those rules. For example, according to von Hayek a government *should not* say, 'Company A will now obtain six tonnes of wood from company B and company C is to deliver eight tonnes of gravel to company D.' The free market is going to be much better at doing that than a command economy.

Even if we accept von Hayek's arguments for the superiority of the free market as a means of allocating resources, we are still a long way from having a moral justification for economic rationalism. Recall that the central idea of economic rationalism is that the primary aim of government activity should be to maximise economic efficiency. Von Hayek's claim that the free market is much more efficient than command economies does not constitute a *moral* justification of the free market unless we add the extra claim that efficiency is a morally good thing. More importantly, even if we do agree that efficiency is a morally good thing, von Hayek's ideas still do not constitute a moral argument for a *totally unfettered* free market, since von Hayek's position is compatible with governments controlling the rules by which the free market operates, such as taxing the rich to help the poor, prohibiting the sale of certain products or stipulating minimum wages.

CONSERVATISM AND ECONOMIC RATIONALISM

For economic rationalists, the primary aim of governments should be the maximisation of efficiency. This emphasis on *efficiency* is, in fact, in considerable tension with a general conservative position. Traditionally, governments have had many jobs to do other than just maximise efficiency or move society closer to an 'ideal market'. They have also looked after the poor and the unemployed, provided public goods, education, medical services, the police force and the army, and have passed laws which are not merely designed to increase economic efficiency but are in some way related to justice. To modify or eliminate all these traditional activities of government so that it has just the one aim of maximising economic efficiency would be to carry out a very radical change in the way things have been done. Recall that from a conservative point of view, we ought to be very reluctant to carry out reforms to a society. Conservatives say society is so complicated, and we are in a state of such ignorance concerning how it manages to function, that even well intentioned attempts to modify society are likely to backfire in unexpected ways. Since the reforms proposed by economic rationalists are very radical, a conservative is much more likely to oppose economic rationalism than support it.

SOME EXAMPLES OF UNFORESEEN CONSEQUENCES OF ECONOMIC RATIONALIST REFORMS

We can illustrate the point made above by considering a few examples of how economic rationalist plans have had unintended consequences. In the 1980s in Britain, Prime Minister Margaret Thatcher tried to make the hospitals more economically efficient. One way in which she tried to do this was to make each hospital compete with other hospitals for patients: the amount of funding that a hospital got would, according to Thatcher's scheme, depend on the number of patients they managed to attract. This was a way of making the environment in which hospitals operated more like the environment in which private companies operate. So, of course, hospitals tried to attract as many patients as they could. On the face of it, it might seem as though this would be a good thing; surely, it might be thought, hospitals would thereby be motivated to provide a better service to their patients. Unfortunately, this was not quite how things worked out. Many hospitals throughout the world are infected with a micro-organism known as *Staphylococcus aureus* (golden staph). Patients who go into a hospital for some other reason can be in danger of being infected by golden staph, which can prove fatal. Now, of course, a patient who is able to choose which hospital they go to will rationally try to avoid hospitals infected with this disease. If the news gets out that a hospital is infected with it, the number of its patients can be expected to decrease radically. Consequently, British hospitals infected with golden staph tried to conceal the fact; if it were to become widely known that they were infected then their number of patients, and hence their funding, would be radically reduced. But of course, in concealing from patients the fact they were infected, hospitals were thereby placing the unknowing patients at risk of infection by this disease. The *intention* behind forcing hospitals to compete for patients was to make them more efficient; it may have done this, but it also had the unintended consequence of increasing a patient's chances of exposure to a potentially fatal disease.

The next example of an 'unintended consequence' of the pursuit of economic efficiency comes from Australia and frequently features in reports in the media. One aim of the deregulation of the banking industry in Australia was to force Australian banks to compete with foreign banks, and to thereby make them more efficient. To some extent this happened: banks were forced to become more efficient, but this increase in efficiency had certain unintended consequences. It can be very difficult to profitably run a branch of a bank in a very isolated area where it may only have a few customers; thus, branches in isolated areas may often run at a loss. Prior to deregulation, the banks tolerated this, using city branches to support ones in isolated rural areas. However, when deregulation forced them to work in a more intensely competitive environment, supporting rural branches become a luxury they could no longer afford. Consequently, many bank branches in rural areas were closed down. This is, of course, an unintended consequence of deregulation, but it is only the beginning of the story. Once a bank is closed down in a small rural town, the bank staff are likely to move out of the town to find work. Also, people living in the district who would have used the bank now have less incentive to go into town. If they go into the town less frequently or start to do their banking and shopping elsewhere, shopkeepers in the town will have less business. Those shops which were only just surviving prior to the closure of the bank are now likely to be forced to close. This sets in train a process in which the whole town may go into decline.

This process was, of course, an *unintended* consequence of making banks more efficient by exposing them to competition, but it illustrates the idea that reforms to society — including the reforms advocated by economic rationalists — are likely to have all sorts of unintended consequences. So conservatives will say we should at least be very wary about such reforms. Conservative thought is more likely to oppose the reforms of the economic rationalist rather than embrace them.

We will look at one more area in which the pursuit of economic efficiency can have unintended consequences. This area is scientific research. The way to maximise economic efficiency is to minimise the costs that are directed towards some activity, while maximising the economic benefits that are likely to flow from it. In the area of scientific research, this means minimising the amount of funding directed towards scientific research, while concentrating that research on the development of forms of technology that are likely to, fairly quickly, result in saleable products.

On the face of it, the pursuit of economic efficiency in scientific research might seem sensible, but we do not have to look very far into the history of science to see what the consequences of such an approach would have been, had economic rationalist policies been adopted in the past. The basic idea can be brought out by considering an anecdote concerning the great nineteenth century English experimentalist Michael Faraday. After giving a public lecture on electricity, one member of the audience said to Faraday, 'This is all very interesting, but tell me this: what *use* is electricity?' Faraday's famous reply was, 'Madam, what use is a baby?' The surprising fact is that, up until the mid-nineteenth century, electricity was simply a laboratory curiosity with no foreseeable useful applications. Even so, scientists had been studying its properties and behaviour — they had been engaging in what we would now call 'pure research'. A person who, in the year 1800, was trying to develop new means of communication, or lighting, or heating, would never have considered that obscure laboratory curiosity *electricity*. If they had been trying to develop a means by which one part of the country could quickly communicate with another, they might have looked at a system of horses and riders, or perhaps steam engines. But the idea that an immeasurably faster means of communication could be developed using thin strips of wire and magnets would not even have occurred to them as a possibility. It would not have seemed an idea even worth investigating. If economic rationalist policies had guided scientific research and development from the year 1800 to the present, scientists would not have investigated the properties and behaviour of electricity, and so the myriad of devices we now have that use electricity would never have been developed. If economic rationalist policies had governed research from 1800, perhaps the fastest way we would now have of communicating between Melbourne and Sydney might be some particularly fast type of steam train, rather than telephone, fax or e-mail.

Amongst scientists, and in universities and other institutions, there is a long-standing tradition of looking for the underlying laws of nature. Such investigations may, or may not, turn out to have practical applications, but it is not possible to tell *in advance* whether they will have practical applications for the simple reason that it is not possible to tell whether a law of nature will be useful until you have discovered what the law actually is. For example, you cannot tell whether electricity will be useful until *after* you know how it behaves, and it took centuries of research to discover that. Until the mid-nineteenth century nobody, even the scientists themselves, could see how electricity would prove useful. The unintended consequences of focussing only on research and development that seemed likely to produce saleable products, and neglecting research on electricity, would have had a huge — and, I think most would say, undesirable — impact on how people subsequently lived their lives. It would appear, therefore, that if in the present day we focus only research and development into quickly saleable products and neglect pure research, we run the risk of missing out on the really big or fundamental advances in technology that we otherwise would have made.

The three examples we have looked at: making hospitals more competitive, the deregulation of banks and concentrating research and development on saleable products, all illustrate the idea that reforming a particular sector with the aim of increasing economic efficiency is likely to have unforeseen and negative consequences elsewhere in society. In the long term it can even lead to a decrease in economic efficiency.[6]

ECONOMIC RATIONALISM AS ANTI-CONSERVATIVE

Conservatives tend to be very sceptical of the idea that the institutions of society should be remodelled according to some overall plan or rationale. The economic rationalist programme of remodelling the institutions of society so as to maximise their economic efficiency is therefore a form of anti-conservatism *par excellence*.

Of course none of this need be an argument *against* economic rationalism. Whether or not it is an argument against it will depend on whether there is good reason to believe in conservatism. It is beyond the scope of this book to consider whether or not conservatism is correct. However, there does seem to be at least an element of truth in one aspect of conservative thought. Conservatives stress the *complexity* of society. They say it is so complex no single human being can understand it all and that, as a consequence, any attempt to improve on society as a whole would probably end up making matters worse. This is the complexity thesis of conservatives. Now, we do not have to agree with the conservatives' thesis to agree that society is very complex indeed. Changes to society are likely to have many unforeseen and unintended consequences. Therefore, it does seem reasonable to say that any proposed major changes to society ought to be examined very carefully — they ought to be discussed in great detail and their consequences carefully considered. However, economic rationalists advocate very major changes to society. The idea that all institutions of society should be remodelled so that they maximise economic efficiency is perhaps as great a change to society as the suggestion that all industry be nationalised. So it is at least the case that all aspects of the reforms advocated by economic rationalists should be thoroughly examined and a cautious approach adopted.

CONCLUDING REMARKS

The aim of this chapter has been to consider the relations between economic rationalism and conservatism. It is often assumed that economic rationalists are conservative about economic matters and the main aim of this chapter has been to argue that this is not so. Economic rationalism is a strongly *anti-conservative* movement. Of course whether the reader is inclined to see this as a point in favour of economic rationalism, or a point against it, may depend on whether they are inclined to be sympathetic to conservatism. Even if the reader is inclined to reject conservatism, the considerations raised in this chapter at least show we ought to be very cautious in the implementation of economic rationalist policies. Economic rationalism is highly *reformist*, and history has shown that great reforms to society are likely to have unforeseen and unintended consequences: some of these may be good, others bad. It would be foolish to assume economic rationalism will be an exception to this rule. A conservative is likely to see this as a sufficient reason for not implementing at least the most extreme of the economic rationalist reforms, but we do not have to be conservatives to agree that we should at least be very careful and thorough in working out what the consequences will be before going ahead with what the economic rationalist wants us to do. We should also remember that if economic rationalist policies had been adopted in the past, particularly in areas such as scientific research, there is good reason to believe the world would have ended up much poorer than it is now.

11
SUMMARY AND
CONCLUSIONS

Let us now attempt to gain an overview of the conclusions we have arrived at in part two of this book. We have examined a wide range of the moral arguments for economic rationalism and the free market, and there are three very general conclusions we can draw.

1   All the arguments we looked at are flawed in some way or another.

2   Although they are all flawed, none of them — with the possible exception of the social Darwinist argument — are completely worthless. All of them establish *something*. They make a case for the free market under special conditions, or the free market constrained in certain ways. However, the moral cases for extreme free marketeerism and pure economic rationalism are confronted with many difficulties.

3   More specifically, it repeatedly emerged that the position that was *actually* supported by the arguments was not extreme free marketeerism or pure economic rationalism, but a position in which governments supplemented the activities of the free market to bring about a greater degree of equality in the distribution of wealth than that which would be obtained in either of the other positions.

The first moral argument for economic rationalism that we considered was the argument from utilitarianism. We recall that the moral theory of utilitarianism is the theory that the morally correct course of action is the one that brings about the greatest happiness for the greatest number. Economic rationalists tell us that if we get society close to an ideal market, then there is a special sense in which the total amount of wealth in a community will be at a maximum. (This 'special sense' in which the wealth will be at a maximum is technically known as 'Pareto-optimality'.) The argument from utilitarianism claims that to get a society into a Pareto-optimal state is to bring about the greatest happiness for the greatest number, which, according to utilitarianism, is the morally best state for a society to be in. However, there were a number of faults with this argument. First, it really is very doubtful whether Pareto-optimality would maximise human happiness. One important reason for doubting this is that there is no reason why wealth would be evenly distributed in a Pareto-optimal state. In fact, intense competition tends to bring about a larger gap between rich and poor. It was argued that a society in which wealth is more evenly distributed, but in which there is less overall wealth, might easily produce more human happiness than a society with more overall wealth but in which that wealth was very unequally distributed. Therefore, the claim that Pareto-optimality maximises human happiness is unsound. We also noted that the theory of utilitarianism itself seems to be questionable. It is doubtful that the course of action which maximises human happiness is morally correct if it also causes significant suffering to some person or group of persons *who have done nothing to deserve that suffering*. This led to the question: does economic rationalism, or the operation of the free market, cause suffering to those who have done nothing to deserve it? The next chapter addressed itself to this question.

Briefly, the argument from desert is that the free market confers rewards upon individuals to the extent that they deserve those rewards. According to this argument, people who grow rich in the free market deserve their riches and those who are poor deserve their poverty. If this argument is sound, then there is nothing wrong with the gap between rich and poor produced by economic rationalism — in fact it is precisely how things *should* be. It gives to each person just the amount of wealth they deserve. We noted that there are really two versions of the argument: the first is that the free market rewards those individuals who show qualities such as intelligence, industry and creativity, while it does not give rewards to the lazy, dull and profligate. The second version of the argument says that the free market rewards people to the extent that they make available for sale to the public products that the public wants that are cheap and/or good. The first thing we noted about both versions of the argument from desert is that they both have a certain measure of truth to them. At least as a rough first approximation, it does appear that the rewards the free market confers upon people would appear to be roughly correlated with both their meritorious qualities and the extent to which they give people just what they want. However, we also noted there are many counter-examples to the general claim that the free market *always* conferred rewards according to desert. Some things, such as luck, wealthy parents, duplicity, ruthlessness and bullying behaviour, might make success more likely but we would hesitate to say that the subsequent success is *deserved*. There are also a range of occupations — specifically those which involve the creation of items which could be used by many people without being *used up*, such as the creations of scientists, artists, poets, writers, inventors and researchers — whose rewards from the free market are systematically less than the benefits they confer on the community.

Finally, it was argued that since low status is a positively bad thing, those who have low status in a free market but are nevertheless performing some valuable service to the community, are not getting what they deserve: they are getting the 'negative' of low status despite performing a useful job. This is not a trivial thing. There is medical evidence which seems to indicate that status is such an important thing to human beings that low status increases proneness to disease. All these points show that the free market does not always confer rewards according to desert. We also considered a fundamental assumption behind the argument from desert. The argument assumes that if a person has done nothing to deserve a particular good, it is morally permissible for them not to receive that good. However, we noted that this principle seems to have some highly counter-intuitive consequences: for example, that if a drowning stranger, whom you can easily save at no risk to yourself, has never done anything good to you it is morally permissible to just let them drown. But such a conclusion seems a long way from commonsense. Such a person has not done anything to deserve being saved, but still, anyone who, on those grounds, does not save them has acted wrongly. Likewise, even if jobless, starving people have not performed any valuable service for the community, and therefore have not done anything to deserve money or food, it is at least controversial to claim that it is morally right that they should be without money or food.

The next major argument for the free market that we considered was the social Darwinist argument. Although not so popular now, this argument was once very important. Briefly, the social Darwinist argument sees the operation of the free market as analogous to Darwinian natural selection: the fit and strong prosper and the weak die out. Social Darwinists reason that since this process is *natural*, it is therefore *good*. They come to the conclusion that the survival of the economically strong and the failure to survive of the economically weak, which occurs as a part of the free market, is actually a good thing. There are many things wrong with this argument, but perhaps the main point to note is that its assumption, 'if it's natural, it's good', is untenable and is a version of the *naturalistic fallacy*.

Chapter eight is a discussion of Robert Nozick's controversial and influential attempt to provide a moral justification of an extreme version of the free market. Nozick said that if a person had gained their wealth through strictly voluntary exchange, then they thereby had a right to that wealth. This means, according to Nozick, that no government has the right to take that money from them (in the form of taxes) and give it to the poor. However, we found Nozick's claims to be rather questionable. In particular, a person may not have a right to wealth gained in this way if the other person involved in the strictly voluntary exchange would suffer from the exchange not taking place at all. If people *are* to have a right to the wealth they gain in the free market, it must have been gained in just exchanges. And exchanges may not be, and in fact are rather unlikely to be, just if the other party to the exchange would be caused to suffer from it not taking place at all. Wealth acquired by voluntary exchange between two people is at least more likely to be justly acquired wealth if neither person involved in the exchange would starve, lose their homes or have themselves or their family undergo serious medical difficulty were they not to participate in the exchange at all. Therefore, providing benefits such as food, shelter and medical care for those without a job helps to ensure that the voluntary exchanges in the free market that do take place do not result in the unjust acquisition of wealth.

The next chapter considered a range of 'political' arguments for the free market. The first argument was that the free market is simply democracy applied to the economic realm. Yet, it was argued that the free market lacks one of the main qualities that we especially value in democracy: that of 'one person, one vote; one vote, one value'. If the economic democracy argument is to be taken seriously, its proponents would have to advocate putting as much energy into ensuring each person had the same buying power as is put into ensuring that each person's vote is worth no more and no less than anyone else's vote.

The argument for the maximisation of liberty which we next considered said that the free market maximised the *total* amount of freedom in a society. It claimed that if the free market, with its *economic* freedom, is introduced into society, then other forms of freedom, such as political and religious freedom, and freedom of speech, will follow. We noted that while this claim is to some extent true, it is not always so. More specifically, while a moderately free market did seem to encourage the other freedoms, a society which had a completely unfettered free market was rather more likely to act against, for example, political freedom, freedom of organisation and freedom of speech.

We also considered the argument that governments are not justified in using taxes to produce a more equitable distribution of wealth than that which comes from the free market alone, because to do so would be to *impose* their own values on the rest of the community. There are a number of things wrong with this argument, but one feature worth recalling here is that the argument seems to be based on a false premise. It seems to be false that when governments try to bring about a more even distribution of wealth, they are *imposing* their own values; rather, that the poor should at least be given a decent standard of living seems to be a value that is *already present* in society. It is not something imposed on society by a government. It was also argued that increasing the evenness of the distribution of wealth, far from involving the imposition of values on a society, can increase the total freedom people have to lead their lives according to their own values.

Finally, we considered the argument that the free market produced order with minimal coercion. However, we noted that it is unclear whether either extreme free marketeerism or pure economic rationalism would use only minimal coercion. There is, rather, good reason to believe that a free market which ensures those at the bottom of the system still enjoy a satisfactory standard of living is likely to minimise overall coercion.

In chapter ten we considered the relations between economic rationalism and conservatism. It is often thought that economic rationalism is a form of conservatism applied to the economic realm, but we saw this is almost the opposite of the truth. If economic rationalism is seen as the doctrine that all the institutions of society should be either remodelled on, or else abolished altogether, then it is a form of anti-conservatism par excellence. This in itself, of course, is an argument neither for nor against economic rationalism, but if there is an element of truth in the complexity thesis of conservatives, then people advocating major changes to society need to examine very carefully the consequences those changes are likely to have. A number a cases were examined in which changes brought about by economic rationalists had unforeseen consequences that were very bad.

So, serious problems emerge when we try to give a moral justification of economic rationalism from a utilitarian perspective, from the point of view of desert, as an ensurer of property rights, as a maximiser of liberty or from the perspective of conservatism. Moreover, the attempts to give it a moral justification from all these different moral frameworks fail for similar reasons: pure economic rationalism may maximise total wealth, but it also tends to increase the gap between rich and poor, and fails to provide an assurance that those at the lowest economic levels of society enjoy a satisfactory standard of living. It may maximise our total wealth, but may make it harder to ensure that we can obtain other aspects of life that are also of value, such as security and freedom from stress, and a balanced life that includes enough time for leisure, hobbies and relationships. We should also not overlook the fact that a person's status is often closely tied to the amount of money they have. In a society in which there is a big divide between rich and poor, it is as though the rich are paid twice: they receive a lot of money *and* the high status that goes with it, while the poor not only receive little wealth but also suffer the *negative* effects of low status. We have also seen that this can be so serious that life expectancy is affected. Economic rationalism adds to our wealth, but it also takes away from justice, from fairness, and many aspects of the quality of life. From an ethical standpoint, it is hard to see that it is justified.

NOTES

1 WHAT IS ECONOMIC RATIONALISM?

1 This is actually something of an oversimplification. The *overriding* aim of economic rationalism is to maximise economic efficiency. For economic rationalists this overriding aim will always be what determines the level of government activity. We can get some kind of a grasp of how economic rationalists would use considerations of efficiency to determine levels of government activity by considering a simple example. How many police should there be? If there were no police, then perhaps theft would be so rampant, and such a threat, that everybody would have to spend a lot of their time in such unproductive activities as guarding their possessions. If there were no police then many people might decide their best bet was to become thieves themselves. We would have an increased number of people engaged in theft rather than in some other more productive activity. So it seems as though having *some* police might help the overall productivity of society. But, going to the opposite extreme, it would be no good to have everyone in society in the police force, because then no-one would be engaged in productive work. So, *how many police* should there be? The way economic rationalists approach this puzzling question is as follows. Suppose a society began with absolutely no police, resulting in many thieves, and much time spent on guarding things. Add a single police officer to this society and both benefits will be gained and costs incurred. The benefits, let us say, are that fewer people will decide to become thieves, less time will be spent guarding and so more time will be spent on productive work. But there will also be costs as everyone will have to pay the police officer's wages out of their taxes. Let us assume, though, that society as a whole is better off with this police officer. We then add another police officer to society and again there will be benefits and costs. Let us assume that the benefits outweigh the costs once more. However, the benefits will not go on outweighing the costs indefinitely, no matter how many police we add to society. The economic rationalist says we should have N police officers, where, if we had N + 1 police officers the benefits that would come to society from having that extra police officer would be less than the costs of having to pay their wages. Thus, we have the number of police that maximises the total productive output of society — no more police than that and no less. For the economic rationalist, the same principle will be used to determine the levels of all governmental activity.

2   Implementing pure economic rationalism would involve eliminating all government activity that did not help to improve economic efficiency. So it would, very likely, eliminate all government assistance to those people who were unlikely to ever find a job, as well as to the disabled. It may involve removing any kind of minimum wage. It would also involve removing all forms of protection to the environment that did not have some economic pay-off. It is unlikely that an elected government would do all those things.

3   Distinguishing between *pure*, or *strict* economic rationalism, and economic rationalism as a *tendency*, helps us to sidestep the issue of just how economic rationalism is to be defined. The question of how it is to be defined has generated considerable heat. Michael Pusey, who coined the term 'economic rationalism' in his book *Economic Rationalism in Canberra: A Nation-Building State Changes its Mind* (Cambridge University Press, Cambridge, 1991), said that an economic rationalist was someone who believed the market value of a thing was always the only way of determining its real value, and that markets always do things better than governments (Michael Pusey, 'Reclaiming the middle ground from new right economic rationalism', in The University of Melbourne Conference on *Economic Rationalism?: Economic Policies for the 1990s*, University of Melbourne, Melbourne, 1993, p. 4.). However, Michael Warby reports that, according to one prominent public servant, there may be no economic rationalists at all in Canberra in that sense. (Michael Warby, 'Scapegoating and moral panic: political reality and public policy versus anti-rationalism', in Chris James, Chris Jones & Andrew Norton (eds), *A Defence of Economic Rationalism*, Allen & Unwin, Sydney, 1993, pp. 132–42; especially pp. 137–38.) James, Jones and Norton say the core belief of economic rationalism is that 'competitive markets are likely to improve efficiency' (James, Jones & Norton, *A Defence of Economic Rationalism*, p. xxiii), but surely almost anyone will accept *that* — perhaps we are all economic rationalists in that sense. However, opponents of economic rationalism may reject the *importance* of maximising efficiency compared to other aims, such as maximising equality. The approach adopted here is to accept that perhaps no-one is a *pure* economic rationalist. The *substantive* question is: ought we to move in the direction of pure economic rationalism, and, if so, how far?

4   James, Jones and Norton, *A Defence of Economic Rationalism*, p. v.

2   THE FOUNDATIONS OF ECONOMIC RATIONALISM IN CLASSICAL ECONOMICS

1   See, for example, Milton Friedman & Rose Friedman, *Free To Choose: A Personal Statement*, Macmillan, Melbourne, 1980, pp. 19–20.

2   Quoted on the title page of Adam Smith, *An Inquiry into the Nature and Causes of the Wealth of Nations*, 6th edn, ed. Edwin Cannan, 3 vols, Methuen, London, 1950.

3   Smith, *The Wealth of Nations*, vol. 1, pp. 2 & 10.

4   Elmer Sprague, 'Adam Smith', in Paul Edwards (ed.) *The Encyclopaedia of Philosophy*, vol. 7, Collier-Macmillan, London, 1967, p. 463.

5   Smith, *The Wealth of Nations*, vol. 1, p. 475.

6   Smith, *The Wealth of Nations*, vol. 1, pp. 477–78.

7   B Toohey, 'What do the figures mean?', in Donald Horne (ed.) *The Trouble with Economic Rationalism*, Scribe Publications, Melbourne, 1992, p. 53.

8   Smith, *The Wealth of Nations*, vol. 1, p. 18.

9   Smith, *The Wealth of Nations*, vol. 1, pp. 8–9.

10   Smith, *The Wealth of Nations*, vol. 1, pp. 22–23.

11   Smith, *The Wealth of Nations*, vol. 1, pp. 21–25.

12   Smith, *The Wealth of Nations*, vol. 1, p. 25.

13   Smith, *The Wealth of Nations*, vol. 1, pp. 478–79.

14 Friedrich Nietzsche was a nineteenth century German philosopher who thought that there were two types of 'morality', which he called 'master morality' and 'slave morality'. According to slave morality, moral goodness consists of qualities such as kindness, generosity, forgiveness, obedience, gentleness and sympathy. Master morality, on the other hand, valued qualities such as charm, strength, the ability to dominate and manipulate others, and even cruelty and brutality — provided they were used to gain power. Nietzsche himself preferred master morality. He also believed that what is wrong with our society is that most people accepted slave morality. He wanted to see our society adopt master morality instead.

15 The gross domestic product of a country is the value of its national production.

16 Smith, *The Wealth of Nations*, vol. 2, pp. 184–85.

17 Smith advocated the construction of public works such as roads and canals because they facilitate transport. He noted that the construction of roads, in particular, had been opposed by those who held a monopoly in some area. See, for example, Smith, *The Wealth of Nations*, vol. 1, p. 165.

18 Smith, *The Wealth of Nations*, vol. 1, p. 478.

19 What is uncontroversial is that the free market will, as a matter of fact, work out *some* uses for skills and resources. But this need not mean that it will work out the *best* uses for those skills and resources. That is a controversial matter. This whole book is a discussion of whether the free market will work out the *best* uses for the skills and resources of a society.

20 Friedrich von Hayek, *The Road to Serfdom*, Routledge & Kegan Paul, London, 1976.

3 ECONOMIC RATIONALISM, EFFICIENCY AND THE FREE MARKET

1 A proof of this theorem can be found in Allan M Feldman, *Welfare Economics and Social Choice Theory*, Martinus Nijhoff, Boston, 1980, pp. 47–51. A more extended proof can be found in chapter 16 of Charles E Ferguson & John P Gould, *Microeconomic Theory*, 5th edn, RD Irwin, Homewood, Illinios, 1980. However, in the opinion of the present author, the clearest and most accessible exposition of the basic ideas of the theorem is to be found in Kurt W Rothschild, *Ethics and Economic Theory: Ideas, Models, Dilemmas*, Edward Elgar, Aldershot, Hants, UK, 1993, pp. 59–62. It should be noted, however, that Rothschild's presentation of the 'proof' is rather informal.

2 In fact the two terms have almost opposite — or, rather, almost complementary — meanings. A theorem is a proposition that has been established to be true by a mathematical proof. Once something is a theorem, it is no longer a conjecture, or something that just might be true, it is established to be true with certainty. However, one definition of a theory describes it as 'just a conjecture' — something that might be true, but has not been proved.

3 It is worth briefly noting the implications of the term *distortion* used here. To say that something is 'distorted' is to say that it has been 'pulled' or 'twisted' out of its natural or correct shape, or that it has been misrepresented or downgraded. The term generally has negative connotations. To say, for example, that a person has *distorted* someone else's argument is to say that they have misrepresented that argument or changed it *in a bad way*. (If, on the other hand, A had *improved* B's argument, it would not be considered a distortion.) However, in the jargon of economists, any alteration of the price of a good from that which would occur in the free market is a 'distortion' of that price. This suggests that it is implicit in the choice of language used by economists that the market price for something is its 'correct' or 'natural' price. This in turn suggests that it is implicit in the language of economists that the market is 'natural' and that the natural is good. This idea is explored further in chapter seven.

4   RH Coase, 'The problem of social cost', *Journal of Law and Economics*, vol. 3, 1960, pp. 1–33.
5   We should note, however, that this way of removing externalities runs up against a difficulty. Suppose Smith owns a fish farm. A creek runs through Smith's property and the cheapest way of raising fish means that some by-products flow into the creek. The creek then flows into Brown's property. What should Smith do? If the by-products are harmful, then Brown might sue him for violating his property rights. But if the products aren't harmful and instead carry nutrients that would increase the fertility of Brown's soil then Brown might be grateful for them. So, what is Smith to do? Pretty clearly, he needs to *find out* if the by-products flowing into the creek are harmful or not. This may be an elaborate business requiring the employment of ecologists, biologists and chemists to determine what he is putting into the creek, and whether it is likely to be harmful to Brown. Obviously enough, this may all be fairly expensive: he will need to *pay* the biologists, ecologists and chemists. This money will have to come from somewhere, so Smith would need to raise the price of his fish.
        Now, let us suppose that at the end of their investigation, the scientists discover that the material Smith is discharging into the stream is not harmful at all. It would then be quite safe for him to keep using the cheapest method of raising fish, but the cost of *discovering* this fact might have been quite appreciable. Perhaps Smith had to pay a lot of money for the expertise of the scientists. Under these circumstances, it seems everyone would have been better off if Smith had just gone ahead raising fish in the cheapest way. That way, Brown would have received the nutrients, Smith would not have had to pay for the services of the scientists and so would have been able to sell his fish more cheaply, passing on the benefit of cheaper fish to his customers.
        What this example illustrates is that it will often *cost something* to find out if a producer is violating the property rights of others. This creates a difficulty since in some cases it may be that everyone would have been better off if producers had not incurred this extra cost. Consequently, an additional assumption needs to be made if we are to achieve Pareto-optimality by introducing the appropriate property rights. It needs to be assumed that the cost of finding out whether a company is violating the property rights of others is itself zero. But plainly, in the real world, this assumption is often going to be false.
6   It should be emphasised that the way of defining perfect competition given here is not the only possible way. Professional economists look for the simplest possible way of stating the conditions for perfect competition, or a way of proving the First Theorem from the smallest number of simple assumptions. For economists, any definition will do, so long as it enables them to prove the First Theorem; but this does not always produce an intuitively illuminating way of explaining the notion of perfect competition. The definition given here, although in some ways unnecessarily lengthy, has been used because it helps to give an intuitively clear understanding of the notion.
7   In writing this account, I have been greatly assisted by the (relatively!) highly accessible sketch of the proof given by Rothschild in *Ethics and Economic Theory*, pp. 59–62.
8   Galbraith argued for this in his book *The New Industrial State*, Houghton Mifflin, Boston, 1967.

4   RATIONALITY AND MORALITY
1   It is even more misleading to describe opponents of economic rationalism as the 'irrationalists', but unfortunately there are some people who have done just that. (See James, Jones & Norton (eds), *A Defence of Economic Rationalism*, especially the Foreword by John Hyde, p. v.)

2   I must emphasise here that I am not suggesting that professional economists deny this point. On the contrary, they say that what has value for a person, or what has 'utility' for them, is crucially important in determining what is rational for that person to do.

3   Again, I should emphasise, this resistance does not come from economists. They do consider what is of value, or utility, to a person as having a necessary role in determining what choices are rational for that person to make. But, in the author's own experience, it is quite common for people to think that being rational involves *disregarding* your own desires, values and preferences. For example, suppose a person is deciding what type of fence to buy to put up around their property. I think that many people might say that 'being rational' involves disregarding questions such as: What type of fence would look nice? What type of fence would I personally like to look at? and *only* considering questions like: 'what type of fence would most effectively do the job fences are supposed to do (keeping strangers out)? However, economists are quite prepared to allow that the sheer fact that the fence looks nice can be a rational reason to prefer that fence.

4   There are some rather unusual cases in which it can be argued that what is rational to believe does depend on your desires or values. Suppose, for example, I must cross a raging river by walking along a slippery log. I have never tried this type of thing before, so I don't know if I can do it. But, arguably, I should do my best to believe I can, because that way I may increase my chances of actually doing it successfully. (If I go on to the log thinking, 'I can't do this, I'm going to slip off', then I may actually be more likely to slip off.) In this case, my desire to cross the river (arguably) makes it rational for me to believe I can cross. But, apart from rather odd cases like this, it seems that what is rational to believe is independent of what you hope to be the case.

5   Indeed, it is not even clear how this notion of rationality would *apply* to decisions made on behalf of a number of people. If a woman buys a car for herself, it seems quite clear that the rational thing to do is to maximise the number of her own aims and desires that are satisfied, while minimising the cost. But suppose she is buying a car that will be used not just by her, but by other members of her family as well. Here it becomes much less clear what it even means to say that a decision is *rational*. Or again, what would it mean to say that a particular decision made by Rob and Chris was the most rational decision for them to make? Somehow, the concept of rationality does not seem to be the right concept to use here. To say this is not to say that Rob and Chris should be irrational, or even that it is permissible for them to be irrational. Rational *considerations* surely enter into the picture when they are deciding what to do. They ought to debate the matter rationally, but it seems as though what they should rationally debate is not: what is the rational thing to do on behalf of their children? but: what is the morally right thing for them to do on behalf of their children?' Rational means are used to settle a fundamentally ethical question. What is the *rational* thing to do for our children? does not seem to be the right question to ask.

5   UTILITARIANISM

1   Although Epicurus is often cited as a precursor of utilitarianism, it is probably more accurate to say that he held that 'the good life' was a life full of pleasure, rather than that *moral* goodness consisted of maximising the amount of pleasure in the world. Although Epicurus wrote many books, his writings now survive only in fragments. (Much of his work was destroyed when Vesuvius erupted in AD79.) The classic study of Epicurus is Cyril Bailey, *The Greek Atomists and Epicurus: A Study*, Russell & Russell, New York, 1964. The English word 'epicure' is derived from 'Epicurus'.

2 Bentham's writings are gathered together in *The Works of Jeremy Bentham*, ed. John Bowring, 11 vols, Russell & Russell, New York, 1962.

3 Mill's utilitarian views are developed in his essay simply called *Utilitarianism*, which was first published in *Fraser's Magazine*, vol. 64, 1861, pp. 391–406. Details of a more modern edition can be found in the Bibliography.

4 Smart's views are developed in his book *An Outline of a System of Utilitarian Ethics*, Melbourne University Press, Melbourne, 1961. Perhaps Peter Singer's best known book is *Animal Liberation: A New Ethics for our Treatment of Animals*, New York Review, New York, 1975. This book is, among other things, a defence of vegetarianism from a utilitarian point of view. Also well known is his *Practical Ethics*, Cambridge University Press, Cambridge, 1979.

5 Here we are assuming that it is possible to measure the total quantity of happiness associated with some course of action. This assumption is, of course, questionable, and some people have used this as an argument against utilitarianism. We discuss this type of objection to utilitarianism later in this section.

6 This way of mathematically calculating the amount of happiness associated with a course of action was devised by Jeremy Bentham. He called it the 'hedonic calculus'. Bentham's way of calculating happiness was actually rather more sophisticated than the very simple example used here, but the basic idea was the same.

7 A statement of the law of diminishing marginal utility, and a discussion of it, is given in Paul A Samuelson, *Economics*, 11th edn, McGraw-Hill, New York, 1980, pp. 408–409. Samuelson explains the law of diminishing marginal utility as follows: 'As you consume more of the same good, your *total* (psychological) utility increases. However, let us use the term "marginal utility" to refer to "the extra utility added by one extra last unit of a good". Then, with successive new units of the good, your total utility will grow at a slower and slower rate because of a fundamental tendency for your psychological ability to appreciate more of the good to become less keen.' By '(psychological) utility', Samuelson means something like 'happiness' or 'pleasure'. Roughly, the law implies that if you give a man who has no loaves of bread one loaf, he will become a lot happier. Give him another, and he will again become happier, but his happiness is likely to be increased *less* by the second loaf than it was by the first. Give him a third and his happiness will still be increased, but by an even smaller amount, and so on.

8 Ruut Veenhoven, 'Happy life expectancy: a comprehensive measure of quality of life in nations', *Social Indicators Research*, vol. 39, 1996, pp. 1–58.

9 Ruut Veenhoven, *Happiest nations — Sweden, the Netherlands and Iceland*, Global Ideas Bank, accessed 5 July 2001, <www.globalideasbank.org/crespec/CS-121.HTML>.

10 The figures for happiness as a subjectively felt experience were obtained from *World Database of Happiness*, Erasmus University, Rotterdam, directed by Ruut Veenhoven, accessed 5 July 2001, <www.eur.nl/fsw/research/happiness/>. The database contains the results of many different types of surveys given to people in a wide range of different countries. In order to obtain a consistent basis for comparison, the present author obtained the figures for that survey in which people were asked to rate their happiness on a scale of '1'(least happy) to '4'(most happy). This type of survey was the most commonly used throughout the world. The figures were then converted into percentages. In this way, results were obtained for sixty-two countries. It should be noted that the survey does not include all the countries in the world. No information was obtained from many Islamic countries, from many of the poorest African countries, and from many of the world's very small nations.

11 Ruut Veenhoven, *Happiest nations — Sweden, the Netherlands and Iceland*.

12 John R Hicks, *Value and Capital: An Inquiry into some Fundamental Principles of Economic Theory*, Clarendon Press, Oxford, 1939.

13 Hicks, *Value and Capital*, p. 18. Hicks gives two more reasons why economics ought to be done without assuming that there is some quantity 'utility' or 'happiness' which people have in degrees that can be compared with the amounts that other people have. He says economics ought to be done without assuming utilitarianism because utilitarianism is a controversial theory. He also says that the assumption of the existence of 'utility' or 'happiness' ought be rejected because it is possible to explain the behaviour of markets without assuming that it exists and *it is simpler to assume that it does not exist.* He then appeals to 'Ockham's Razor', a principle which says that the simpler explanation is to be preferred. However, here we can, I think, protest a little against Hicks's argument. Of course, Ockham's Razor is usually a very sensible principle for choosing between competing rival hypotheses, but there seems to be something very odd about applying it to the mental life of our fellow human beings. To take a very clear example, I can perhaps explain everything about the behaviour of the people around me by saying that they are automata devoid of consciousness, and that the firing of their brain cells is not accompanied by any conscious experience. This would be the simpler explanation, but it seems to be verging on madness to suggest that it is thereby more probably true. Of course, what Hicks is denying or disputing is not the existence of conscious experience, but the existence of some quantity 'happiness' of which it can be meaningfully said that one person has more or less than another. However, the sheer fact that we can explain the behaviour of markets without postulating the existence of such a quantity does not seem to be very good reason, in this case, for saying that such a quantity does not exist.

14 It is worth briefly noting a (slightly technical) distinction here. The question: is it possible to measure *quantities* of happiness — that is, can we say A has 3 units of happiness while B has 4 units? is actually a different question from the question: can we say person A has more happiness than person B? Quite possibly, we might be able to say A has *more* happiness than B without being able to put precise numbers on how much happiness either of them has, but Hicks thought *neither* question could be answered with scientific rigour. The question of whether it is possible to compare one person's happiness with that of another is called by economists *the problem of interpersonal comparisons of utility*.

15 Rothschild, *Ethics and Economic Theory*, pp. 86–87. Actually, Rothschild discerns four main types of objection to the problem of 'interpersonal comparisons of utility'. I have rather drastically simplified Rothschild's account.

16 See Robert A Solo's *The Philosophy of Science, and Economics*, Macmillan, Basingstoke, Hampshire, 1991, especially p. 110.

17 This is (a slight modification of) an example originally due to JJC Smart. See John JC Smart & Bernard Williams, *Utilitarianism: For and Against*, Cambridge University Press, Cambridge, 1973, pp. 69–73. Smart, himself a utilitarian, agrees that it is indeed a consequence of his position that the police officer (Smart's original examples used a sheriff rather than a police officer) should frame the person whom he (the officer) knows is in fact innocent; but he argues that it nonetheless does not refute utilitarianism.

18 Karl Popper, *The Open Society and its Enemies*, 3rd edn, Routledge & Kegan Paul, London, 1957, vol. 1, ch. 5, note 6.

19 For a development of rule-utilitarianism see Stephen Toulmin, *An Examination of the Place of Reason in Ethics*, Cambridge University Press, Cambridge, 1951. Some authors have claimed that the distinction between act- and rule-utilitarianism is unclear. For a development of this line of thought see Richard M Hare, *Freedom and Reason*, Clarendon Press, Oxford, 1963.

6   THE ARGUMENTS FROM DESERT

1   The discussion of the arguments from desert in this chapter are in part derived from Allen E Buchanan, *Ethics, Efficiency and the Market*, Rowman

& Allenheld, Totowa, NJ, 1985, especially pp. 51–53. What is perhaps the 'classic' statement of the argument from desert is John B Clark, *The Distribution of Wealth: A Theory of Wages, Interests and Profits*, Kelley & Millman, New York, 1956.

2 That the free market may produce great inequalities of wealth is accepted by both friends and enemies of the free market. Perhaps the most high-profile of the defenders of the free market is Milton Friedman. In the first chapter of his book *Free to Choose* (co-authored by Rose Friedman), Friedman readily agrees that the free market can produce a vast gulf between the 'haves' and the 'have-nots'. Surprisingly, he even concedes that this is not fair, but he goes on to argue that, despite its unfairness, it is still a good thing. He says simply, 'Life is not fair' (p. 168). He also says that a world in which everyone was the same would be a boring world in which to live. The implication the reader is evidently meant to draw is that a world in which there was no inequality of wealth would be a boring world, too (pp. 166–72).

3 This statement requires a little qualification. If a country were to move from a feudal system of organisation to economic rationalism, then there may be an increase in the degree of equality of distribution of wealth. But, at least as far as the present author knows, what no-one has ever disputed is that if a society moves from a society in which there is a high level of government spending on social security, education and health, to economic rationalism or free market economics, then the gap between rich and poor is likely to increase.

4 Timothy M Smeeding & Lee Rainwater, *Globalisation, Inequality and the Rich Countries of the G-20: Updated Results from the Luxembourg Income Study (LIS) and other Places*, Syracuse University, 5 August 2002, <www-cpr. maxwell.syr.edu/faculty/smeeding/papers/index.htm>, especially figure 1 'Changes in income inequality'.

5 The average income of Australia's richest 20 per cent was, in 1999, about ten times that of its poorest 20 per cent. This was greater than the gap found even in the United States. See Peter Townsend, 'Poverty, social exclusion and social polarisation: the need to construct an international welfare state', in Sheila Shaver (ed.), *Social Policy for the 21st Century: Justice and Responsibility*, Proceedings of the National Social Policy Conference, University of NSW, July 1999, vol. 2, UNSW: Social Policy Research Centre, Sydney, pp. 1–23, especially p. 1.

6 Timothy M Smeeding & Lee Rainwater, *Comparing Living Standards Across Nations: Real Incomes at the Top, the Bottom and the Middle*, Syracuse University, accessed 5 August 2002, <www-cpr.maxwell.syr.edu/faculty/ smeeding/papers/index.htm>, especially figure 1 '"Social distance": relative income comparisons across 21 nations in the 1990s'.

7 Smeeding & Rainwater, *Comparing Living Standards Across Nations*, figure 2 'Social distance and real standards of living'.

8 The distinction between the merit and service versions of the argument is due to Buchanan, *Ethics, Efficiency and the Market*, pp. 51–52. However, the terminology *merit version* and *service version* is the present author's.

9 Rembrandt lived his latter years in poverty, despite being very highly regarded as an artist. Some other examples of famous artists who were poor in their own lifetimes are: Cézanne, Uttrillo, Modigliani, Samuel Palmer, Chaim Soutine and William Pinkam-Ryder. If an artist's name is found in *The Oxford Companion to Art*, they have, presumably, been judged by history to be significant and their works now often sell for considerable sums of money. A random browse through *The Oxford Companion to Art* seems to indicate that of a number of these significant artists, more were poor than rich. That artists themselves do not get a fair deal in the free market is given further support by the familiar fact that the prices of artistic works *increase* in value when the

artist *dies*. Obviously, however, the artists themselves cannot receive any benefit from the increased prices of their work. (Harold Osborne (ed.), *The Oxford Companion to Art*, Clarendon Press, Oxford, 1970.)

10 We should note that there is another reason why it might be thought wrong to take money from some producers and give it to others. This is because the producers from whom we are taking the money have obtained that money by *strictly voluntary exchange* and so have a right to that money. We discuss this important argument in chapter eight.

11 According to Wallace Peterson, in real terms the average weekly income of a worker in the United States went down by 19.1 per cent from 1973 to 1991. He also says that, over the same period, the average incomes of the top 10 per cent went up by 16.5 per cent in real terms, while the incomes of the bottom 10 per cent went down by 14.8 per cent. (Wallace Peterson, 'The silent depression', *Challenge*, July–August, 1991, pp. 30–31.)

12 Richard G Wilkinson, *Unhealthy Societies: The Afflictions of Inequality*, Routledge, London, 1996.

13 Wilkinson, *Unhealthy Societies*, pp. 5–6, 70, 72 & 75, and intermittently throughout chapter five (pp. 72–109).

14 How wealthy must a country be to be 'wealthy enough' in this sense? Wilkinson says that a country becomes wealthy enough, in this sense, when it crosses the 'epidemiological transition'. This happens when the public health systems of a country become so well developed that infectious diseases cease to be the main cause of death, taken over by diseases of affluence, such as obesity, stroke and heart-attack. So, in essence, a country becomes 'wealthy enough' when it can afford a public health system extensive enough to make infectious disease an unlikely cause of death. Wilkinson goes on to note that, paradoxically, the members of affluent societies who suffer most from the diseases of affluence are not the rich but the poorer members of the affluent societies. (Wilkinson, *Unhealthy Societies*, pp. 43–44.)

15 These themes are explored in chapters nine and ten of Wilkinson, *Unhealthy Societies*.

16 Wilkinson, *Unhealthy Societies*, p. 176.

17 Wilkinson, *Unhealthy Societies*, p. 195.

18 Eric Brunner, 'The social and biological basis of cardiovascular disease in office workers', in David Blane, Eric Brunner & Richard G Wilkinson (eds), *Health and Social Organisation: Towards a Health Policy for the Twenty-First Century*, Routledge, London, 1996, pp. 272–99. (Quoted in Wilkinson, *Unhealthy Societies*, pp. 195–96.)

19 Wilkinson, *Unhealthy Societies*, p. 196.

7 SOCIAL DARWINISM

1 Richard Hofstadter, *Social Darwinism in American Thought*, G Braziller, New York, 1959, chapter five: 'Evolution, Ethics and Society', especially pp. 90–92.

2 Herbert Spencer, 'A theory of population, deduced from the general law of animal fertility', *Westminster Review*, LVII, 1852, pp. 499–500. The publication date of 1852 means that Spencer's article appeared seven years before Darwin's *Origin of Species*, which was published in 1859. Actually, many people, including Darwin's grandfather Erasmus Darwin, had formulated versions of the theory of evolution prior to Charles Darwin himself. Like many ideas, it can be traced back to the Ancient Greeks. What Darwin was the first person to do was to discover the *mechanism* (natural selection) by which organisms gradually evolved over time.

3 Or, to give the essay its full title: *An Essay on the Principle of Population, as it Affects the Future Improvement of Society; with Remarks on the Speculation of Mr Godwin, M. Condorcet, and Other Writers*, privately printed, London, 1798.

4   Andrew Carnegie, *The Autobiography of Andrew Carnegie*, Houghton Mifflin, Boston, 1920, p. 327.

5   William Ghent, *Our Benevolent Feudalism*, Macmillan, New York, 1929, p. 29.

6   Herbert Spencer, 'The Study of Sociology', in *The Works of H Spencer*, 9th edn, vol. 12, Otto Zeller, Osnabruck, 1880.

7   William G Sumner, *The Challenge of Facts and Other Essays*, ed. Albert Keller, Yale University Press, New Haven, CT, 1914.

8   The Scottish philosopher David Hume (1711–76) is generally credited with being the first to clearly see that it is a fallacy to attempt to derive 'ought' from 'is'. (David Hume, *A Treatise of Human Nature*, ed. LA Selby-Bigge, Clarendon Press, Oxford, 1960, vol. III, part I, section I.) Some modern scholars think that Hume was not actually claiming that it is always impossible to derive 'ought' from 'is'; rather they think that all he was saying was that many authors had attempted to derive 'ought' from 'is' without giving any justification of that inference.

9   The expression 'naturalistic fallacy' is due to George E Moore (1873–1958). He developed his ideas in *Principia Ethica*, Cambridge University Press, Cambridge, 1929, especially pp. 10–14. For an explanation of just why this is thought to be a fallacy, see Michael Ruse, *Taking Darwin Seriously: A Naturalistic Approach to Philosophy*, Basil Blackwell, New York, 1986, especially pp. 86–90.

10   For a brief discussion of Spencer's idea that evolution is an inexorable process which it is folly to try to arrest, see, for example, Hofstadter, *Social Darwinism in American Thought*, especially pp. 43–44; and for Sumner on the same theme, see *The Challenge of Facts*, pp. 60–61.

11   'Eugenics' is the attempt to produce a perfect human being by selective breeding and the control of inherited qualities. The Nazis attempted to produce a 'perfect Aryan' by means of eugenics.

12   Thomas H Huxley & Julian S Huxley, *Evolution and Ethics*, Pilot Press, London, 1947. Huxley writes: 'Let us understand, once and for all, that the ethical progress of society depends not on imitating the cosmic process, still less in running away from it, but in combating it.' (p. 82).

8   THE ARGUMENT FOR THE FREE MARKET FROM THE NOTION OF VOLUNTARY EXCHANGE

1   For an exposition of Nozick's arguments that we will be concerned in this chapter, see: Robert Nozick, *Anarchy, State and Utopia*, Basil Blackwell, Oxford, 1975, pp. ix–x, 160–64 & 178–82.

2   See, for example, John Rawls, *A Theory of Justice*, Clarendon Press, Oxford, 1972, especially pp. 136–41 & 251–57.

3   This remark needs qualification. Rawls is prepared to allow that a society that gives more rewards to those with special abilities may be just if doing so helps to minimise the suffering of everyone in that society. So, for example, a self-interested person, from behind the veil of ignorance, might choose to live in a society in which medical doctors were paid a lot if this ensured that people of high ability were attracted to the medical profession, and this guaranteed that the sick in the society received competent treatment.

4   See, for example, the article on Rawls by Thomas Nagel in *The Oxford Companion to Philosophy*, ed. T Honderich, Oxford University Press, Oxford, 1995, pp. 745–46.

5   Buchanan, *Ethics, Efficiency and the Market*, p. 71.

6   According to figures released by the Australian Tax Office, the majority of those people earning $500 000 or more per annum gave nothing at all to charity in the financial year 1997–98. (Daniel Dasey, '905 people earned more than $1m last year: 362 of them didn't give a cent to charity', *Sun-Herald*, 30 January 2000, p. 10.)

9 ECONOMIC DEMOCRACY AND THE MAXIMISATION OF LIBERTY

1 See Milton Friedman, *Capitalism and Freedom*, University of Chicago Press, Chicago, 1962, especially p. 15. Friedman writes: 'the [free] market ... is, in political terms, a system of proportional representation. Each man can vote, as it were, for the colour of tie he wants and get it.' He goes on to claim, 'he [the tie-buyer] does not have to see what colour the majority wants and then, if he is the minority, submit'.

2 People who do not have enough money to buy their own home typically rent one. However, house builders sell homes to home buyers, rather than rent them out directly — although some of these house buyers may then proceed to rent them out. So it is the preferences of house buyers that determine what type of houses get built.

3 See, for example, Friedman, *Capitalism and Freedom*, especially chapter one: 'Economic freedom and political freedom'. See also Friedman & Friedman, *Free To Choose*, pp. 77–78. Another statement of this argument can be found in Buchanan, *Ethics, Efficiency and the Market*, especially pp. 78–79. However, perhaps the most well known advocate of the point of view that economic freedom ensures other types of freedom is Friedrich A von Hayek. He developed this idea in his book *The Road to Serfdom*, Routledge & Kegan Paul, London, 1976. Von Hayek's ideas are discussed in the next chapter.

4 Friedman & Friedman, *Free to Choose*, p. 32.

5 Friedman, *Capitalism and Freedom*, pp. 19–21.

6 Friedman, *Capitalism and Freedom*, p. 18.

7 Popper, *The Open Society and Its Enemies*, vol. 2: 'Hegel and Marx', pp. 124–25.

8 Popper, *The Open Society and Its Enemies*, vol. 2: 'Hegel and Marx', pp. 124–25.

9 The term *liberal* has, unfortunately, many different meanings. In Australia, if you call someone a 'liberal' it would most probably be assumed that they supported the Liberal Party. In America, a 'liberal' is someone who supports government assistance to the poor and other forms of social welfare, while opposing strict censorship laws. In Britain, the term 'liberal' seems to mean something like the account of it given in the main text above or to a position which, while a bit to the left of the Tory Party, is still well to the right of (old) Labour. The account of 'liberal' given in the main text is, I think, a fair account of the way that term is used by political theorists. It is also a fair enough account, I believe, of what Friedman means by the term. For an account of the complexities of the use of 'liberal' see Alonzo W Sparkes, *Talking Politics: A Wordbook*, Routledge, London, 1994, pp. 219–26.

10 Anne Godfrey-Smith et al. (eds), *The Oxford Australian Reference Dictionary*, Oxford University Press, Oxford, 1986.

11 The idea that even well intentioned governments impose their values on the community, and thereby reduce their liberty, runs through the first chapter of Friedman's *Capitalism and Freedom*.

12 Friedman, *Capitalism and Freedom*, p. 13.

10 CONSERVATISM, THE FREE MARKET AND ECONOMIC RATIONALISM

1 Roger Scruton, *The Meaning of Conservatism*, 2nd edn, Macmillan, London, 1984, pp. 21–22.

2 The expression 'complexity thesis' comes from Kenneth Minogue. See his article 'Conservatism' in Paul Edwards (ed.), *The Encyclopaedia of Philosophy*, vol. 2, Collier-Macmillan, London, 1967, p. 195.

3   Edmund Burke, *Reflections on the Revolution in France and on the Proceedings in Certain Societies in London relative to that Event*, ed. Conor Cruise O'Brien, Penguin, Harmondsworth, Middlesex, 1976; quoted without page number reference in Kenneth Minogue, 'Conservatism', *The Encyclopaedia of Philosophy*, vol. 2, p. 195.

4   The argument to be presented here comes from Friedrich A von Hayek, *Individualism and the Economic Order*, Chicago University Press, Chicago, 1948, pp. 119–208.

5   Friedrich A von Hayek, *The Constitution of Liberty*, Chicago University Press, Chicago, 1960, pp. 223–58.

6   For example, virtually every industry now in existence would have been much less efficient than it actually is if it had had to develop without electricity.

BIBLOGRAPHY

Bailey, Cyril (1964) *The Greek Atomists and Epicurus: A Study*. Russell & Russell, New York; originally published in 1928.

Bentham, Jeremy (1962) *The Works of Jeremy Bentham*, ed. John Bowring, 11 vols. Russell & Russell, New York; originally published in 1838–43.

Blane, David, Eric Brunner & Richard G Wilkinson (eds) (1996) *Health and Social Organisation: Towards a Health Policy for the Twenty-First Century*. Routledge, London.

Brunner, Eric (1996) 'The social and biological basis of cardiovascular disease in office workers'. In David Blane, Eric Brunner & Richard G Wilkinson (eds) *Health and Social Organisation: Towards a Health Policy for the Twenty-First Century*. Routledge, London, pp. 272–99.

Buchanan, Allen E (1985) *Ethics, Efficiency and the Market*. Rowman & Allanheld, Totowa, NJ.

Burke, Edmund (1976) *Reflections on the Revolution in France and on the Proceedings in Certain Societies in London relative to that Event*, ed. Conor Cruise O'Brien. Penguin, Harmondsworth, Middlesex; originally published in 1792.

Carnegie, Andrew (1920) *The Autobiography of Andrew Carnegie*. Houghton Mifflin, Boston.

Clark, John B (1956) *The Distribution of Wealth: A Theory of Wages, Interests and Profits*. Kelley & Millman, New York; originally published in 1899.

Coase, RH (1960) 'The problem of social cost'. *Journal of Law and Economics* 3: 1–33.

Darwin, Charles Robert (1968) *On the Origin of Species by Means of Natural Selection*, ed. JW Burrow. Penguin, Harmondsworth, Middlesex; originally published in 1859.

Dasey, Daniel (2000) '905 people earned more than $1m last year: 362 of them didn't give a cent to charity'. *Sun-Herald*, 30 January, p. 10.

Edwards, Paul (ed.) (1967) *The Encyclopedia of Philosophy*, 8 vols. Collier-Macmillan, London.

Feldman, Allan M (1980) *Welfare Economics and Social Choice Theory*. Martinus Nijhoff, Boston.

Ferguson, Charles E & John P Gould (1980) *Microeconomic Theory*, 5th edn. RD Irwin, Homewood, Ill.

Friedman, Milton (1962) *Capitalism and Freedom*. University of Chicago Press, Chicago.

Friedman, Milton & Rose Friedman (1980) *Free to Choose: A Personal Statement*. Macmillan, Melbourne.

Galbraith, John K (1967) *The New Industrial State*. Houghton Mifflin, Boston.

Ghent, William (1929) *Our Benevolent Feudalism*. Macmillan, New York; originally published in 1902.

Godfrey-Smith, Anne, et al. (eds) (1986) *The Oxford Australian Reference Dictionary*, Oxford University Press, Oxford.

Hare, Richard M (1963) *Freedom and Reason*. Clarendon Press, Oxford.

Hicks, John R (1939) *Value and Capital: An Inquiry into some Fundamental Principles of Economic Theory*. Clarendon Press, Oxford.

Hofstadter, Richard (1959) *Social Darwinism in American Thought*. G Braziller, New York.

Honderich, Ted (ed.) (1995) *The Oxford Companion to Philosophy*. Oxford University Press, Oxford.

Horne, Donald (ed.) (1992) *The Trouble with Economic Rationalism*. Scribe, Melbourne.

Hume, David (1960) *A Treatise of Human Nature*, ed. LA Selby-Bigge, 3 vols. Clarendon Press, Oxford; originally published in 1817.

Huxley, Thomas H & Julian S Huxley (1947) *Evolution and Ethics*. Pilot Press, London, originally published in 1893.

James, Chris, Chris Jones & Andrew Norton (eds) (1993) *A Defence of Economic Rationalism*. Allen & Unwin, Sydney.

Malthus, Thomas R (1798) *An Essay on the Principle of Population, as it Affects the Future Improvement of Society; with Remarks on the Speculations of Mr Godwin, M. Condorcet, and Other Writers*. Privately printed, London.

Mill, John Stuart (1969) 'Utilitarianism'. In JM Robson (ed.) *Collected Philosophical Works of John Stuart Mill*, vol. 10. University of Toronto Press and Routledge & Kegan Paul, Toronto, pp. 203–60; originally published in 1861.

Minogue, Kenneth (1967) 'Conservatism'. In Paul Edwards (ed.) *The Encyclopedia of Philosophy*, vol. 2. Collier-Macmillan, London, pp. 195–98.

Moore, George E (1929) *Principia Ethica*. Cambridge University Press, Cambridge; originally published in 1903.

Nagel, Thomas (1995) 'Rawls, John'. In Ted Honderich (ed.) *The Oxford Companion to Philosophy*. Oxford University Press, Oxford, pp. 745–46.

Nozick, Robert (1975) *Anarchy, State and Utopia*. Basil Blackwell, Oxford.

Osborne, Harold (ed.) (1970) *The Oxford Companion to Art*. Clarendon Press, Oxford.

Peterson, Wallace (1991) 'The silent depression'. *Challenge*, July–August: 30–31.

Popper, Karl (1957) *The Open Society and its Enemies*, 3rd edn, 2 vols. Routledge & Kegan Paul, London.

Pusey, Michael (1991) *Economic Rationalism in Canberra: A Nation-Building State Changes its Mind*. Cambridge University Press, Cambridge.

—— (1993) 'Reclaiming the middle ground from new right economic rationalism'. In The University of Melbourne Conference on *Economic Rationalism?: Economic Policies for the 1990s*, University of Melbourne, Melbourne.

Rawls, John (1972) *A Theory of Justice*. Clarendon Press, Oxford.

Rothschild, Kurt W (1993) *Ethics and Economic Theory: Ideas, Models, Dilemmas*. Edward Elgar, Aldershot, Hants.

Ruse, Michael (1986) *Taking Darwin Seriously: A Naturalistic Approach to Philosophy*. Basil Blackwell, New York.

Samuelson, Paul A (1980) *Economics*, 11th edn. McGraw-Hill, New York.

Scruton, Roger (1984) *The Meaning of Conservatism*, 2nd edn. Macmillan, London.

Singer, Peter (1975) *Animal Liberation: A New Ethics for our Treatment of*

Animals. New York Review (distributed by Random House), New York.

—— (1979) *Practical Ethics*. Cambridge University Press, Cambridge.

Smart, John JC (1961) *An Outline of a System of Utilitarian Ethics*. Melbourne University Press on behalf of the University of Adelaide, Melbourne.

Smart, John JC & Bernard Williams (1973) *Utilitarianism: For and Against*. Cambridge University Press, Cambridge.

Smeeding, Timothy M & Lee Rainwater (2002) *Comparing Living Standards Across Nations: Real Incomes at the Top, the Bottom, and the Middle*. Center for Policy Research, Maxwell School, Syracuse University, accessed 5 August 2002, <www-cpr.maxwell.syr.edu/faculty/smeeding/papers/index.htm>.

—— (2002) *Globalisation, Inequality and the Rich Countries of the G-20: Updated Results from the Luxembourg Income Study (LIS) and other Places*, Syracuse University, accessed 5 August 2002, <www-cpr.maxwell.syr.edu/faculty/smeeding/papers/index.htm>

Smith, Adam (1950) *An Inquiry into the Nature and Causes of the Wealth of Nations*, 6th edn, ed. Edwin Cannan, 3 vols. Methuen, London; originally published in 1776.

Solo, Robert A (1991) *The Philosophy of Science, and Economics*. Macmillan, Basingstoke, Hampshire.

Sparkes, Alonzo W (1994) *Talking Politics: A Wordbook*. Routledge, London.

Spencer, Herbert (1852) 'A theory of population, deduced from the general laws of animal fertility'. *Westminster Review* LVII: 499–500.

—— (1880) 'The Study of Sociology'. In *The Works of H Spencer*, 9th edn, vol. 12. Otto Zeller, Osnabruck.

Sprague, Elmer (1967) 'Adam Smith'. In Paul Edwards (ed.) *The Encyclopaedia of Philosophy*, vol. 7. Collier-Macmillan, London, pp. 461–63.

Sumner, William G (1914) *The Challenge of Facts and Other Essays*, ed. Albert Keller. Yale University Press, New Haven, CT.

Toohey, B (1992) 'What do the figures mean?' In Donald Horne (ed.) *The Trouble with Economic Rationalism*. Scribe Publications, Melbourne, pp. 46–55.

Toulmin, Stephen (1951) *An Examination of the Place of Reason in Ethics*. Cambridge University Press, Cambridge.

Townsend, Peter (1999) 'Poverty, social exclusion and social polarisation: the need to construct an international welfare state'. In Sheila Shaver (ed.) *Social Policy for the 21st Century: Justice and Responsibility*. Proceedings of the National Social Policy Conference, University of NSW, July 1999, vol. 2, UNSW: Social Policy Research Centre, Sydney, pp. 1–23.

Veenhoven, Ruut (1996) 'Happy life expectancy: a comprehensive measure of quality of life in nations'. *Social Indicators Research* 39: 1–58.

—— *Happiest nations — Sweden, the Netherlands and Iceland*, Global Ideas Bank, accessed 5 July 2001, <www.globalideasbank.org/crespec/CS-121.HTML>.

—— *World Database of Happiness*, Erasmus University, Rotterdam, accessed 5 July 2001, <www.eur.nl/fsw/research/happiness>.

von Hayek, Friedrich A (1948) *Individualism and the Economic Order*. Chicago University Press, Chicago.

—— (1960) *The Constitution of Liberty*, Chicago University Press, Chicago.

—— (1976) *The Road to Serfdom*, Routledge & Kegan Paul, London; originally published in 1944.

Warby, Michael (1993) 'Scapegoating and moral panic: political reality and public policy versus anti-rationalism'. In Chris James, Chris Jones & Andrew Norton (eds) *A Defence of Economic Rationalism*. Allen & Unwin, Sydney, pp. 132–42.

Wilkinson, Richard G (1996) *Unhealthy Societies: The Afflictions of Inequality*. Routledge, London.

INDEX

act-utilitarianism 95–97, 99
akrasia 162
Albania 155
anarchism 14
arguments from desert 100, 102–103,
    112–14, 121–22, 182–83, 193–94
  charity work 111
  ethical assumptions of 119–21
  fundamental assumption 183
  merit version 102, 103–107, 109,
    121–22
  service version 102, 103, 104,
    107–12, 121–22
  status 112
Armenia 86
artist, occupation of in free market
    109–110
Arts, the vii, 11, 12, 13, 81, 83
assistance, to struggling producers
    112–13
assurance problem 8, 162
Australia vii, 16, 35, 54, 86, 101,
    154, 169
  amount given to charity 149
  divorce laws 170–71
  gap between rich and poor 101,
    194
  pursuit of economic efficiency
    176–77
Australian Competition and Consumer
    Commission (ACCC) 54

Bailey, Cyril 191
balanced life, and economic rationalism
    55, 81–84

Bangladesh 85
banks (in Australia), and economic
    rationalism 176–77
Belarus 86
Belgium 101
Bentham, Jeremy 75, 192
Britain see United Kingdom
Brunner, Eric 110, 118, 195
Buchanan Allen 148, 193, 194, 196,
    197
Bulgaria 86
Burke, Edmund 19, 168, 198

Canada 86
Carnegie, Andrew 126, 195
Catholic Church 105
Chamberlain, Wilt 141, 149
Chile 157
China 27, 86, 154
Clark, John B 194
Coase, RH 189
Colombia 86
command economies 155, 156, 164,
    165, 172–73, 175
communism 86, 156–57
compensation 94
competition viii, 25, 61, 98–99
  Adam Smith on 30
  causing
    decreased wages 158
    gap between rich and poor 182
    town closures 177
  for scarce resources 126–27
  importance of 30–31
  in an ideal market 56–59, 70,

82–83, 87, 97, 190
role of governments to preserve 131
complexity of society, (stressed by conservatives) 167–73, 176–79
conservatism 167–80 *passim*
and economic rationalism 170–78
consumer, as sovereign in ideal markets 44
corporatisation 53
creation of demand 60
Czech Republic 102

Darwin, Charles 20, 125
Darwinism, social *see* social Darwinism
Dasey, Daniel 196
democracy,
free market as an economic form of 151–55
one vote, one value as feature of 152–53
deregulation 54
desert (deservingness) concept of 100, 100–22 *passim*, 182
omitted by utilitarians 97
desert, arguments from *see* arguments from desert
desires (and rationality of action) 65
differentiation of products (and competition) 56–57
diminishing marginal utility, law of 79, 87
distribution of wealth 140–41
division of labour 24–26
manufacture of pins 24–25

economic efficiency 39, 40
and rationality 5–6
definition 2
maximising 5–6
pursuit of in Australia 176–177
economic rationalism
Adam Smith and 29–31
and competition 59
and conservatism 167–80
and ideal markets 39
and scientific research 177–78, 180
and unforeseen consequences 176–78
concept of 13–17
consequences of 17
definition 15
ethical dimension of decision to adopt 17
interpretation by typical Australians 2–3
pure 15, 16, 188

non-economic aspects of 61
reformist nature of 179
economic rationalists (and ideal markets) 53–55
economics
neo-classical 19, 37, 38
as explanatory science versus source of recommendations 90–91
education 10
Edwards, Paul 197
egalitarianism 154
Egypt (ancient) 27
Epicurus 75, 191
equality
and maximisation of happiness 80–81
versus maximisation of wealth 67–70
Estonia 86
ethical concepts, as unscientific 91
ethics ix, 17
externalities 45–48
negative 46–48
pollution 48
positive 46–48
extreme free marketeerism 14, 131, 164

fairness 72
Faraday, Michael 177–78
Feldman, Allen 189
Ferguson, Charles 189
Finland, 101
First Fundamental Theorem of Welfare Economics 38, 39
and maximisation of happiness 77
fitness, as a variable quality 130
Ford Motor Co. 60
France 85
freedom
and liberalism 159–60
free market as encourager of 155–61
notion of, as involving notions of both right and power 163
free exchange, and creation of wealth 32
free market 13–16
as economic democracy 151–55
as minimiser of coercion 164–65
economics 18
resources, efficient use of 22–23
unfettered, and distribution of wealth 143
see also artist; extreme free marketeerism; libertarian argument; liberty

free-rider problem 8, 12
Friedman, Milton 151, 156, 160–61,
    165, 188, 197
Friedman, Rose 188

Galbraith, JK 59, 60, 190
gap, between rich and poor 70,
    100–102
Gates, Bill 130
General Motors 60
Getty, John Paul 130
Ghent, William 196
glitter toothpaste 57
global economy 16
  and ideas of Adam Smith 30–31
Godfrey-Smith, Anne 197
golden staph (*Staphylococcus aureus*) 176
Gould, John P 189
government assistance, as 'rewarding
    inefficiency' 112–13
governments
  Adam Smith and the role of 33–36
  Australian 53, 101
  British 101
  bureaucrats, unable to efficiently
    perform tasks in free market 35
  power required to control economy
    36
  role to preserve competition 131
gross domestic product (GDP) 30

happiness
  difficulties in comparing degrees of
    88–89
  effects of distribution of wealth on
    78–79
  levels in different countries 84–87
  utilitarianism and 76
Hayek, FA von 36, 171–75, 198
Hicks, J 88, 192, 193
Hitler, Adolf 131
Hofstadter, Richard 195
hospitals, funding for 176
housing market, and economic democ-
    racy 153
Hume, David 196
Huxley, Julian S 196
Huxley, TH 137, 196
Hyde, John 190

Iceland 85
ideal markets 39, 41–49, 60, 77
  and Pareto-optimality 52–53
imitation, of work practices 170
imposition, of values on a community
    161–64, 185

India 27, 86
inequality, as inevitable according to
    social Darwinism 132–33
information, required for planned
    economy 35, 171–75
inheritance 103
inventions, as source of income in a
    free market 110–11
invisible hand 21, 38
irrationality 65
'is/ought' fallacy 129
Italy 85
  gap between rich and poor in 101

James, Chris 188, 190
Japan 102, 154
John Birch Society 14
Jones, Chris 188, 190
justice 72
  in distribution of wealth 140–41

Korea 154

Latvia 86
liberal
  meaning of in various countries 197
liberalism 159–61
libertarian argument
  first 155–61
  second 161–64
liberty 184
  and the free market 151–66
  and justice 147
'lifeboat ethics' 136
lipoproteins 118
low status, as a negative concept 114
luck, and success in free market
    103–104

McCarthy era 157
Major, John (British Prime Minister)
    101
Malthus, Thomas 125
market anarchy 14
markets, adaptability of 42–43
maximisation of wealth, versus equality
    67–70
Mexico 86
Microsoft 58
Mill, John Stuart 75
Minogue, Kenneth 197, 198
Moldova 85, 86
money, and status 115
monopoly 41, 59
  trade unions as a form of 54
Moore, GE 196

morality, general nature of 64–73
   passim

Nagel, Thomas 196
natural advantage 30
naturalistic fallacy 130, 183
natural, and the morally good 128–31
natural selection 124
neo-classical economics 19, 37, 38
neo-liberalism 17
The Netherlands 102
Nietzsche, Friedrich 29, 189
North Korea 155
Norton, Andrew 188, 190
Nozick, Robert 138–41, 184, 196
   and property rights 144–45

Ockham's Razor 193
oligopoly 41, 59
Origin of Species (Darwin) 125
Osborne, Harold 195
'ought' implies 'can' 131
outsourcing 54

Pareto-optimality 52–53, 60, 73, 77,
      90, 97, 138, 182
   as capable of existing with great dis-
      parities of wealth 78
patents 12
peppered moth, as exemplifying evolu-
      tion 133–34
perfect competition *see* competition, in
      an ideal market
perfection, human, and social
      Darwinism 133–35
Peterson, Wallace 195
Pinochet, General Augusto 157
police, numbers of 187
   see also public good
pollution, as negative externality 48
Popper, Karl 94–95, 158–59, 193,
      197
preference, versus notion of utility 92
price, knowledge of 43
privatisation 53
progressivism 167–68
promise-keeping, ethics of 95–96
property rights 48
   Nozick on 144–45
protection, Adam Smith on 28–29
public goods 7, 9, 45
   army 10
   lighthouse 6–7
   police 10
pure economic rationalism 15, 16,
      188

pure research, and economic rational-
      ism 178
Pusey, Michael vii, 188
Rainwater, Lee 194
rationality 64–73 *passim*
   and decisions affecting groups
      67–70, 72
   and economic rationalism 70–73
   of action 65, 66–67
   of beliefs 65
Rawls, John 146–48, 196
   see also 'veil of ignorance'
Reaganomics, viii
Rembrandt 194
research
   medical/scientific 11
   reluctance of private companies to
      finance 11
   scientific, and economic rationalism
      177–78
resources, and efficient use of in free
      market 22–23
revised sequence (Galbraith) 60
rich and poor, gap between 70,
      100–102
right wing market anarchy 14
Rockefeller, John D 126
Romania 86, 155
Rothschild, Kurt W 189, 190, 193
rule-utilitarianism 95–97, 99
Russia 86

Samuelson, Paul A 192
Scruton, Roger 197
self-interest 21
   and justice 148
Singer, Peter 75, 192
skills, and efficient use of in free mar-
      ket 23
Slovakia 86
Smart, JJC 75, 92, 192, 193
Smeeding, Timothy M 194
Smith, Adam 18–37 *passim*, 38, 188
social Darwinism 123–137 *passim*, 181
   see also inequality; perfection
Solo, Robert 92, 193
sovereign
   consumer as 59
   duties of 33–36
Soviet Communist Party 105
Soviet Union 86, 155
Spencer, Herbert 125, 126, 136, 195
Sprague, Elmer 188
Staphylococcus aureus (golden staph) 176
status 113–116
   and money 115

effects on health of 118
importance of 116–19
in civil servants 118
low, effects of 183
Sumner, William Graham 127, 196
survival of fittest 131
as an irresistible force of nature 132
Sweden 101, 102

tariffs, Adam Smith on 28–29
taxation 8
imposition of values on a community
162–63
Nozick on 149
Thatcher, Margaret 100, 101, 176
Thatcherism viii
Toohey, Brian 188
Toulmin, Stephen 193
trade, and the creation of wealth 27
tradition, and conservatism 170
transport, importance of in creation of
wealth 26–28

Ukraine 86
unforeseen consequences, and conservatism 169
unions 54
United Kingdom viii, 20
gap between rich and poor in
100–102
hospitals 176
see also liberal; Thatcherism

United States of America 86
gap between rich and poor in 101
unnatural, as that which is morally bad
129
utilitarianism 74–99 *passim*, 191
act- versus rule- 95–97
justice or fairness 92–95
see also act-utilitarianism, rule-utilitarianism

values, and rationality of action 65
Veenhoven, Ruut 84, 192
'veil of ignorance' (Rawls) 147–48
voluntary exchange 20, 49, 138–50
passim
strictly 139

Warby, Michael 188
wealth
creation of 24
just distribution of 140–41
maximisation of 31–32
Wealth of Nations, The 19, 21
Wilkinson, Richard 117, 118, 122,
195
Williams, Bernard 193
win–win exchanges 20, 49

Xland 6–9, 12, 13–14, 28–29

Yland 28–29